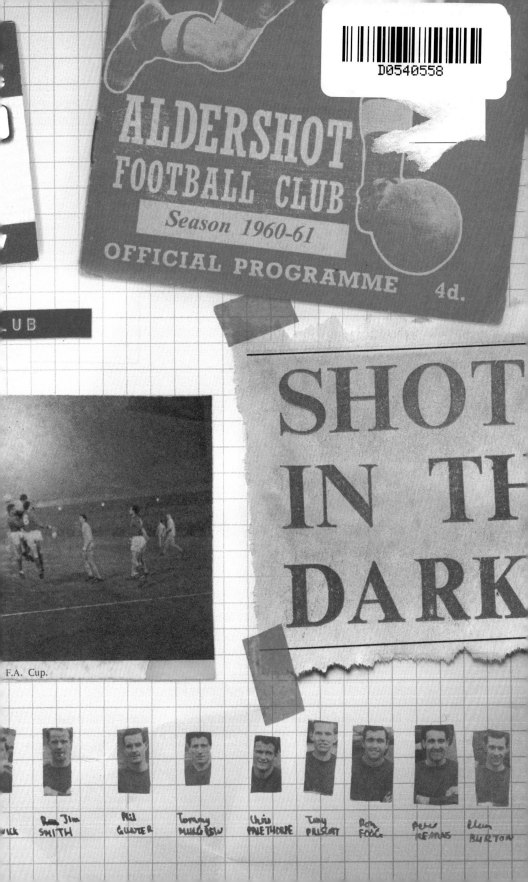

SHOTS IN THE DARK

King Labour: The British Working Class, 1850–1914
The Secretary of State
The Chancellor of the Exchequer
Bobby Abel, Professional Batsman
Archie's Last Stand: MCC in New Zealand, 1922–23
The Financial Times: A Centenary History
WG's Birthday Party
Cazenove & Co.: A History
The City of London, Volume 1: A World of Its Own, 1815–90
The City of London, Volume 2: Golden Years, 1890–1914
LIFFE: A Market and Its Makers
Phillips & Drew: Professionals in the City (with W. J. Reader)
The City of London, Volume 3: Illusions of Gold, 1914–45
The City of London, Volume 4: A Club No More, 1945–2000
City State: How the Markets Came to Rule Our World
(with Richard Roberts)
Siegmund Warburg: A Centenary Appreciation
Austerity Britain, 1945–51
Family Britain, 1951–57
Modernity Britain, 1957–62
The Lion Wakes: A Modern History of HSBC
(with Richard Roberts)
Till Time's Last Sand: A History of the Bank of England,
1694–2013
Arlott, Swanton and the Soul of English Cricket
(with Stephen Fay)
Engines of Privilege: Britain's Private School Problem
(with Francis Green)

SHOTS IN THE DARK

A Diary of Saturday Dreams and
Strange Times

David Kynaston

BLOOMSBURY PUBLISHING
LONDON · OXFORD · NEW YORK · NEW DELHI · SYDNEY

BLOOMSBURY PUBLISHING
Bloomsbury Publishing Plc
50 Bedford Square, London, WC1B 3DP, UK

BLOOMSBURY, BLOOMSBURY PUBLISHING and the Diana logo are
trademarks of Bloomsbury Publishing Plc

First published in Great Britain 2020

A catalogue record for this book is available from the British Library

ISBN: HB: 978-1-5266-2302-7; EBOOK: 978-1-5266-2304-1

2 4 6 8 10 9 7 5 3 1

Typeset by Newgen KnowledgeWorks Pvt. Ltd., Chennai, India
Printed and bound in Great Britain by CPI Group (UK) Ltd, Croydon CR0 4YY

To find out more about our authors and books visit www.bloomsbury.com
and sign up for our newsletters

This book is dedicated to the memory of my mother,
Gisela Hunt (1923–2019)

A diary is a diary, full of partial judgements, overheated reactions and rash predictions – the faintly malicious delight for future historians. This diary, written between July 2016 (the fiftieth anniversary of England winning the World Cup) and May 2017 (the day after Aldershot Town Football Club finished their season), is no exception. The footnote-s, mainly for the purpose of elucidation and/or updating, have all been added over the last few months. Preparing this diary for publication has reminded me of what feels in retrospect like a somewhat larger-than-life time. But perhaps, compared to the inconclusive muddle of the present, that's what the past always does feel like.

November 2019

Saturday 30 July 2016

Sixty-five today (information not gleaned from the *Guardian's* birthdays list).

I remember my sixty-first birthday – a biopsy at St George's, Tooting (non-Hodgkins lymphoma, fortunately treatable).

I remember my fifty-first birthday – stupidly going at deep mid-off for a thunderous drive, finger spurting blood, spending the night at A&E.

I remember my forty-fifth birthday – escorting my eleven-year-old daughter to a Boyzone concert at Wembley Arena, too dark to read the book I'd brought along.

I remember my thirtieth birthday – the day after the Charles/Di wedding, watching a Chandler film on TV that evening.

I remember my twenty-second birthday – going to my grandfather's funeral in Shrewsbury.

I remember my twenty-first birthday – waking up stiff and cold on the bank of the Po.

I remember my eighteenth birthday – waking up less stiff, less cold on the roof of a youth hostel at Delphi.

And I remember my fifteenth birthday…

4 Baker Avenue, RAF Benson, near Wallingford (though my father was not in the RAF but the Army, apparently specialising in dropping things – not bombs – from aeroplanes, or so he once told me). My father, my stepmother and me. Apart from all the usual stuff, three specific memories of that almost mythical afternoon:

1. Near the end of normal time, with England holding on 2–1 and missing a chance to clinch it, Kenneth Wolstenholme – of course we watched it on BBC, the alternative would have been unthinkable – said something like 'it doesn't matter now'. At which point my father (only forty-one, but already a man deeply rooted to his armchair) stood up, gesticulated angrily at the TV and shouted, 'Of course it fucking matters.'

2. At the halfway point of extra time, with England 3–2 up, I could bear it no longer and went upstairs to my bedroom to listen to a side of Nancy Sinatra's first album, reckoning that its fifteen minutes or so (pop albums were generally short in those days) would take me and England safely through to the final whistle. I came downstairs just seconds before Geoff Hurst completed his hat-trick with the final kick. It all seemed so chaotic that it took me a moment to realise it actually counted as a goal.

3. After the presentations, after the on-the-pitch celebrations, it was all quickly wrapped up by the pundit-free BBC. I reckon that within half an hour of the final whistle we were in the company of David Jacobs and his *Juke Box Jury*. One of the new singles they played – and I half think gave that rude noise to – was Nancy Sinatra's 'Friday's Child'.

Well, Wolstenholme dead, Jacobs dead, my stepmother dead, my father dead. It somehow makes me particularly happy that Bobby Charlton is still alive. And this afternoon, at the family gathering, the plan – my plan – is to watch a DVD of the match in real time. Everyone so far surprisingly tolerant.[1]

---

[1] 'Everyone' comprised: my wife Lucy, daughter Laurie, sons George and Michael, son-in-law Graham, grandson Wolfie.

Monday 1 August

A quicker, more open game than I'd remembered. With the younger generation watching, I'd expected to feel a sense of embarrassment – but actually it was pretty skilful, and with both defences tending to fall back, a much less clogged midfield than we're now used to, and enjoyably end to end. Difficult to make out a revisionist case for Wolstenholme as a commentator – one of my sons wondering at one point if some other sport was really his speciality, and he was just filling in as a football commentator for this particular occasion – but undeniably at the death he did rise to that world-historic moment.

Tuesday 2 August

Why a diary? And, specifically, why a football-oriented diary?

Because I use diaries a lot in my own work and I'm curious to see what it's like writing one; because I've always imagined – conceited confession – that, rather like David Cameron about why he should become PM, I'd be rather good at it; because I'm getting old; because it might help to make the present more real and to stretch out time; because football, for better or worse, has been a significant part of my life; because of the fiftieth anniversary of that fifteenth birthday; because of another football-related fiftieth anniversary later this year; and because there seems a serious possibility that the team I support, Aldershot, might be moving ground some time in the next few years – which would be a huge blow, whatever the economic logic of leaving a rather tired 1920s ground that has become costly to keep going.

Like an autobiography, a diary has implicit rules. Mine are that this is essentially not about family and friends, nor my day job; that it is not just about football (how could it be otherwise at this extraordinary political moment?); and that although I can amend an entry while I am still writing it, there is no subsequent (other than purely cosmetic) rewriting. So, in the spirit of Charles Pooter – why not me? – here goes.

Will and Cheye on the case

Friday 5 August

Season starts tomorrow. Shots away to Barrow in the Vanarama National League – that's what it's called now, used to be the Conference a bit ago. I've never been to Barrow and have long wanted to go – partly the distant location (I live in New Malden, an outer London suburb), partly because the diarist Nella Last lived there, partly because this was the fixture (though at Aldershot) on the afternoon of Churchill's funeral – we were more robust then – cf. cancellation of all fixtures on day of Diana's funeral.

Some real pre-season anticipation this time round, after a dismal few seasons. A quick recap:

> 2012/13 – A stirring FA Cup run, with Danny Hylton (an idiot on the pitch sometimes, but our idiot) well ahead as leading goalscorer in the entire tournament that season. But dismal in the league, ending in relegation to

the Conference (i.e. non-league), followed immediately by severe financial crisis and administration. A critical weekend in early July – would the club be saved? My recollection is that £60,000 had to be raised immediately. After some keen debate at home, I took down to the club a cheque for £1,500 – not huge, I know, but a lot of intense emotion. Anyway, the club saved, albeit starting the next season on minus 10 points.

2013/14 – Under a rather dour manager, Andy Scott, relegation averted to next tier down (Conference South).

2014/15 – A Cup highlight (epic 2–2 draw at Portsmouth, followed by 1–0 win in replay), but otherwise drab. Scott sacked in January, with the crowd dipping below a thousand. His temporary replacement, as player-manager, was Chris Barker: steady, experienced defender, & quite a favourite – something about his work ethic, & implicit belief in essential justness of his cause, always faintly reminded me of [Orwell's] Boxer.

2015/16 – New, unexpected appointment as 'permanent' manager: a Scotsman called Barry Smith. I was hopeful (after all, the land of Busby, of Shankly, of Stein), but ultimately his dourness & lack of imagination got me down. And a pretty awful season, especially at home (what felt like numberless defeats), with relegation avoided but not much else.

So, time surely for something better... Smith left at the end of the season to return to Scotland and almost at once the board appointed Gary Waddock. A real boost, because almost a decade ago it was Waddock who got the Shots out of the Conference and back into the League. Something of the cheeky chappie about him – he has a sense of humour, seems essentially optimistic & his hair always makes me think a little of Tintin.

He's assembled what is largely a new squad, with just four left from last season – right-back Cheye Alexander (young & quick going forward, but a bit slight), central defender Jack Saville (knows what he's doing), striker Charlie Walker (top scorer last season, perhaps not quite good enough holding up the play, currently injured) and my favourite of the four, midfielder Jake Gallagher. He came at the start of last season – sent off three times by November – & then emerged as the heartbeat of the team, with a flair for surging runs from deep. The rest of the squad are of course just names. There's such a high turnover these days, plus of course all those often inconsequential loan signings during the season itself. It seems to take me until about October to master who's who, & I do miss the continuity of the old times. Oh my Jack Howarth, my Richard Walden, my Len Walker of long ago.

Anyway, I guess this has to be prediction time. I'll put a small bet on anyway, but I doubt if we'll get in the play-offs. Yet surely a better season – 8th perhaps as finishing place. My favourite (lucky?) number…

While in the rather bigger, marginally more important world, who will be in the White House by the time that is resolved? Clinton or Trump? If the latter – a liar & a bully – it might seriously threaten democracy, fragile and shallow-rooted already. Goethe once said that men always have a tendency to overestimate the importance of the times they live in. That's probably right. But this really does seem a serious moment. And one has to trust, if not quite predict, that a horrendous, grotesque wrong – exploiting the bad we all have in us – won't prevail.

P.S. Bet now placed. £10 at 20/1 for promotion. (Only two go up, in a league of twenty-four.)

Saturday 6 August

No pioneer trip to Barrow. Probably wouldn't have happened anyway – a very long way to go – but as it happens we're looking after our two-year-old grandson this weekend.

Football-wise, a bitty sort of afternoon. Shots started the day as league leaders (alphabetical, admittedly). Saw an early scoreline on the internet – one down after seven minutes – & in the as-it-stands table we'd plunged to 23rd.

Then out for some shopping, then back for last half-hour or so on local radio via internet. Struggled to locate the commentary on BBC Radio Surrey (though Aldershot is in Hampshire), but found it on BBC Radio Cumbria. Perfectly congenial, with friendly remarks about the visitors like 'We'll see worse outfits here this season.' But the score staying obstinately 1–0, with Shots thwarted by a 'miracle' clearance off the line, plus missing a golden chance in injury time. Still, it sounded a perfectly decent performance, so continuing to travel hopefully. While also travel-wise, grateful enough not to be somewhere on the M6 this evening, though I've an idea there's a very distinctive motorway services near Lancaster, which one day – like Barrow itself – I'd like to clock.[2]

Wednesday 10 August

First home match last night – against newly promoted Maidstone United. Kind of perfect in a way. Summer evening, floodlights coming on as the sky darkens above the trees, the pitch looking a smooth green treat (I try to forget that it comes via the munificence of Abramovich's Chelsea),[3] & a late, well-deserved winner, with the Aldershot sub Bernard Mensah thumping home the only goal of the game.

Last season the football was so uninspiring, from the Shots anyway, that I seemed to watch much of it in a dream – remembering better, more engaging times, thinking about different stages of my life. But last night I was gripped, and I also found myself admiring that mixture of speed and muscularity, if not always control or creativity, that characterises modern football – a remarkable mixture even at this quite lowly level.

[2]   I was thinking of Forton Services, with their 'iconic' but sadly now closed tower-cum-restaurant (the Pennine Tower) attached to the northbound building. The Beatles were reputedly among the restaurant's earliest customers.
[3]   Chelsea at this time were using Aldershot's ground for their Development Squad matches.

So, a first win, and back home to discover not only that the Shots are now in the top half of the table (just) but that Trump, compounding his recent acts of self-harm (we must hope/assume), has implicitly talked of an assassination attempt on Clinton by the gun lobby if she becomes President. Though actually it's another sobering moment, as just like the 1930s – the devil's decade, with its many pre-echoes of where we may now be heading – the inconceivable becomes the conceivable. In the micro, one generally looks around & trusts to the decency/non-fanaticism/tolerance of people; but in the macro, well, things are pretty terrifying. I'll try over these coming months not to bang on too much (as someone once said in another context).[4]

Saturday 13 August

Shots at home to Wrexham later today – & the start of the Premiership. Why am I instinctively so grumpy-old-man about it?

1. Because, inevitably, of the money-not-talking-but-swearing aspect. Whether transfer fees/agents' cuts/players' salaries/clubs' admission prices & merchandising, it all shouts 'money' in the face – about something that is a) a sport & b) intrinsically doesn't matter very much. In an era of food banks...

2. Because of the complete abandonment of any roots/identity, whether in terms of players/managers or supporters. On the latter, the Aldershot fans' chant of 'Fuck off back to Guildford', directed at the away support for Man U in a League Cup match a few years ago, was for me the last word. And on the former, it fails to engage me when I look at a team comprising wholly, or almost wholly, foreigners. Sometimes of course they're wonderful – my two favourite players of the Premiership era have been Zola & Hazard

[4] David Cameron to 2006 Tory conference, explaining why his party had lost last three elections: 'While parents worried about children, getting the kids to school, balancing work and family life, we were banging on about Europe.'

(despite my visceral dislike of Chelsea under the owner-ship of the Russian oligarch) – but collectively they become meaningless to me. Curious, I occasionally reflect with a degree of queasiness, that UKIP have never taken up this issue. Or am I just completely off-beam?

3. And the final 'because': the football itself. Hugely skilled/disciplined/athletic etc. – but not enough whimsy, not enough fallibility, not enough expression of character. I also badly miss the old-style muddy pitches – vividly evoked in those clips at the start of the Clough/Taylor film.[5] Plus the crunching tackles. Actually, that compelling encounter between Chelsea & Spurs at the end of last season, giving the title to Leicester, was a real throwback – but very much the exception.

All of which said, I can't deny a flicker of interest. Hard not to get a little sucked into the psychodrama of that handful of top managers – Mourinho, Guardiola, Klopp, Wenger, Conte – & after all, Leicester did win the title last year – by some 10 points. So, I'll keep an eye on it, but – a puritan to the last – try not to get too sucked in. Oh yes, & prediction: Spurs – why not?

Sunday 14 August

To the Recreation Ground yesterday for home to Wrexham.[6] Same fixture on a Saturday in August 1968: one all with about a quarter of an hour to go – Aldershot player-manager Tommy McAnearney, midfielder, put in a decent long-range effort that the keeper tipped over – somehow that gave momentum – & the winner came a bit later. I have only ever talked with two or three professional footballers, & he was one of them. Around 1967 – when sometimes I went to reserve matches – & at the start of

---

5   *The Damned United* (2009).
6   Officially in recent years it's been called the EBB Stadium. But for me it'll always be 'the Rec'.

the second half I was sitting immediately behind the dug-out, trying to finish a passage in the book I was reading. 'What's that? A thriller?' he asked as he glanced at me. My memory is blank as to how I replied. I hope nothing too smart-arse. The book was Samuel Butler's *The Way of All Flesh*. I still think very warmly of Tommy Mac – Aldershot's best manager (in two different spells), certainly of the pre-1992 era, & a Scot, but not a hard-man Scot. Plus amazing eyebrows.

One other Wrexham association. My best friend at New College, Oxford in the early 70s was Pete McQuay, a sardonic northerner. 'I can tell you this, David,' he said to me once, 'the Sixties never happened in Blackburn.' Football was the rock of our friendship, & we played together in the College team – he a gritty midfielder, buzzing around his opponents' ankles. In December 1972 we won the league, 2–1 at home to Wadham, & as I walked towards him at the final whistle he was already taking off his boots – the afternoon's work done – and he said to me (seriously? ironically? you could never tell), 'I suppose that makes me one of the best eleven players in the university.' (Note to someone: the last time I looked, the Oxford Univ football website said that Wadham won the league in the 1972/3 academic year. They didn't, New College did.) Anyway, why Wrexham? Because Pete was convinced that he was going to end up as an average teacher in an average school in Wrexham – a place (where I've never been) that for some reason he identified as the acme of averageness. Well, I'm sure he didn't. But I haven't seen or heard from him since 1985.[7] About five years later, I was in Beverley when I read in the *Independent* that Player's No. 6 was stopping production. Absolutely Pete's cigarette – not a Marlborough man, to put it mildly – & with him in mind I bought a packet. Still unopened.

I'd been slightly dreading the match yesterday. Tuesday evening a high, & instinctively I anticipated a lacklustre performance in boiling heat. But far from it. The weather perfectly pleasant, & the Shots looked good. An early goal – clinched

---

[7] I've recently been in touch with his sister Elizabeth, and the sad news is that Pete, who lives in northern Thailand, has been incapacitated with brain damage since 1999.

about quarter of an hour into the second half – & the home goal seriously threatened only once. Wrexham definitely one of the bigger Conference clubs, so the mood by the end of the game distinctly optimistic. 1–0, then 2–0: two solid home results this week, & 8th in the table. 'The Wadfather: Part II', as an East Bank banner rather neatly put it on Tuesday evening in tribute to the returning Gary Waddock, & for all my customary pessimism I continue to travel hopefully.

Tuesday 16 August

Away at Bromley this evening, & I'm planning to go. Bromley quite a special place for me. For two or three years, 1955 or 1956 to 1958, we lived fairly near by, at Grove Park, an unremarkable suburb – if to me the world – in south-east London; and the two places that were somehow the *big* places, yet conceivably attainable (unlike London itself, of which I had only the faintest conception), were Bromley and Lewisham – I suspect that occasionally I saw buses that had one of them as the final destination. I don't think I ever did as a child actually get to Bromley or Lewisham – I certainly don't remember it. But the frisson still there – & it was a bit of a thrill to discover, maybe a few years after leaving Grove Park, that the Prime Minister, Harold Macmillan, was MP for Bromley.

I still think of 'the Grove Park years' as in some sense the happiest of my life. We lived in a flat surrounded by other Army families; I was in a gang; my parents were together (not that any alternative had ever crossed my mind); I watched *Watch with Mother* with my mother ('The Woodentops' my favourite, a stronger narrative line than the others; 'Rag, Tag and Bobtail', which somehow always seemed to be on an indistinct, spotty sort of screen, by some distance my unfavourite); and enjoyed starting school (Coopers Lane Primary School, which for a time I misheard as Private School), except for a couple of bad moments: one when, having just got the hang of reading, I raced ahead with the book &, when I went up to her desk to show her where I'd got to, the teacher refused to believe me, I think reducing me to tears of frustration about the essential unfairness; the other when, long after everyone else had left the dining room, I was compelled to go on sitting there, trying as best I could to finish my semolina – almost impossible, the stuff sticking in my gullet, however much jam (or what called itself jam) I added. Over the next half-century, I did my best to avoid rice pudding & tapioca as well as semolina. Until 2005, when I was sitting in a small dining room somewhere near the top of HSBC's monster building at Canary Wharf, having (with a colleague, Dick Roberts, and two of the archivists) lunch with the bank's chairman, John Bond, essentially so that he could give Dick and me the once-over before commissioning from us a history of the bank. A sophisticated lunch – nouvelle cuisine, etc., not my kind of thing – culminated in a sweet that, however fancily disguised, was, *au fond*, rice pudding. A bad moment as it was put in front of me, with the chairman immediately to my right at the end of table. I gazed beyond him to that view below of east London stretching miles into the distance, took a deep breath, thought of the money & just about managed to eat it. But a close-run thing.

Back briefly to Bromley. The time I did definitely set foot there was in 2002 – the day that England were knocked out of the World Cup by Brazil (Beckham's feeble non-tackle, Seaman's rash positioning) at about 7 or 8 o'clock in the morning. I went up to town, met my mother at Waterloo & we set out for Grove Park to have a look at where we had once lived. Found the right road – but the flats had gone, only a couple of years before (we were told). A flat feeling, compounded by going to Coopers Lane & finding a school that bore no resemblance to my memory of it. So we caught a bus to Bromley, looked at the plaque on a department store marking where H. G. Wells was born, got something to eat & went on in pursuit of the cemetery not so far away where W. G. Grace is buried, a more successful quest. Wells himself quite a hero for me, albeit flawed by a) his being so wholly in the wrong in that exchange with Henry James about life/art late in James's life, an exchange that almost makes one weep for the stricken James; & b) his equally wrong-headed approach to

Stalin in the 1930s – far from alone of course, but compare him with Muggeridge.[8] My favourite Wells – despite its silly name – is *Tono-Bungay*. He really could write. Indeed, J. B. Priestley once remarked that, of all the Edwardians, Wells was naturally the best, most creative writer – even though, in his mind, the main purpose of his novels was message etc. rather than literary as such. Put another way, 'palpable design' can have its merits. And if it has to be an absolute choice (which it wasn't in the Wells/James case) – life without art? or art without life? – I know which I'd go for. And I'm reminded of that moment in Martin Amis's *Experience* when he recalls a dinner party where the subject of general conversation/chatter became 'Leavis or Bloomsbury?' All but one – Amis himself – plumped for Bloomsbury. On this, as perhaps relatively little else, I'm with Amis.

Wednesday 17 August

Something else about the Bromley man. During the summer of 1996 I was researching/writing a history of the London financial futures exchange. At the place where people ate ('the Pit Stop'), the traders in their coloured jackets were usually either slumped – knackered – over their meal, or reading the *Sun*, or playing cards. One day, on the other side of the large, populous room, I noticed that a trader was reading a book. I went round behind him to see what it was. Answer: H. G. Wells's *A Short History of the World*. A moment that would have cheered that autodidact – who would

---

[8]   Wells attacked James ('his vast paragraphs sweat and struggle') in *Boon*, published in July 1915, seven months before James's death. James, who had shown nothing but kindness to the younger writer, reacted with a very natural sense of hurt. Wells in a letter sought to justify himself, asserting that 'to you literature like painting is an end, to me literature like architecture is a means, it has a use'. James's reply was both moving and unanswerable: 'I live, live intensely and am fed by life, and my value, whatever it be, is in my own kind of expression of that … It is art that *makes* life, makes interest, makes importance … and I know of no substitute whatever for the force and beauty of its process.' As for the Stalin aspect, Wells's verdict after interviewing him in 1934 was that 'I have never met a man more fair, candid, and honest.' By contrast, Malcolm Muggeridge earlier in the decade had already been fearlessly reporting on the Soviet regime (including the Ukraine famine) for the *Manchester Guardian*.

also have enjoyed, if perhaps not applauded, the vitality & lack of hypocrisy of those Essex boys.

Bromley itself last night – a perfect summer's evening. Longish walk from Bromley South station – until almost the last moment, prosperous outer London suburbia – then a small road, with horses in a field just before getting to the ground. Hot dog (no onions, alas) + chips + Diet Coke: not great, but did the job. Bromley pointless & goalless after three matches. Shots two up after some 25 minutes & playing with both zip & elegance. Only one outcome surely. But Bromley clambered back, scored just before half-time, then midway through the second half, & in the end 2–2 fair enough. Some of that early-season optimism felt a little premature... 9th in the table.

Two other things about the game. First, there was some ruthless physical targeting by the home side of the Shots 'danger man', winger Bernard Mensah – unpunished bad tackles, no protection from referee, until he limped off just before the equaliser. It made me think of a Second Round Cup replay in December 1970, away at Bristol Rovers, when the Shots left-back Len Walker – honest journeyman – systematically took out without punishment the Rovers right-winger, the hugely skilful Ray Graydon, who would become a favourite player. For all my desire that the Shots won (which they did), I remember feeling faintly embarrassed.

The other thing is my mixed feelings when the Shots were cruising at 2–0. A bit of me wanted a cricket score. A bit of me wanted a contest. A bit of me felt sorry for Bromley. What I really didn't want was a flat, semi-meaningless second half, as the Shots efficiently, methodically shut their opponents out & killed the game. Well, I didn't get that.

Saturday 20 August

A semi-detached sort of day, Shots-wise. Away at Braintree, but big family get-together means I barely follow it, except a couple of times via Twitter feed – OK? – of Michael (the most on-the-ball, knowledgeable Shots supporter in the family). One down early on – dominating possession, but creating few chances – a break-away for Braintree near the end seals it. Waddock not a happy bunny in post-match interview, barely a trace of usual buoyancy. 13th in the table. Back to that familiar, depressing bottom half.

Wednesday 24 August

First of the Shots 'anniversaries'. Five years ago, away at West Ham in League Cup, with the match having been delayed by a couple of weeks because of the riots.

A certain sense of unfinished business. In the 1990/1 season, the Shots were drawn at home to West Ham for the Third Round of the FA Cup – but chose, to my annoyance, to play it at Upton Park (the choice was allowed then). I really think we could have won at home. Anyway, a creditable & relatively comfortable goalless draw; but of course, with that having been theoretically 'at home', the replay was also at Upton Park – & predictably enough, the Shots crashed out, 6–1. A little over a year later, Aldershot – in severe financial straits – left the League before the season had ended (& subsequently reformed as Aldershot Town, requiring five promotions in sixteen years in order to regain League status, for only five years as it turned out). I've always felt it was some sort of punishment for the craven – however 'sensible' – decision not to bring West Ham to the Rec when the opportunity was there. *The Glory Game* Hunter Davies called his wonderful early 70s book on Spurs (with the young Steve Perryman imagining that all his team-mates were Labour voters, when in fact he was the only one), & he was right. Otherwise, why bother? Though of course, one sometimes needs a broad definition of what 'glory' means.

Anyway, in August 2011 it was to Boleyn Road for the third time to see the Shots, taking Michael (sixteen) with me. A wonderful evening, sitting (but mostly standing) behind the goal where almost all the key action was. Shots one down at half-time – a bit unlucky, but hanging in well. A West Ham player sent off early in the second half – Shots then building up pressure – equalising with about 11 minutes to go – & then Danny Hylton threading home the winner just after the 90 mark. When the equaliser went in, a tap-in after a fairly feeble effort by the home keeper, Michael was amazed by how excited I got. And next morning, in the *Guardian*'s rather splodgy photograph, I was just about identifiable. The whole thing was almost unutterably thrilling: the Shots away to a big club (admittedly just relegated from the Premiership) – & *winning*. While the stubborn ill-grace after the match of the West Ham manager Sam Allardyce – whom on the whole I respect, even admire, & who is now the England manager, with I think a good chance of things working out – somehow just added to the pleasure. But of course one swallow doesn't make a summer. In the intervening five years, West Ham have returned to the Premiership, left Upton Park & gone to the Olympic Stadium (courtesy the British taxpayer); while the Shots have been relegated from the Football League & look like being out of it for a fair time to come.

The evening also included what was for me a significant epiphany. I'd become increasingly preoccupied since 2008 by questions of social mobility & equality/inequality of opportunity &, above all, private education. I was of course well aware of Michael Young's counter-meritocracy argument – i.e. the danger of arrogant, self-serving 'meritocratic' elites valuing the brain above the heart, the pursuit of academic prizes above the rose-growing, & assuming that they deserve & are fully entitled to their good fortune – but in my own mind, because of my increasing vexation (even fury) at the sheer unfairness of our education system, I'd started to downgrade it.[9] My epiphany was provoked by being surrounded by

[9]   In *The Rise of the Meritocracy* (1958), his dystopian warning against a rampant, IQ-driven, intolerant meritocracy, Michael Young includes these two haunting sentences in the 'Chelsea Manifesto', issued by a local group of the Technicians Party (as the Labour Party has been rebranded) in 2009, a quarter of a century before the 'populist' revolution of 2034: 'Were we to evaluate people, not only according to their intelligence and their education, their occupation, and their power, but according to their kindliness and their courage, their imagination and sensitivity, their sympathy and generosity, there could be no classes. Who would be able to say that the scientist was superior to the porter with admirable qualities as a father, the civil servant with unusual skill at gaining prizes superior to the lorry driver with unusual skill at growing roses?'

Shots supporters who realistically – even if our society became genuinely meritocratic, e.g. private education abolished – were never going to come within sniffing distance of life's glittering prizes. I felt a rush of warmth & admiration towards them – & suddenly the force of what Young had said back in 1958 really hit me. Half a decade on from that epiphany, I still think that greater equality of opportunity is worth pursuing – indeed, I'm hoping next year to co-write a book about 'the 7% problem', i.e. private schools[10] – but I'm keen this time not to forget Young. Peter Hennessy a couple of years ago came up with the apposite phrase 'a well-tempered meritocracy', i.e. as the ideal. And perhaps at some level this diary is my tribute to the rose-growers.

Thursday 25 August

Last night, caught last part – 80 mins onwards, watching at home – of Accrington Stanley v Burnley in the League Cup.

A resonant fixture. Six miles apart – & first competitive encounter since the old Stanley folded near the end of the 1961/2 season. (Then the thirty-year gap until Aldershot, with no other clubs doing the same.) Stanley's demise often attributed to Bob Lord, 'the Burnley butcher', who abused his larger position in football & put the interests of his own club first. And in the post-war history I've been writing, I drop in every now and then the Stanley story between 1945 & that melancholy end – not least the late 1950s episode of how they acquired at great expense a stand from Aldershot (but the military tattoo rather than the football club) that proved a fateful white elephant. So, one way or another, a soft spot for Stanley (symbolic of course of northern industrial decline) – & when the Shots got back in the League in 2008, it was fitting their first match was there (though sadly not the old Peel Park).

Anyway, it was pretty good stuff, & fairly even, with Burnley – regrettably but inevitably – fielding virtually a reserve eleven.

[10] *Engines of Privilege: Britain's Private School Problem*, co-written with Francis Green, was published in February 2019.

Goalless when I turned on, & it was quickly clear that the commentator was reserving particular praise for the Accrington central defender Omar Beckles – who was at Aldershot last season & was voted Player of the Year by the supporters, usually a good sign. I was sorry he left but couldn't begrudge him a move up a division – meritocracy & all that... Close to penalties, still goalless – & then a scramble in the Burnley penalty area, with Beckles intimately involved, before another player neatly drilled it home. Stanley away to West Ham in the next round, so it all seems meant.

Saturday 27 August

Home to North Ferriby United – a team/place I hadn't heard of until the fixture list came out. Turns out to be near Hull, on the other side of the Humber Bridge. Lucy & I couldn't go, but Michael went with a friend. Heard the odd snatch of commentary, but no more. A comfortable enough 2–0 win, taking the Shots to 7th place. 100% record so far at home, but only 1 point out of 9 away. Meanwhile for North Ferriby – including the thirteen away supporters – a long journey home. When I was younger, & the Shots had lost to a team from the industrial North, I would sometimes try to console myself with the thought that it had almost been an act of charity, i.e. cheering up those poor souls in those grim places.

No act of charity more big-hearted than that on a midweek evening in February 1969. Shots, top of the table in the old Division Four, away at Doncaster Rovers, lying second. My last year at school, & we'd been taken to a Shakespeare at the Oxford Playhouse, I think *Romeo and Juliet*. Obviously, I'd brought my transistor radio with me; equally obviously, I sneaked out to the Gents to hear the result – after a news bulletin, at around 10.30, on Radio 2? A bit of a shock as it came through: Doncaster Rovers 7 Aldershot 0. And over the next couple of months, the Shots fairly comfortably failed to get promoted.

Earlier this year, Lucy and I were in Concord, Massachusetts. We visited the Old Manse – home at different times to Emerson & Hawthorne. The guide showing us round was English – my sort of age, or a little younger. We got talking. It transpired that in his youth he'd been a Doncaster fan. And that he'd been there that night at Belle Vue. And that, in his words, 'it could have been more'.

Monday 29 August

A Bank Holiday afternoon spent listening to the Dover v Aldershot commentary on BBC Radio Surrey. It sounded a terrific match. Shots dominant during first half – two up shortly before the interval – Dover pulling one back with last kick – Bromley all over again? – but Shots managing to hold on during the second half & come out 2–1 winners. Sorry not to have gone, but work making it difficult, plus the word from Heather – who sits in the row in front of us & goes to all the away games – was that it's not one of the great venues for an away supporter. Fifth in the table, first time since relegation from the league in 2013 that we've been in one of the play-off places. Genuinely exciting. And my only worry is that if it turns out to be a successful season, this diary may not be a wholly representative document of the archetypal Shots experience. In which case I may have to show Churchillian magnanimity &, yes, accept life over art.

Wednesday 31 August

Two things I spotted in today's *Times*:

1. A lengthy notice about the start tomorrow of the autumn term at King's College School, Wimbledon – one of the oppressively many public (i.e. private) schools near to where I live. All the usual stuff: 'results were again excellent' (55 pupils winning places at Oxbridge; 96% of GCSE grades at A* or A); planning to act as consultant for two schools in China; 'building of the new music school and concert hall is now underway [*sic*]'; and 'our new

classroom building was opened in March by the Rt Hon Nicky Morgan MP, Secretary of State for Education and Minister for Women and Equalities'. Equalities!

2. The increasing prevalence of musical playlists being handed to funeral directors. Frank Sinatra's *My Way* top of these particular pops.

For the record (as it were), & assuming I'm allowed two choices, I'd like: Bob Dylan/'Every Grain of Sand' + Fairport Convention/'Meet on the Ledge'. Forty-seven years ago today, incidentally, I was at the Isle of Wight to see (in a manner of speaking) Dylan, a speck in the distance. As the huge crowd waited impatiently late into the evening for him to come on, one of the Foulk brothers implored, 'Please keep the level of your cool.'[11] Ultimately, it was a disappointing (if underestimated) performance – and, for me, the end of the Sixties, rather than Altamont and the Stones a few months later. The day before, Saturday the 30th, I saw the Shots at home to Newport County – a tame 1–1 draw – & then in the evening went up from my mother/stepfather in Farnborough to go to the ICA and watch for the first time *Don't Look Back*, the Pennebaker documentary about Dylan's 1965 tour of England. A great film, halfway through the Sixties albeit 'the Sixties' barely visible, but in retrospect I wish I'd gone to Les Cousins to see Roy Harper (who did a semi-affectionate take-off of 'Girl from the North Country').[12]

---

[11] Ronnie and Ray Foulk were two of the Festival's three rather improbable organisers, the third being Rikki Farr. But it may have been Farr, who certainly at the following year's IoW Festival acted as compere.

[12] Les Cousins was a folk and blues club in Greek Street, Soho. A double live CD of Harper's performance that evening was released in 1996. The cover reveals that admission was 5 shillings, one-twelfth of the cost of my Isle of Wight ticket.

Bernard flying

Thursday 1 September

More from the press – p. 3 of *The Times* (not my daily paper, but I buy it quite often, mainly in case there's a good obit). Two stories.

Top of the page. Those ten self-possessed Etonians who went to Moscow & got an audience with the Russian monster. 'Guys,' posted one, 'we truly gave Putin a deep impression of us and he responded by showing us his human face.' Aka Putin's useful idiots, as another Russian non-democrat might have put it.[13] The story made me think of August 1968 & the Wellington College school trip I went on to Russia. At the Russian border – a Sunday evening, eight days after that Tommy Mac moment versus Wrexham, coming from Warsaw, where a few of us had seen Legia in action (1–0?) the evening before – we had to get off the train & spend the night at a small station called Terespol. My suitcase was searched by an official. 'Anti-Russian?' he asked, holding up a copy

---

[13] The disparaging term is always attributed to Lenin, though documentary evidence is thin.

of *A Passage to India*. 'No, anti-English,' said the cocky seventeen-year-old, & he sort of smiled. We got to Moscow some twenty-four hours late, on the Tuesday. That day, Russian troops invaded Czechoslovakia. I've always assumed that the hold-up was because the railway network was getting the soldiers to the right places. Two days after that, on the Thursday, we were shown around the Kremlin. We never saw a British paper during our trip – even the *Morning Star* had come out against the invasion – but on returning home I discovered we'd been in the Kremlin the same day as Dubcek, as that poor man was being hauled over the coals. The following year, editing the school magazine, I included a poem about Jan Palach[14] by someone called Gerald Hine-Haycock – first time I've thought about him for years. It included the accusatory line to its readers, 'Because you're sunk in an apathy as deep as a highball'.

Bottom of the page: a social-mobility story, about City discrimination against would-be entrants who come from the wrong side of the tracks – & make that painfully clear by turning up for the job interview wearing brown shoes... It reminded me of the three maxims attributed in the 1960s to a partner (Cedric Barnett) at the well-bred stockbrokers Cazenove & Co. 'Shoes have laces'; 'cars are black'; and, of course, 'jelly is not officer food'. For the last quarter-century or so, my own everyday footwear has been brown. I was in Kingston one day, walking to a shoe shop (right down there with going to the dentist as a favourite occupation), when I suddenly thought of the title of a Frank Zappa number – 'Brown Shoes Don't Make It'. There & then, I decided that for the rest of my life I'd always wear brown shoes – unless, of course, I was going to the City.

Meanwhile, I'm looking forward a lot to Saturday's match. Home to Tranmere Rovers – historically not happy. I think I've been to the fixture four times. In early 1966 the Shots were in the middle of a dreadful run, but with a quarter of an hour to go were one up. The visitors then scored three. In August 1973, I foolishly truncated a holiday to see the opening game of the season, with the Shots having

---

[14] Palach, a young Czech student, died in January 1969 after publicly setting fire to himself in Prague as his protest against the forcible ending of the Prague Spring.

just got promoted from Division Four. A sterile goalless draw. And more recently, a 2–1 Cup defeat &, in spring this year, another goalless draw. Playing for Tranmere in that match was a grey-haired, rather overweight-looking central defender called Steve McNulty. I watched him closely – massively competent and assured, he really knew what he was doing. Anyway, he's still there, &, top of the table, they have so far taken 19 points out of 21 – six wins & a draw. It feels like a big, big encounter. If the Shots could win it, we actually could be contenders. So yes, excited but nervous. Ridiculous really.

Gerald H-H, by the way, once described Dylan's voice to me as like 'sandpaper dipped in honey' (possibly with specific reference to *Blonde on Blonde*?). I've occasionally wondered whether he got it from somewhere else.

Sunday 4 September

Well, an utterly gripping afternoon at the Rec as the rain belted down. Shots off to a flyer with an early goal (nice bit of interplay down the right, then scrambled home) – Shots largely on top over next 20 mins or so – then Tranmere starting to take control (McNulty pulling the strings from the back – 'you big fat bastard' the inevitable chant from the East Bank) – equalising after about half an hour – Shots happy to get to the interval at 1–1 – Tranmere then still on top for next 20 or 25 mins – some desperate defending, though the odd chance created at the other end – Iffy Allen (reserve winger – young, black, quick) coming on as a sub & soon winning a penalty, calmly put away – & then soon after, with about 10 mins to go, Shots clinching it with a genuinely thunderous volley (one of the most thrilling goals I've ever seen) from a central defender, Will Evans.

So, a famous victory against a team that hadn't lost away since last November. The Shots move up a place to 4th. Hope now seems a rational emotion. Of course, of course – I know that Frayn/Cleese line from *Clockwork*.[15] But, with the season

---

[15] 'It's not the despair, I can take the despair. It's the hope I can't stand.'

just about to hit the one-month mark, hope is now the official policy.

This weekend, meanwhile, has two anniversaries. That day of brilliant sunshine in 1939, obviously; but also, marked by various events in and around the City, the 350th anniversary of the Great Fire. My thoughts turn to a rather wacky boy called Thornton, who was with me at prep school in Shrewsbury in the early 1960s. One day during a history lesson, he stuck his hand up & said: 'The best way to remember the date of the Great Fire of London? Dial 999 for fire and turn the numbers the other way up.'

He & I were never particularly friends. But a very old & good friend, Harry Ricketts, over from New Zealand & staying with us, tells the story this morning of how his godmother, who knew Valerie Eliot, went to dinner with the Eliots in about 1959. While Valerie prepared the meal, she had the daunting experience of chatting with him [Tom]. After a bit, he put on the record-player something he had recently acquired – an advance recording of *My Fair Lady*. Eleven or so years later, my first year at Oxford, I went to the music shop on the High Street &, on its first floor, picked up an LP of Eliot reading *Four Quartets* & took it to the counter. The girl looked at it & kindly said, 'You know it's mono?' I seldom play it, but it's one of the last records I'd leave behind if there was a great fire closer to home.

Monday 5 September

Sitting this afternoon on a bench by the Waitrose car park in St Albans[16] – trying to cool down after a long, sweaty walk from the main station – suddenly from the radio in a parked open-roof car came pretty much my all-time favourite pop song: Petula Clark, 'Don't Sleep in the Subway'. Wonderful tune, wonderful chorus, wonderful arrangement/production – but also that nasal

---

[16] Where Laurie and her family were living (and in November 2019 still are, including another child, my granddaughter Larkspur).

delivery & that bit about life being all compromise... Not that I was ever specially keen on her, certainly compared to Dusty or even Sandie. And Dusty's 'I Just Don't Know What to Do with Myself' runs it close – a song I often find myself singing silently as I walk along. I do, incidentally, think that some of the great 60s pop songs were *objectively* better than virtually anything else that followed, i.e. not just a case of that happened to be when I was growing up. Perhaps down to first-mover advantage? – i.e. a generational freshness/release, reacting against those 50s constraints, etc., that could never quite be replicated.

And sort of related: a lengthy obit in today's *Guardian* of Richard Neville. Never my favourite person. Partly because I always assumed that he had a phenomenally successful sex life (one can be wrong in these things – I was spectacularly/painfully so about Nick Drake), partly because the irreducible puritan in me disapproved of the very concept of *Playpower*. 'Life is real! Life is earnest!' said Longfellow – & that's how I always saw it, even if I pretended (sometimes to myself) otherwise, & how I still do.

Talking of play. Highlights are up on Shots website – a full 10 mins – of Saturday's match. I would happily watch many times that winning volley flashing in. But like a party strategist before a by-election, time perhaps for a bit of expectations management... After all, just the thirty-eight games to go.

Thursday 8 September

I like the sound of Howard Colyer's haikus – a para about them by James Campbell in today's *TLS*, & apparently comprising 225 haikus-as-match-reports covering Millwall's last thirteen seasons. A couple of samples: first, home to Wolves in 2014, with the visitors three up:

'We're taking the piss,'
they chant, urged on we score,
once, twice, then again.

And second, after a 2–0 defeat in 2011 at home to Swansea:

'Please stay off the pitch,'
the announcer announces,
the invasion starts.

I have the faintest shadow memory of my father taking me to Millwall when I was about six – not so far from Grove Park, so not wholly implausible – & Millwall winning 5–0, but I've never tried to check it.[17] Much more recently, November 2008, the Shots were away at Millwall in the Cup. I went with George, & my dominant memory is of coming down the stairs at South Bermondsey station, turning a corner & having to walk past a huge phalanx of policemen – unnerving rather than reassuring. The rest of the afternoon stayed oppressive, until at last, after the return journey, getting off the train at London Bridge & merging back into the non-football crowd. The match itself a fairly comprehensive 3–0 defeat, with only the odd flicker to suggest it might be a different story. And I remember thinking during much of it that I'd like to have been time-machined back to the Den in the 1960s, & watching Harry Cripps et al. – at least, anyway, just to have seen what it was like – & realising regretfully that I had of course long ago missed my chance. As indeed with so much else. Trite, I know, but true. Still, a notable anniversary to mark tomorrow – when I *was* there.

Friday 9 September

On this day forty-six years ago. Shots at home to Man Utd in the League Cup. Packed of course – at least 17,000. Man U somewhat on the wane as a team, but Best, Charlton & Law were all there, plus Nobby Stiles. I was between Wellington & Oxford, & about to go to Germany to stay with my grand-father (reading in a German headline about the death of

---

[17] I have now, alas struggling to find a likely match, so shadow indeed.

Hendrix). A friend, James (later Jack) Ozanne, came with me to the match – perhaps his first?[18] Anyway, just after we passed through the turnstiles, I said that he should perhaps keep an eye on his pockets. 'I don't think anyone will be taking this,' he said, plucking out of his jacket pocket a paperback of *A Room of One's Own*.

We stood on the north side, more at the East Bank end and reasonably close to the pitch. If I could watch again 45 minutes of football, it would be those 45 minutes, as the Shots dominated, with wave after wave of attacks towards the High Street end, culminating in a goal shortly before half-time. Richard Walden – right-back, local, my co-favourite (with Jack Howarth), wonderful surging down the right and crossing, not always so good defensively – indeed surged forward, but instead of crossing he powered towards the penalty area & from either just outside or just inside it, with the defence retreating, shot low & hard across Jimmy Rimmer in goal. An ecstatic moment.

Two or three minutes later came the match-turning roll of the dice. A loose bouncing ball, near the part of the touchline I was close to, & a little inside the Shots half. The two balding midfield captains went for it – Bobby Charlton for Man U, Jimmy Melia for the Shots. (Melia, player-manager, was a classic working-class footballer: brought up in the Scotland Road, Liverpool, one of twelve children, played under Shankly & a couple of times for England, before going to Southampton in the mid-60s). It was a completely 50–50 ball – pure chance which way it would break – & it broke Charlton's way. He took it forward a few yards, then swung over a left-foot cross. Somewhere central, perhaps back a bit from the penalty spot, Law rose high & glanced it on to an unmarked Best, who despatched it comfortably. Moments later, the ref (Clive Thomas) blew for half-time.

Predictably, the second half was all United. After about a quarter of an hour, Best was apparently pinned down near the left-side corner flag, with defenders surrounding him. Out of the

[18] Comprehensively wrong, it turns out: he had years before, under his father's tutelage, become a veteran of Highbury and White Hart Lane.

corner of my eye I saw an unmarked Brian Kidd at the far post. It all seemed to take an eternity, but eventually Best wriggled free and crossed, where Kidd – still unmarked – nodded home. The Shots never looked like getting back. And not long before the end, Law sealed it – I have a memory of a tap-in after a parried shot, but maybe because that's so archetypal Law.[19]

A coda came forty-one years later – October 2011 – when the Shots, following wins at home to Carlisle & Rochdale after the Upton Park triumph, were again home to Man U in the League Cup. An exciting occasion of course, but ultimately not much of a match. Lucy, George & Michael all generously stood with me at a spot as near as possible to the 1970 spot. Ferguson – two days after a 6–1 defeat to Man City – fielded a second eleven, but still including Owen & Berbatov, plus Pogba coming on as a sub. An earlyish goal from Berbatov, clinically opening up a static defence – not long before the break, a mishit shot by Owen that the keeper should have stopped – a third soon after the interval. The Shots had the odd moment – an early turn of pace by Danny Hylton leading to a booking for that implacable, take-no-prisoners Serbian central defender whose name I now forget (Vidic, perhaps?)[20] – but the outcome was never seriously in doubt, thoroughly decent effort by the Shots though it was.

Anyway, back to 2016, & it's home to Chester tomorrow. Last season the equivalent fixture was in January, & one of the few really enjoyable home matches. 3–1 to the Shots, a fine goal for Chester by Wayne Rooney's brother John, torrential rain – &, a week or two before his death, the last Shots match watched by Frank Burt, a centurion who in 1927, as a twelve-year-old boy, had cycled to the very first Aldershot match. 1927 to 2016… Almost ninety years, & he went out with a good one.

---

[19] Almost right. 'In the 71st minute,' reported Albert Barham in the *Guardian*, 'Charlton burst through and hit one of his rasping shots on the run. Hollins could not hold it and Law provided the *coup de grâce* with a negligent nod of the head.' For *The Times*'s Geoffrey Green (lushest of football writers), the star of the evening was Best, whose 'powers of comprehension and invention were at last unfurled [after a poor run of form] as he broke loose in his full poetic flow'.
[20] Yes, Nemanja Vidic.

I should probably add that a few weeks later last season, the Shots went on a Tuesday evening to Chester for the rearranged return. After a quarter of an hour, I checked the score on the computer. 2–0 to Chester. We were watching something, but after about 5 or 10 minutes I thought I'd better see that it wasn't going to be a rout. 2–1, so that was OK. Then got absorbed in whatever it was (a *West Wing* episode?), but thought to check again at half-time. 6–1. Listened to some of Radio Surrey's black-humour second-half commentary, & it finished 8–2. Heaviest Shots defeat I could remember. And Chester had scored precious few goals before, would score precious few goals later. So I guess that gives tomorrow a bit of 'previous', but in truth this season already feels so different from last that it doesn't really matter.

Sunday 11 September

A resonant date. Fifteen years ago now. A truly awful event, of course, with momentous, ill-conceived consequences, but I've occasionally thought that its perpetrators never quite got the credit – if that's the right word, which in some moral sense it clearly isn't – for the sheer audacity of execution of what they did. Rather like, in a more minor key, Murdoch's Wapping coup in 1986 – cynical, deceitful, etc., but quite something to pull it off. I am not – repeat not – seeking to justify 9/11, however much one does feel at odd moments, e.g. flicking through the TV Cable channels, that the West has it coming (as the *New Statesman* under Peter Wilby bravely if ill-advisedly put it at the time); while, as for Wapping, the experience at around that time of writing the *FT*'s history did make me not unsympathetic to the management perspective vis-à-vis the print unions. And out of Wapping came of course the *Independent* – in its prime a fine paper, until that long, slow death begun by ... Murdoch. And now he's married to someone who lived for so long with a street-fighting man.

Anyway, on this sunny Sunday morning, with a brief, unexpected heatwave predicted, I'm sitting in Bingsoo – a newish Korean café in New Malden High Street. It's the name I love, but

I quite like the café itself too. Some exotic-looking cakes, etc., but so far I've been conservative – the odd panini, & today a slice of carrot cake with my coffee. NM of course is the great European centre for Koreans – over 20,000 living here, generating plenty of restaurants, shops, etc., which is a major plus. A few years ago, when Lucy & I were in Paris, and around 1.30 or perhaps later left a museum & felt very hungry, we spotted a Korean restaurant & went in. Were they still serving lunch? Reluctant noises were made. I played my only – but trump – card, viz. that we were from New Malden. And everything changed.

Well, I guess all this is to delay recording the inconvenient fact that yesterday, after the previous Saturday's richly flavoursome match, was vin ordinaire. A goalless draw – not the worst of its kind, but even so... And that, if either side deserved to win, it was undoubtedly Chester – on top in the first half, including a thunderous strike against the woodwork. Shots picked up in second half, missed a good early chance & generally had the edge, though not the cutting-edge. So, down two places in the table, to 6th, 4 points behind the new leaders, Lincoln City, with both Tranmere and Forest Green losing.

All that said, it still felt good. The seats around us significantly more crowded – I sat next to a nice, knowledgeable guy in his late thirties who now lives in Camberley but who grew up in New Malden, going to the same primary schools as our children – & the mood positive, even when mistakes were made. In short, that continuing collective sense of travelling hopefully.

Plus the programme – which is excellent & actually worth the £3 – had a couple of nice bits. One was a piece by Matt Badcock, of the weekly *Non-League Paper* (which I don't read but am thinking I should), that touched on his irritation with the patronising coverage when FA Cup First Round day comes around. '"Oh look, the postman managed to score from outside the box, round of applause everyone." It grinds my gears.' Quite apart from the justifiable sentiment, what a phrase... & one I hadn't come across before. The other bit was in Jack Rollin's regular historical column. I've long had mixed feelings about him. A veteran football writer/ statistician/editor – clearly a thoroughly decent person – & a very long-standing Shots allegiance. The problem is that his words only seldom come off the page, to my mind anyway, & indeed I usually skip his column, not least because it often doesn't touch on the Shots. But this one had a fascinating few paras about the story – completely new to me – of Borough United of the Welsh League North. The product of a merger between two bust clubs – Llandudno Junction and Conwy Borough – they won the Welsh Cup in 1963 (defeating Newport County of the Football League Division Four); then, in the following season's European Cup Winners' Cup, defeated a Maltese team before going out to Slovan Bratislava; but by the late 1960s were reduced to playing in the Conwy and District League & soon folded. I've always found myself very drawn to those clubs which flicker briefly & then are gone. Thames, New Brighton, Middlesbrough Ironopolis – those are my three favourites. And didn't the twelve founder-members of the Football League include Darwen as well as Accrington Stanley?[21] I guess I should be grateful that the Shots, in one form or another, look like embracing my lifetime.

Monday 12 September

I watched quite a lot of Premiership football over the w/end, courtesy BBC/Sky. Some of it exciting, though moments of really caring only sporadic. Highlights of Man U/Man City on Saturday showed near the end – with United 2–1 down – a rather haunting shot of Ferguson, looking deeply fed up, even disenchanted. Because of the score? Because of Mourinho's tactics? Because he was no longer running the show? Impossible to tell. After United won that dramatic treble in 1999 – the European final on the day that we moved into our current house, with George & I watching those closing minutes as we sat on packing cases – my fantasy was that he would leave United, where he could hardly top what he'd achieved, & go to a small, deserving club (not necessarily Aldershot). Somehow I doubt it was ever a serious possibility.

---

[21] Close but no cigar: Darwen not a founder-member in 1888, but did join three years later.

Shots away at Boreham Wood tomorrow evening, & planning to go. I've never been there – place as well as ground – though the place takes up a couple of pages of my 1950s history, *Family Britain*. Essentially it was one of the rather drab LCC out-county estates built soon after the war, in Borehamwood's case (two words or one?)[22] largely housing skilled working class from London. I plunder the diary of Cyril Dunn, a rather puritanical *Observer* journalist who lived there for a while, believed strongly in 'community' but didn't particularly like people – working-class people anyway. 'I am not at all convinced that the Estate people *want* an organized community life,' he reflected disappointedly – & disapprovingly – at one point. I borrowed the diary from his son, Peter Dunn, also an *Observer* journalist, but a much nicer man – who, sadly, died a few years ago. He & his wife lived in Dorset, near Bridport, & they gave me quite a lot of info, largely negative, about Kenneth Allsop – a star of *Tonight* when it was absolutely my favourite TV programme & a rather glamorous semi-literary, semi-intellectual figure, if ultimately perhaps someone for whom life soured. I associate *Tonight* especially with when I was about seven or eight: living in 'Chip Chase' in Headley Down – my parents still together – & all that… Just starting to get some sense of the world at large, through the eyes of unflappable, young-uncle-like Cliff Michelmore, suave Alan Whicker, grumpy Fyfe Robertson & those singers I liked so much – Cy Grant, Robin Hall, Jimmie MacGregor. The BBC when it was really the BBC. Life seemed simpler then – but maybe just because I was a child who, by & large, felt happy & secure.

Tuesday 13 September

On the face of it, a rather ho-hum performance & ho-hum result this evening. One apiece, with both goals (Shots equalising) coming midway through the second half, & taking the game as a whole Boreham Wood would have been the more deserving winners – though Shots a shade unlucky not to steal it at the death. But

[22] Definitive ruling: one word for the town, two for the club.

getting back home, & watching Waddock's post-match interview on the Shots website, it all seemed rather less ho-hum, because there's clearly been a bug passing through the team. 'Iffy's on the toilet now,' he said – & given that Iffy Allen was perhaps the Shots' best player, taking on opponents & making things happen down the left wing, that was doubly eloquent. There were several other Vanarama draws this evening, so no one's got away & the Shots remain 6th, still 4 points behind Lincoln.

What really made the evening was less the football – though it was quite compelling in a full-bodied sort of way – than a mixture of the weather (the end of an astonishingly hot day, apparently the hottest September day since 1911, when Asquith & Lloyd George were engaged in protracted guerrilla warfare with the House of Lords) & the company, viz.: Lucy & all three 'children' & Laurie's husband, Graham, & a publishing friend, Nick Humphrey, who supports Macclesfield & seems to enjoy coming along to the odd new non-league ground in southern England. The seven of us all sat in a row, & it was a good feeling. A less good vibe came from a group of Aldershot fans. Targeted abuse of one of the home players, plus constant chants of 'You're fucking shit' directed at the Boreham Wood team & supporters generally: thoroughly witless, thoroughly unpleasant &, as Lucy says, it makes one feel a bit less good about being one of the red-and-blue army.

I guess this is all sounding a bit Cyril Dunn. The walk from the station, incidentally, did provide a glimpse of the old out-county estate, with some of those 50s houses, never that wonderful in the first place but blessedly possessed of hot & cold running water & indoor lavs, now looking distinctly the worse for wear. I'd like to have had a proper look round, but it wasn't possible. Still, I'll be surprised if both teams aren't in the Conference (as I continue to think of it) again next season – so perhaps another chance, DV.

Wednesday 14 September

Boreham Wood's player being targeted was their right-winger, the home player regularly nearest during the first half to the away section. He was black. Was that a coincidence? The more I've thought about it, the more uncomfortable I've felt. Of course over the years I've heard a lot of foul-mouthed stuff at football matches, but at the age of sixty-five do I really want to go on hearing it? More importantly, we're living in a world in 2016 that has become very frightening – more frightening than I can remember. For whatever mixture of reasons, nationalism & intolerance really are on the march – think of Trump, think of Russia, think of Eastern Europe, think of France, think (I'm afraid) of Germany & yes, think of here & Brexit. Most of the very worst things that have happened in the world in the last century & a half – & arguably they've been worse things than ever happened before – have been because of nationalism. A minimum degree of liberalism & tolerance – of, in essence, European enlightenment values – are not just luxuries, they are absolutely indispensable if the horrors are not to return.

George (about to return to the States) & I talked about it this evening. He remembered Orwell's 1945 essay about football as war without the guns (or whatever the exact phrase was) & how, for *Austerity Britain*, I'd found a reader of that *Tribune* essay who the following week had criticised him for his ignorance about what football crowds were really like & had concluded that Orwell hadn't had much fun in his life.[23] For myself, I used to think that football foul-mouthery served an unattractive but not unhelpful escape-valve purpose. Now I'm not so sure. It kind of gives a licence – rather like the spike in hate crimes following the Referendum result – & who knows where that licence might go? I didn't think about the possibility at the time, but if I had,

---

[23] What Orwell actually wrote was: 'Serious sport has nothing to do with fair play. It is bound up with hatred, jealousy, boastfulness, disregard of all rules and sadistic pleasure in witnessing violence: in other words it is war minus the shooting.' And obviously he's not completely wrong, to put it mildly. Yet earlier this year (July 2019), a memorable counterpoint occurred at Lord's as cricket's World Cup Final moved to its unbelievably nail-biting climax: England's Ben Stokes clubbed the ball high towards the Warner Stand and New Zealand's Trent Boult took what seemed a fine catch – only for his nearest colleague, Martin Guptill, immediately to signal a six, realising that Boult had stepped, if only for a nanosecond, on the boundary line. In short, a wonderful and instinctive act of sportsmanship – but more likely, I'd accept, to happen in cricket than football.

would I have had the guts to go over to the yobs & ask them to desist? Almost certainly not. Alternatively, write to the Aldershot chairman? (Shahid Azeem, a good man I'm sure.) Maybe. Or even submit a piece to the next match-day programme? Perhaps unlikely, for a mixture of reasons I'd probably rather not explore.[24]

I appreciate that I may be in mountain & molehill territory, but the whole thing is troubling. I realise – of course – that the starting-point of realism about society is that not everyone plays together nicely. Also that tribalism runs deep in our natures, that everyone is a daily jostling mixture of good & bad instincts, & that the notion of someone having not a jot of racism in their bones is for the fairies. But to give those bad instincts free play? To allow football grounds to be places where vile abuse, impossible to be expressed in any other public place, can be shouted & chanted with impunity? I appreciate the quasi-impossibility of knowing where exactly to draw the line – & that many other people have unsuccessfully wrestled with the issue. But sometimes there are evils that are not necessary evils.

Friday 16 September

Away at Southport tomorrow. Between 1968 & 1970 my father and stepmother lived about six miles away – in Freshfield, near Formby, where I'd be for part of school holidays. Deep in adolescence – summer '68 when I properly became aware of Dylan & Cohen (in both cases through CBS's *The Rock Machine Turns You On* – 15 shillings I think, & a record I'd love to still have a copy of) – & long moody walks along the beach, having walked through the wood where – reputedly – red squirrels lived. Freshfield was where I was on moon-walking day – grumpily getting up to watch it on TV, at my father's (correct) insistence. Liverpool in one direction on the railway line, Southport in the other – & I went to the odd Fourth Division match at Haig Avenue (starring the bustling,

---

[24] In retrospect I suppose I should have spoken to a steward, but somehow it didn't occur to me.

37

bulky Eric Redrobe up front for Southport), though never saw the Shots there. I remember walking from the ground one evening & feeling a strong stab of envy for a friend, Pete Bevington, who I knew was at the Festival Hall at that very moment listening to Pink Floyd – April '69 I'm sure.[25] Southport's also where I bought *Bringing It All Back Home*, saw on the big screen *2001* (only later discovering why Hal is called Hal – 'H' before 'I', 'A' before 'B', 'L' before 'M') – & that's about it. Never, in any sub-Proustian sense, one of my 'places'. For the first time since 1970, I went back a few years ago, & it generally struck me as a bit dispiriting, English-seaside tawdry.

Southport themselves have been out of the League for what feels like a long time, though maybe I blinked at the wrong moment & they were briefly back?[26] This season they're struggling, have already sacked the manager & in theory are ripe for the taking. An authentic top-five team would go there, win clinically 2–0 (one in each half) & barely break sweat. I'm pretty sure the Shots aren't that sort of team. For a nanosecond, Lucy & I have thought of making the trip tomorrow, but workwise apart from anything else it's not really realistic. And I sort of feel, after Tuesday's mixed emotions, that I could do with a break anyway.

Saturday 17 September

A last-minute decision to go on this afternoon's pro-refugees march in London – partly to keep Lucy company, partly also coming out of Tuesday plus that growing feeling/realisation that some critical mass has been reached this year that seriously threatens conventional assumptions of tolerance, diversity & liberal democracy. We got to Green Park tube & walked up towards Hyde Park Corner, from where the march was just starting. As it came past us, we waited on the pavement scrutinising faces – surely

[25]   Correct, 14 April 1969, with the score (I remember nothing about the match) Southport 1 Luton Town 1.
[26]   They weren't. After failing to get re-election to the Football League in 1978 (still the era before automatic relegation), Southport have been non-League ever since.

there'd be a friend we could join – & there was. So we stepped in line with Julian, a good feeling. Lucy's been on marches before, including Iraq '03, but for me – I must now unavoidably admit it – it was my first march. Always held back, I guess, by a mixture of nervousness & dislike of group activities, plus somehow not wanting to be pigeonholed – & have always felt vaguely guilty. Anyway, as with every loss of virginity, a mild sense of triumph as we made fairly stately progress down Piccadilly. But in all honesty I only half enjoyed it – a certain sense of claustrophobia – & those moments when the march suddenly stopped, for no apparent reason, well, it was too much for comfort like that bit in Eliot about the tube train stopping between stations & that mixture of vacancy and anxiety on the part of the passengers. Throughout the hour or so, before I peeled off at Trafalgar Square (Lucy kept going until Parliament Square & the speeches – including one by Vanessa Redgrave, so prominently emblematic in those early 60s CND demos) & headed home, I kept looking out for UKIP or UKIP-type counter-demonstrations, but there didn't seem to be any. And of course, thinking later about their absence, the reason is depressingly simple: they've already won. 'We've lost our country,' Paddy Ashdown says (or words to that effect) in today's *Guardian*, & he's right. Impossible I know to write all this & not sound intolerably sanctimonious-cum-arrogant. And I'm reminded how, though listening endlessly to Dylan, I could never really take Pete Seeger or Tom Paxton or even Woody Guthrie – admirable though of course their sentiments invariably were. But really, what's the alternative?

I was back in time for most of the second half at Southport – no longer called Haig Avenue, but instead Merseyrail Community Stadium. I struggled to get Radio Surrey commentary, so followed it – a tantalising mixture of text updates on the screen plus odd snatches of commentary – on what seemed like a very local radio station – I couldn't quite work it out. The pattern of the match rather similar to Boreham Wood. No goals in the first half – Southport taking the lead – Shots equalising (Will Evans, rapidly becoming my favourite, apparently storming into the penalty area & smashing home a cross) – one all at full time. Waddock gave a critical post-match interview, in effect accusing the team of not being brave enough to play the sort of pressing, creative football he believes in, & the Shots down (I think) to 7th in the table, with Dagenham & Redbridge the new leaders.

Wednesday 21 September

Voting closes today for Labour leadership election – incumbent Corbyn versus challenger Smith. 'Registered supporters', paying £25 each, able to vote. I registered, & voted for Smith. The near certainty is that he will lose – & lose heavily.

The extraordinary turn of events in Labour since last year's general election has generally been on my mind a lot, & at times I've felt very conflicted. At odd moments I've travelled hopefully with Corbyn, though not all that often since his Conference speech a year ago. I made a point of watching it live & thought it was dreadful – less because of the delivery (poor though it was) & lack of structure, more because it seemed so intellectually barren. Here was a man who'd been on the backbenches for over thirty years – had very much ploughed his own furrow, especially of course during the New Labour period – had utterly unexpectedly become leader – was now addressing the nation as well as his party – & had nothing interesting to say, no coherent structure of the polity/economy/society he hoped to bring into being, but instead just an ill-assorted collection of platitudes.

That said, I've belatedly come to realise that Corbyn himself – good leader, bad leader, whatever – is not the issue. Ultimately, it's down to beliefs. Corbyn, McDonnell & those around them, plus probably most of the new members, plus almost all of Momentum, in essence believe in pure-milk socialism (in McDonnell's case with a strong Marxist strain), i.e. out-&-out egalitarian/anti-capitalist, sceptical of liberalism (? even antagonistic), wanting to take control of the economy's commanding heights & perhaps not believing in the primacy of the democratic parliamentary process (? how else to explain a leader staying on when three-quarters of his MPs explicitly no longer have confidence in him).

Those are not my beliefs – they once were, as expressed in my first book, *King Labour*, published forty years ago next week – but no longer – & presumably that's the case with many of the 172 no-confidence MPs, many pre-2015 Labour members & a huge swathe of non-Tory voters.

Or put it this way. For much of its life, Labour has been the pantomime donkey – two ill-fitting parts, uneasily spatchcocked together through too much fudge & mudge. Of course I appreciate the inexorable logic of the first-past-the-post electoral system (cogently explained, as ever, by Polly Toynbee in yesterday's *Guardian*), but I still think that we would all be healthier & happier if there was a split – if not now, when? And it doesn't really matter which of the two groups/parties is called 'Labour'. What matters is intellectual honesty. Not least because a new party explicitly of the centre-left that believes in a reformed capitalism – which is essentially where I am – needs to do some really hard mental graft (never really done I'm afraid by Miliband/Balls in the 2010–15 period, admiring though in some ways I am of them) if it is to work out & then explain what it means by those two crucial words. I also think a new centre-left party has to have a degree of realism in its social liberalism – in particular, less aggressively/intolerantly certain of the moral certainties of its beliefs. Yes, 'you're fucking shit' chanted at a black footballer is outright wrong & should be stopped, forcibly if necessary. But at the same time, more understanding & less condemnation, as someone once said.[27] It's difficult, it really is. Yet ultimately, if confronted by having it one way or the other, I would accept the necessity of managed immigration from *all* parts of the world. We have to go with the grain of human nature – or at the least, not pretend that that grain doesn't exist, however unattractive (including at times your nature & my nature) it may be.

[27] Which is what I believe, though of course the quote I had in mind is the other way round (whether a cock-up on my part or an exercise in irony I can't recall now). Namely: 'Society needs to condemn a little more and understand a little less.' I was right in remembering that it was said shortly after the murder of James Bulger in early 1993, but wrong in mentally attributing it to Tony Blair, shadow Home Secretary. Instead, the 'someone' was the PM of the day, John Major.

Thursday 22 September

Stanley lost 1–0 at West Ham (the 'London Stadium') yesterday evening. Stout resistance for 96 minutes, then at the very death a predictably brilliant free kick by Dimitri Payet. And in the Sky commentary on Northampton/Man U, a slightly unnerving moment with an out-of-the-blue mention – in the context of past Cobblers' financial struggles – of the Shots' demise in 1992.

Home to Gateshead on Saturday, though we won't be going (looking after little Wolfie). I think I've seen the last three equivalent fixtures – & I think in all three, certainly the last two, Gateshead came from behind to win 2–1, so maybe our absence will bring a change of fortune. One of the matches is seared on my memory. Midweek in March – going with Michael – Shots not much above the drop zone – Shots one up earlyish in the second half & playing well – robust challenge by Shots striker Brett Williams on Gateshead player (one J. J. O'Donnell) near the touchline & close to where we were – O'D goes down like the proverbial ton of bricks & lies motionless in near-terminal crumpled heap – red card to Williams – O'D winks at Gateshead trainer attending to him – O'D miraculously gets up, stands by touchline, is waved back on, races across to other side of pitch – within minutes 'the Head' have scored twice... I felt truly indignant for the rest of the evening & the next two days, even contemplated a letter to the Gateshead chairman, who'd written a nice piece in the programme about how he used to watch the Shots back in the Sixties. While Michael, far more balanced & level-headed than me, had a rather good humorous riff about taking O'D aside & saying to him – half stern, half avuncular – 'Now JJ, this really isn't the way to behave, you know, what would your mother think?' & so on. The obvious question was/is whether I'd have been so aerated if it'd been an Aldershot player – as by definition it just as easily might have been – successfully indulging in the same gamesmanship-cum-cheating. I like to think I'd have been at least mildly ashamed – but agitated? Probably not. The episode, incidentally, has a tailpiece. Not that long afterwards, O'Donnell suffered some

rare but serious foot injury, jeopardising his whole career – &
I've an idea he still hasn't played since.

Monday 26 September

Behind with this diary – a mixture of looking after a two-&-a-
half-year-old boy (a sweet child, but still a two-&-a-half-year-old
boy) plus in odd interstices trying to get on a little with the final
chapter of my book (a history of the Bank of England).[28]
Well, Corbyn won on Saturday with an increased majority.
At odd moments I find myself wondering whether I'm missing
something, whether perhaps after all this is the start of something
big & rather amazing & I just need to subdue my qualms & go
along with it. But on the whole the phrase 'it's no joke' comes
increasingly to mind (the title perhaps of a Bowie song? on *Scary
Monsters?*). I've only had the chance to speed-read it, & I don't
have the paper with me (am on a train from St Albans that's just
stopped at Elstree & Borehamwood), but today's *Guardian* has a
letter from a fellow-historian (I didn't recognise the name & now
forget it) to the effect, I think, that it's time for the centre-left to
get real: this is something potentially sinister. And that's broadly
what I feel – but tbc another day.
The Shots also won on Saturday. 3–0, all in the second half,
with apparently a rather spectacular goal – & even more so celebration – by Iffy Allen, who seems to be really coming through.[29]
Everyone else near the top won, so the Shots stay in 7th, 5 points
behind the leaders Dagenham & Redbridge. And it's now seven
games unbeaten. I'm still comfortable with my pre-season prediction (8th), but a side that only concedes once in six games at home
is doing OK.
A quick aside on the Premiership. My tip, Spurs, doing fine at
2nd, but already it looks hard to see anyone catching Man City,

[28] *Till Time's Last Sand: A History of the Bank of England, 1694–2013* was published
almost exactly a year later, in September 2017.
[29] Not so in the event. He would fade during the autumn and be released shortly before
Christmas.

who look a fairly complete team. I admit to some schadenfreude in observing West Ham's misfortunes. Partly because I don't care for the people who run the club, partly because I hate it when clubs leave their grounds (& I imagine in this case it's particularly miserable for a lot of traditional supporters) & partly because they still went ahead & did it even in the knowledge that it would probably kill Leyton Orient.[30] The people's game: in so many ways, & so sadly, it no longer is.

P.S. It's Robert Crowcroft of Edinburgh University. And the passage that struck me reads: 'Moderates should not unite with people who back Britain's enemies abroad and who pursue a style of politics at home that is little more than malice in the guise of virtue. To fixate on unity is a reflection of the same cultural problems that have landed Labour in its current mess: a historical, pathological, and increasingly pathetic fixation with betrayal.'

Tuesday 27 September

Woke up at 2.30 last night, & it was that familiar feeling of needing to go downstairs, turn on the TV & see what was happening. Except this time it wasn't an Ashes contest down under, but the first Clinton/Trump debate.

It was about half an hour in, & Trump explaining (or something) why he'd failed to file his tax returns. Immediate disconcerting impression: for a significantly overweight seventy-year-old man, he looked distinctly youthful, energetic, etc. – more so than she did. I watched the final hour. Clinton predictably articulate, well organised, etc., but only semi-successful when she essayed the odd popular, quasi-demagogic touch. She's head girl really: ultimately a considerable strength – she'd be a pretty good President, I'm sure – but in the 2016 mood a serious problem for her. And Trump? He's quick & intelligent of course, but in the end a coarse huckster who when it comes to it only believes in one

---

[30] It didn't (the two clubs eventually reached a settlement), but it was still hardly a friendly act for a big club to move so close (just over two miles) to a much smaller club.

thing: himself, the non-self-made son of a property man who was once the attacked subject of a Woody Guthrie song. (Is it possible that Dylan will come out & say something anti-Trump before 8 November? He truly ought to, but I doubt he will.) I loathe Trump, from his name downwards. A bully, a braggart, a liar, who has probably never read a novel and quite likely feels no empathy for anyone outside his immediate family. I suspect I'm repeating myself, but never mind. Predictably, watching him, I became convinced he was going to win. Essentially I'm a pessimist – it's much the same when I watch Aldershot – the opposition is bound to have something up its sleeve which we can't counter. It was a relief to discover after the debate that, if either had 'won', it was Clinton. That at least seems to be the conventional wisdom. Until a few weeks ago I'd always assumed that she'd smash him in the debates, but even after last night I'm now far less sure. Am likely to be away on holiday for the next debate – a relief.

I wish inevitably, & this applies to British elections too, that the 'debates' had a quite different format. Why not instead a conversation around a table – with a moderator, yes – but essentially an exploration of values & beliefs rather than prepared set-piece statements about a ragbag of headline 'issues'. I've sometimes fantasised about being the UK moderator, really trying to dig down into *why* & *how* politicians about to assume/reassume 'power' have formed their particular view of the world. It ain't ever going to happen of course – for a thousand/million reasons – but it's one of my more persistent fantasies.

Wednesday 28 September

I feel I should briefly record Allardyce's inglorious demise as England manager. Some mixture I guess of greed/hubris/carelessness. 'Money Changes Everything', Cyndi Lauper once sang, & she was right. Those amounts of money sloshing around at the top end of football are obscene – a much overused word, but really no alternative. I don't want to harp on (& I certainly don't claim for myself any superior financial morality), but the lack of money at the bottom end is surely crucial to making it something one can sign up to, & emotionally embrace, in a kind of way that now seems almost impossible (the odd Leicester-style miracle apart) at the other end.

Thursday 29 September

The Silkmen [Macclesfield Town] winning the other evening = Shots now actually 8th.

Corbyn, Corbyn, Corbyn. Doubts refusing to be stilled about whether I've got it completely wrong. A decent speech yesterday to close Labour's Party Conference – plenty of things in it I'd gladly 'sign up to' – talk of the membership rising to a million. Just at moments I feel rather like T. Fenning Dodworth, hero/anti-hero of a particularly enjoyable Beerbohm story. He is, if I remember rightly, a sententious-cum-portentous political bore who in the pre-1914 period writes sententious-cum-portentous leading articles about the party political scene. He knows everyone, haunts the clubs of Pall Mall & St James's, never doubts his superior knowledge/wisdom. But things change after the war. New men, the rise of Labour, suddenly a rather different political world. And he finds it hard to adjust... But of course, when it comes to it, I don't *think* I'm wrong. Paul Mason, one of the most influential Corbynistas, had a piece in the *Guardian* this week, to the effect that Labour's huge shift leftwards went with the tide of history. 'History!' I found myself wanting to scream. And essentially to say, 'Look, a belief in out-&-out socialism may or may not be a defensible position in the early twenty-first century, but it is only *possible* to adopt it if one has a full knowledge of the consequences of that belief in the twentieth century.' Of course Mason, an intelligent man, knows that grim stuff (I have to assume he does), but do Momentum's youthful followers? I'd guess not – & they should.

Reading this through, I feel a dispiriting mixture of old & impotent – not to mention 'preachy', as Woody Allen puts it early in *Manhattan*. Never mind.

Friday 30 September

Fortieth anniversary today of the publication of my first book – *King Labour: The British Working Class, 1850–1914*. I finished writing it in the autumn of 1975 while living in a Yorkshire village (Elvington, six miles or so from York). And some time that winter, after I'd posted back the proofs & was walking back to the house, I distinctly remember saying to myself, 'Well, that was a young person's book.'

It was, I guess. Strongly influenced by E. P. Thompson's overwhelming biog, its hero was William Morris, its villains were the Fabians (above all the Webbs). Why Morris? Partly because the socialism he espoused was one of the heart & of conviction – as opposed to socialism as expressed through top-down institutional mechanics/processes. ('Your way is wrong, but your way will win in the end,' Morris apparently said to Sidney Webb at one point not long before Morris's death in 1896). But partly also because Morris was – like Pugin, Carlyle & Ruskin before him – reacting so strongly (politically/morally/aesthetically) against Victorian materialism & the ugly dehumanising excesses of industrialism, & that spoke to me strongly. Of course, what really underlay the book was a kind of romantic frustration with the lack of a revolution in mid-1970s Britain – we often talked about the 'R' word... Yet even then, I'm sure looking back, I was conflicted – mainly because I think it was in 1974, certainly around then, that I read Gunter Grass's *From the Diary of a Snail* – in which he extolled, in a way that I know I responded to positively, the virtues of patient, small-scale, 'dogged does it' (a phrase from Trollope, not Grass) incrementalism. And even researching/writing *King Labour*, I recall quite well how I started to grasp that that much criticised 'labourism' – e.g. on the part of the unions – had its definite merits. So in sum, yes, I was mixed up.

As it happens, we're in Yorkshire this evening – partly to collect (& then scatter tomorrow morning) the ashes (or half of them anyway) of Lucy's godmother, partly to see the Shots at Bootham Crescent tomorrow afternoon. I've always had a bit of a soft spot for York City. In 1958/9, my first football season, I was entranced by the progress of Norwich City (Third Division) to the semi-finals of the Cup; & quite likely it was then that I discovered that about five years earlier another team from the Third Division (in fact, Third Division North) had done the same – & that York's main goalscorer on that epic run had been Arthur Bottom, which of course amused a seven-year-old boy. In my year or so at Elvington, where I was reliant on a fairly minimal bus service, I only got to see York once – in the League Cup at home to Liverpool, probably Sept 1975, with the visitors winning comfortably enough, albeit only 1–0. My main memory is of thunder rumbling around the ground for much of the match – & of no one, me not quite included, seeming too worried.

I'm moderately optimistic. York have just come down from the League & have been struggling somewhat. Playing upfront for them has been Richard Brodie, an experienced non-league operator who spent much of last season at the Shots – scoring goals early on, but then completely & painfully drying up, becoming the object of some derision & scorn. He didn't help himself – in my eyes anyway – by his often self-pitying-cum-antagonistic attitude towards referees, who every match seemed to get frequent, largely unjustified earfuls & gestures. If he plays tomorrow, I'll be curious to watch him – while of course dreading that he scores an 87th-minute winner.

Gary upbeat

Sunday 2 October

Driving – or, to be exact, being driven by Lucy – around North Yorkshire on Friday & yesterday brought back playing for Elvington in the 1975/6 season. York & District League, Division Five (the bottom one). We won our first match – away at Market Weighton (or was it Wheldrake? I think Market Weighton), 2–0, with me scoring both – but then barely another, with some pulverising defeats. At one point, on the A64 on the way to Malton, there was a signpost to Westow – a village where we crashed 13–2. At another point, we went past York Racecourse, where on a near-frozen pitch against I forget whom & when one of our players (I'll forbear naming him) refused to play saying it was too dangerous, we lost 15–1 (the one was made by me & crisply finished by a guy in the village who'd become a friend, Steve Pizzey). But most evocative was seeing a signpost to Slingsby, a village near Castle Howard. When we came to play them, away in February, we were next to bottom & they were bottom, still no wins &

with goal difference even more chasm-like than ours. It was a wonderful, memorable afternoon – partly the ding-dong match itself, on a cramped village pitch, partly the enthusiasm of their dogged supporters – & although we lost 3–2 somehow I really didn't mind. About a month later saw the return at Elvington, this time with me in goal. 4–4, with the home custodian at fault for at least one, & again a terrific, chaotic contest. I remember once reading CMJ [Christopher Martin-Jenkins] – about cricket, but surely applicable to football – to the effect that, whether as a team or an individual, it really doesn't matter what the level is, what matters is that all concerned are at roughly the same level. And how I would now rewind the clock to those Slingsby afternoons, especially the first one.

And so to Bootham Crescent. It's pretty central in York, has plenty of character and rundown charm, & of course is going to go in the next year or two. It makes me so cross. And will of course be replaced by some soulless affair, I expect near the outer ring road.[31] It's such a shame – having a pee in the cave-like Gents in the away corner, where the arrangements clearly haven't changed since the ground opened in 1932 (except, perhaps, for the addition of the odd washbasin), felt particularly a moment to savour. The match itself a reasonably rumbustious affair (praise, not criticism), & the Shots won with a first-half goal, calmly scored by Mensah in a one-on-one. The last 10 minutes fairly hairy, & after the referee blew for time a lovely moment as Jake Gallagher led the exultant charge towards our corner. He is, as I've said before, the team's heartbeat – plays with all the rugged enthusiasm he would have had in the playground as a boy – & generally they seem a happy bunch, who don't seem to grumble about each other when things don't come off (which at this level they usually don't). And Brodie? He came on as a sub midway through the second half ('You'll need your earmuffs, ref,' called out someone near me), came close to scoring, & in about the 87th

---

[31]   In the event, it looks as if it'll be in 2020 that the football club moves to the newly built York Community Stadium, to be shared with York's rugby league club. It's sited in Huntington, almost three miles from the city centre.

minute got booked – for complaining too vehemently after a decision went against him. A detail in the York programme pleased me – the pages showing who sponsors the players' kits. The name of the anonymous sponsor for a couple of the team? 'The one and only Arthur Bottom'.

For the Shots it's now eight undefeated. We're staying in a b&b in Nottinghamshire – I'm writing this first thing on Sunday – & I haven't been able to see the table, but surely up a place or two? Next up, though, is a severe test. Home to Forest Green Rovers on Tuesday evening. I'm hoping that a friend, Andy Ward, will be coming along. Unlike me, he's a *real* football person. His father, Tim, played for England & later became a manager, including at Derby just before Brian Clough. He doesn't narrowly support a single team, but has soft spots for clubs that have been at different times part of his life. One of them is Barnsley, where his father was manager through much of the 1950s & about which era Andy & an old friend of mine, Ian Alister, wrote a truly pioneering book (*Barnsley: A Study in Football*) back in the early 1980s. To a remarkable degree, Andy combines in his approach to the game knowledge, sympathy, humour & objectivity. All these qualities are there in his football writings over the years. His current soft spot is for Forest Green, because he lives near by in Stroud, & last season in the equivalent fixture, which FGR won quite comfortably, it was touching how much he wanted the Shots to make a better fist of it. This Tuesday should be a real contest, & I wouldn't – to revert to my own nakedly partisan concerns – be that unhappy with a draw.

Wednesday 5 October

In the autumn of 1972, first term of my last year at Oxford, I edited the arts pages of the university magazine *Isis*. I commissioned my friend Pete McQuay to review the new John & Yoko album, *Some Time in New York City*. His first sentence has always stuck in my mind: 'A pretty savage disappointment.' And that pretty much sums up last night.

I'd spent the day really looking forward to the match. A nice crisp autumn evening – pitch in excellent condition – very happy to be there with Lucy & Andy – & then the slow-motion car crash… I can't quite bring myself to give a detailed account, but in essence here goes.

Forest Green utterly dominant in first 10 minutes, going two up. Shots then hit the bar. After less than 20 minutes, Will Evans sent off (the proverbial off-the-ball incident – I didn't see it). Forest Green score two more before the interval. Second half is more or less water torture, as Forest Green play it around (90 per cent possession, even 95) & Shots understandably enough concentrate on damage limitation – no sort of contest or spectacle. Throughout it all, Andy could not be kinder or less triumphalist, while I try to summon up a modicum of graciousness about Forest Green's impressive performance.

We get home to discover that Forest Green have gone top & that Shots have slipped from 5th to 7th. I am seriously doubtful whether Shots will feature again this season in the play-off zone, though of course keep telling myself it's only one match.[32] Andy is staying with us, & as a form of therapy (for me at least) we indulge in some late-night football anoraking, viz. about record goalscorers in the Football League. We agree it must be Arthur Rowley at the top of the list, & indeed it is – some fifty goals more than anyone else. Mainly for Leicester in the 50s, but also a lot for Shrewsbury in first half of the 60s. That was exactly when I was at prep school in Shrewsbury, & starting to get addicted to newsprint – I'd often get taken out on Sundays by my grandparents, who lived ten miles away at Wem (from where Hazlitt & Coleridge famously walked to Shrewsbury), & while my grandmother made lunch I'd head up to the attic room, where they kept apples & old copies of the *Shrewsbury Chronicle*, in which I'd read about Rowley's exploits. And what made it extra-special about the already legendary goalscorer was not just that he played for the local team, but that he had the same first name as my father. I just

---

[32]   Only 2nd to 5th place finishes qualified that season for the play-offs. From 2017/18 this was expanded to include 6th and 7th places.

wish now I'd got to see him play, but somehow it was never ever a possibility, even though the Gay Meadow was only about 10 minutes' walk from the school. And once a week we'd go past it in a coach on the way to the swimming baths – while somewhere on the opposite side of the road was an advertising hoarding for Hovis that always amused me, saying 'Use Your Loaf'.

Next for the Shots is home to Solihull Moors – newly promoted, doing all right, thumped Southport last night – but we'll miss it, going to Italy that day for a week. It'll be a get-back-on-the-horse match, & I suspect season defining. Fingers crossed, while of course recognising that in the big scheme of things, etc., etc...

Thursday 6 October

Scratching that incurable itch, I found myself last night watching Tuesday's "highlights" (probably needs triple inverted commas) on the Aldershot website. It was remarkable stuff:

First Forest Green goal: definitely offside.
Second Forest Green goal: probably offside.
Third Forest Green goal: started with a palpable foul.
Fourth Forest Green goal: fair enough.

While as for the sending off, it doesn't look as if Evans did anything nearly dramatic enough for the FG player to spend several minutes on the floor doing a very passable imitation of the JJs. On the phone this morning with Michael, who's Twitter-savvy, I gather that it was a slight kick comparable to the Beckham one in '98 that had that Argentinian writhing about. Obviously a foolish thing to do, but perhaps shouldn't have been allowed to wreck a game?

All that said, Forest Green were clearly the better side – well resourced, ambitious & playing a stylish, assured football with a slightly Barcelona feel. My guess is they'll win the Vanarama. But before then, in late Nov, the return match – & it'd be something to savour if the Shots got, as they say, a result. Unlikely, however.

Meanwhile, Theresa May's Conference speech yesterday. Hailed in advance by the *Mail* as an assault on the 'liberal elite', but in truth more complex, with quite a lot of stuff about the need to reform capitalism. This whole question of whether we're moving into a 'post-liberal age' I find sorely exercising, & I might try next week to set down some suitably weighty Home Thoughts from Abroad.

Leaves on the pavement this morning. It's autumn, I suddenly in a visceral way realise. Which used to be my favourite season, but no more. Now I associate it with death & long for spring. But more immediately I'm so looking forward, Goethe-like, to that Italian light next week. For reasons I can't quite explain, & not because I've been there particularly often, it's now become my best country in the world. Maybe a northern European puritan realising in the end that puritanism isn't enough & starting to kick against the pricks?

Sunday 9 October

Well, in Tuscany – just outside (& below) San Gimignano, archetypal hill town. Wondered at odd moments yesterday afternoon, as we made fairly laborious yet somehow very enjoyable progress from Pisa Airport via bus/train/train/bus/cab, how the Shots were getting on. And I still don't know. I think that Juliet (Lucy's friend) may have internet access, but I'm happy enough not to find out. While I guess that if it had been a sensational result (either way), Michael might have texted something through to Lucy. We certainly won't find out locally – it's hardly a *Likely Lads* scenario where Bob & Terry spend the day trying to avoid finding out what happened to England, away somewhere in Eastern Europe, so they can enjoy the highlights that evening – only to discover when they eventually make it through the day (including taking sanctuary in a church) that it had been postponed because of a waterlogged pitch. In the old days, of course, it was usually a case when abroad of going to the railway station, finding an English paper (usually two days old), & trying to sneak a look at the result without having to pay for the too expensive paper itself.

Late on Friday I saw online the *Guardian*'s editorial for yesterday. Only had a chance to speed-read it, but essentially it was about the plight of liberalism in the post-liberal age. It felt like a definitive sealing of the realisation that we are in some sense moving into a new era – or perhaps, rather, that that era has now definitively arrived. I truly wish it were otherwise. But it is also true to say that my own feelings are far from black & white. Of course, when it comes to it, I am on the side of the liberals. Nothing matters more than tolerance; the timber of humanity is probably even more crooked now than in Kant's day, so it is counter-productive & even inhumane not to recognise that; & I believe more or less indivisibly in the sovereignty of the mind to go where it will. But I also know (& am probably repeating myself) that identity matters, that psychological certainty matters, that man is tribal – & in all three respects, that applies to me just as much as the next person. Nor is it just a case of being a life-long supporter of a small football club. It means a huge amount to me when other people acknowledge the worth/value of my life and my work (especially because it doesn't happen all that often, I should hastily add); I would hate to work in an organisation where I felt powerless, could get sacked at any moment, was hot-desking & generally felt an under-appreciated cog in a huge machine that was itself at the mercy of incomprehensible, uncontrollable global forces; & for all my instinctive fear & dread of nationalism, I am Little Englisher enough to feel strongly that England football & cricket teams should 100% comprise Englishmen/women – & that that applies to their coaches/managers also. I am sure too that, when we fly back on Saturday & come down over Gatwick, I will feel my usual quasi-patriotic stirrings as I look down at those wonderfully green Sussex fields.

A book that made a considerable impact on me over a decade ago was Michael Collins's *The Likes of Us*, which I reviewed for the *FT* in 2004. Essentially a historical survey of the white working class, focusing mainly on the Southwark area in south London, it made powerful arguments about the post-war period: first, that in the crucial things that happened between say the 1950s & the 1970s – comprehensive urban redevelopment

& mass immigration – that local white working class had not been consulted even though they were going to be at the sharp end; & second, that considering that, they had been remarkably tolerant. Collins also showed how, during the last quarter of the century, those people in due course largely left Southwark & moved to outer suburbs like Welling & Bexley – precisely those places which, against the larger London trend, voted 'out' in June. The impact of the book was considerable on my understanding – & as a historian as well as citizen I am grateful for it. Multi-culturalism & all that has indeed to be a two-way street, I can entirely see that. But does it mean I have to go further & accept/endorse 'white van' values? Do we all have to be Brexiteers now? The answer is surely not. And travelling in the train yesterday, & looking out of the window, it belatedly struck me like the proverbial punch in the solar plexus that we had – for any number of reasons – made a huge, huge mistake in that mendacious Referendum. Driving through Doncaster last weekend – grim-looking, & Ed Miliband's constituency to boot! – may have brought it home to Lucy & me that the traditional, liberal-minded political class had it coming to them with the June vote. Their remoteness, their arrogance, their virtue-signalling – all that is true. But when it comes to *values*, however imperfectly expressed and/or lived, theirs are the values I would still sign up to. The alternative – let me spit it out at last – is intolerance, philistinism, even the Dark Ages. That seems mildly hysterical, as I look at the words I've just written, but in the fullness of time I wouldn't bet against it.

Meanwhile, in my current rather aggressively liberal mood, I started on the plane Forster's *Where Angels Fear to Tread*, partly of course for its Tuscan setting. Years since I've last read it, probably in my twenties, & all I could remember was the line 'She spoke a platitude as if it was an epigram,' which had much amused me. What I'd completely forgotten, & producing a sharp stab, was that it starts at Charing Cross station, as the travellers set out for the continent. It was at Charing Cross (not Victoria) in August 1960 that my father saw off my mother and me as we left for Germany to stay with my grandparents Omi & Opa. I'd just had my ninth birthday, & it was the last time I saw my parents together. I don't think I'm jobbing backwards to say that the atmosphere seemed strained – a nine-year-old boy does notice the odd thing – & even now, summoning up that moment, I feel myself coming close to crying with self-pity.[33]

Tuesday 11 October

Spotted an *Observer* outside a newsagent/souvenir shop, etc. yesterday. Opened it up as covertly as I could manage & tried to read the Aldershot result, but difficult without my specs. Thought it said 2–0 but couldn't be absolutely sure the 'o' wasn't a '6' – & after Tuesday that didn't seem wholly impossible. So no alternative but to shell out my nearly 5 Euros. And on closer inspection, in better light, it was indeed 2–0 to the Shots. Sounds solid enough, but of course no other details. In any case, up to 6th in the table, outside the play-offs only on goal difference. Quite a relief – a second successive home defeat, after such a good run at home, might have been hard to recover from. Still – just about – travelling hopefully.

Actually, I was pleased to buy the paper & catch up a bit more generally. Especially the main front-page story – about the revelation of Trump's foul-mouthed utterances in 2005 about women, culminating in 'Grab them by the pussy' – the five words that, with any luck, will finally sink him. But I'm still largely in the dark about the debate on Sunday night, apart from a conversation yesterday lunchtime with a New Zealander who was at the

---

[33] This seems the moment for a brief post-1960 update. My parents (Arthur and Gisela, who had met in Germany after the war, with my father persuading her to move to England and marry him, which she did in 1950, a year before I was born) divorced in January 1961. Within a few months they had both remarried: my father to Vivienne Warrington-Strong (daughter of the artist George Studdy, creator of Bonzo Dog); my mother to Bill Hunt (an airline navigator for BOAC). I'm almost certain that for both of them these were happier marriages than their first marriage. My father, who retired from the Army in 1985, died in October 1999, followed by Vivienne in January 2005. Bill died in December 2018; and my mother, sadly suffering from vascular dementia but still quite often recognisably herself, in August 2019, just after her ninety-sixth birthday.

wine-tasting session we went to at the place we're staying. She reported that one question put to Trump & Clinton was asking them to identify the quality in their opponent they found most praiseworthy. Apparently, he praised her persistence; she praised the belief in him that his family had. It reminded me of a favourite political story. When Disraeli died in 1881, the PM was Gladstone, & obviously it fell to him to pay a tribute in the Commons. The problem was that a) Gladstone genuinely believed that Disraeli was a bad man, & b) he was almost constitutionally incapable of telling what he knew to be an untruth. He went through a terrible time, succumbing to sleeplessness & diarrhoea, but eventually came up with the solution: to praise Disraeli for his 'parliamentary courage'.

A couple of things from magazines I want to note. The first, from a profile in the *New Statesman*, I'll do in Q&A form:

Q: Which Premiership manager recently said: 'The only possible moment of happiness is the present. The past gives you regrets. And the future uncertainties. Man understood this very fast and created religion.'

A: Probably not that difficult to guess. It's *Le Professeur*, as his players at first called him – some far from enthusiastically – on his arrival at Highbury twenty years ago.

My own feelings towards Wenger are somewhat ambivalent. His teams over the years have played some wonderful football – above all that amazing 2003/4 team: fast, accurate, on the floor, a type of football combining fluidity & precision in a way never quite seen in this country before. I also like (or anyway admire) that sense of high seriousness he exudes, with those odd & endearing moments of irony. In that charged Wenger/ Mourinho relationship, I am unreservedly in the Frenchman's corner. My ambivalence lies perhaps in the headline to Jason Cowley's profile: 'English football's first cosmopolitan'. True about coaching methods as well as his recruitment policy. And for all the upside (starting with the amazing Thierry Henry), that cosmopolitanism inexorably leads for me to a sense of indifference, an ultimate meaninglessness... I remember Pete McQuay once describing Liverpool's goalie of the 1960s, Tommy Lawrence, as the last of the 'docker' footballers, & even then, early 1970s, that seemed about right – & an absence to lament.[34]

Which neatly takes me to the second magazine item, viz. this opening para from the *Economist*'s 'Bagehot' columnist:

> Mainstream politicos in Britain have long since held these truths to be self-evident. The left won the social battles of the past decades. The right won the economic ones. The ruling consensus combines free-market liberalism with broadly permissive cultural instincts. But on October 5th Theresa May strode up to the podium at the Conservative Party conference, awkwardly waved at the crowd, cleared her throat and unceremoniously drove a bulldozer through those assumptions.

Reading that striking, nicely turned para – I especially like the 'awkwardly' – has reminded me that early last year I wrote a big-picture piece for the *Sunday Times*'s 'Culture' magazine in which, as far as I can remember, I argued that the triumph of *both* those liberalisms – social & economic – was no longer looking so assured. And actually, thinking about it more (& in the knowledge that I'm probably repeating myself – one of the things about writing a diary, I've discovered, is that I almost physically can't bear to look back at earlier entries, a bit like a cat with its sick), I guess that much of the whole thrust of my post-war history has been about the sheer depth & strength of 'Middle England' social conservatism, often ignored or patronised by the 'activators', aka 'liberal elite'. So in that sense, I shouldn't be surprised & shocked by what's now happening. Yet the fact is that I am. Of course I can see the argument, as promulgated by e.g. John Gray, that the notion of 'progress' is a chimera, &

[34] Google 'tommy lawrence bbc interview' for a peculiarly touching (and rightly going viral) chance encounter in February 2015, three years before he died.

often a deeply unhelpful & even destructive one. Yet in the end I find that a counsel of despair – it *has* to be possible, I believe in my bones, for one generation to order things better & more satisfactorily than the previous generation managed. It's kind of the argument, perhaps, of Pascal's famous 'wager' on religious belief: it may well prove mistaken, but ultimately there is no alternative. What I really want, I fully appreciate, is Boris-like to have my cake & eat it.[35] 'Yes' to tolerance of 'the other', to diversity, to 'the liberal imagination' (I'm also just starting this week on Lionel Trilling's celebrated book, a zeitgeist-moulder in its day); but 'yes' also to place, to roots, to the local. 'If you believe you're a citizen of the world,' said May in her speech last week, 'you're a citizen of nowhere. You don't understand what the very word citizenship means.' To which, two (one and a half?) cheers. But – with that Forsterian echo in mind, & to pose the famous Forster question – whom would I betray? My country or my friend? For many years it was axiomatic to me that it would have to be the former – I guess in a way it was my ultimate core belief. And now? It feels a bit more difficult, but in the end I'm a Forster man. And suddenly, chillingly, it doesn't seem altogether inconceivable that we all might one day have to make – in essence – that choice.

Wednesday 12 October

Just back from day trip to Siena (never been before) – weary, but some wonderful moments. The surprise one, in the city's art gallery, was a 1583 portrait of Elizabeth I by a Sienese painter – unregal, unglamorous, felt like the real thing.

Picked up yesterday's *Guardian* while there. 'Senior Republican [Paul Ryan] abandons Trump as outrage intensifies'. First

[35] Why, I've been wondering in 2019 for obvious reasons, is this virtually my sole diary reference to Boris Johnson? I guess the only rational answer is that, even though I was writing soon after the Referendum, there were other self-serving and unscrupulous populists (one in particular) who concerned me more.

national opinion poll since revelation of 2005 tape gives Clinton a double-figure lead. In Blighty, even Jacob Rees-Mogg has withdrawn his support – a shattering blow. As for the debate itself, it apparently hit – by some margin – record depths of unpleasantness, including Trump 'prowling the blue-carpeted stage like a predator, brooding, scowling, skulking, wagging his finger at Clinton, exploding with rage and misogynistic bullying'. On any rational, civilised basis, he's surely done for. And the alternative – the notion of him winning – has shifted from virtually unthinkable as a prospect one can live with to actually unthinkable. Of course, inevitable rider, it's not that I'm crazy about Clinton. I hate the idea, in America of all places, of political dynasties; she clearly has, as [Bernie] Sanders kept saying, been far too close to Wall Street; & *Primary Colors* (a fine novel, brilliantly written, with its haunting, ambivalent ending about whether the political life is worth it or not) nailed her almost as much as it did Bill. But she's a serious politician, she was a highly competent Secretary of State, & it'd be a great thing to have a woman in the White House – never more so than at this very particular turbocharged moment.

The paper also reports the end of the Age of Rooney. Well, not actually, but he's been dropped by England, soon after being dropped by United, & chances are there's no way back. Perhaps just short of greatness, but a very fine footballer who in his decline has acquired a certain nobility. I always felt he was in the noble tradition of street footballers, helped perhaps by that uncanny resemblance to Shrek. And he seems to have been more or less faithful to his adolescent sweetheart. Although his battered body has lost its sharpness, & he's now in his thirties, I suspect he still loves playing. Just possible – if presumably very unlikely given his wealth & global fame – that he'll go on for a fair time to come in English football, gently subsiding down the divisions. Funny if he finished up as player-manager of FC United. Or if, in these (disturbingly) militarised times, he went as a kind of tribute to the club that plays in 'the Home of the British Army'. But I fear this is getting silly – as indeed that Army officer used to say in *Monty Python*.

Thursday 13 October

The others are doing a cookery course, so I've got the flat to myself for a while. I've always had this day in mind for trying to write something more substantial/reflective/autobiographical on the theme of 'football & me'.

Nothing, I'm fairly sure, before 1958. Then come two shadow memories, which may or may not be real. In February 1958 (just after I was six & a half), a sort of dim awareness of the Munich disaster, & a similar shadowy memory of the Cup Final about three months later when Nat Lofthouse bundled over Harry Gregg & the goal was given. But between them, a much firmer memory of looking at the newspaper soon after Munich & being fascinated by the provisional nature of the United line-up – even on the morning of the match, the club not knowing who was going to occupy some of the places. Then in the early months of 1959, excitement about Norwich's Cup progress, my father taking me to Aldershot for the first time, & then the 1959 Cup Final when I passionately wanted Luton to equalise in the second half even though Nottingham Forest only had ten players. Meanwhile, during that year (1958/9) in the village school in Grayshott (near Hindhead), a lot of everyone-chasing-the-ball football in the playground, while at home in the garden I spent a lot of time kicking a ball against a bank & learning, as I kicked the rebounds, to become two-footed.

Two rogue moments from about that time. One was the Millwall match – is it really conceivable that my father took me *before* summer 1958, which was when we moved from Grove Park in south-east London to Headley Down on the Surrey/Hants border? The other is Arsenal versus Blackpool, which he undoubtedly did take me to – Ray Charnley scoring a hat-trick, Stanley Matthews playing, but my only firm memory is of the huge crowd queuing for the tube afterwards – though I don't know when.[36]

---

[36] 29 November 1958 is the answer, so almost certainly my first match; and a crowd at Highbury of 54,629.

Anyway, by the time I was sent to prep school in Shrewsbury in September 1959, I was definitely very keen on football. My earliest memory of my time there is of taking part in a pick-up game in the playground, mainly with older boys, & barely getting a sniff of the ball. I soon had a couple of more or less interchangeable nicknames – 'Sporty' & 'Scruffy'. I associate that time with that song – my song – 'He's football crazy / He's football mad...'[37] Of course, I was an only child & all that, so obviously I loved nothing more than reading newspapers & checking out fixtures/results/tables etc. I remember solemnly deciding that my three favourite teams were Tottenham, Man Utd & Aldershot – & that, of the three, Aldershot were my absolute favourite. All this *predated* discovering that my parents were going to get divorced & then it happening. While on the whole I was happy from the start at my prep school, a much more humane place than many of its type. So I guess that all I can usefully say is that the divorce trauma – which it was – presumably cemented/deepened my attachment to the game.

I'll speed on. Over the next four years (1960–4), I played a lot at prep school (occasionally in goal, mainly upfront), becoming captain of the 1st XI; followed the Shots, though only occasionally getting to matches; & in that pre-*Match of the Day* era, treasured the rare snatches of football on TV – mainly Cup finals, of which my two top ones were '62 (Blanchflower sending Blacklaw the wrong way from the penalty spot) & '64 (the battle of the two teenagers).[38] Nothing problematic in the relationship, & no larger sense of 'football & society'.

---

[37] 'Football Crazy' (clocking in at 2 minutes and 3 seconds, so not outstaying its welcome): a very minor hit (never making Top Twenty) in 1960 for Robin Hall and Jimmie MacGregor after singing it on *Tonight*. But second only to 'Last Train to San Fernando' (Johnny Duncan & the Bluegrass Boys) as the song during childhood I would go around singing.
[38] Preston North End's Howard Kendall (seventeen) and West Ham United's Johnny Sissons (eighteen), the two youngest players ever to play in a Cup final. I've an idea I was fascinated at the time by how the names of seven of the West Ham team began with the letter 'B' (though not of course Geoff Hurst or Bobby Moore, or indeed the goalscoring eighteen-year-old).

Then came Wellington – a deep-dyed rugby-playing school (in the Michaelmas term, with hockey in the Lent term). On my first Saturday afternoon there, a hot September day, we did 'gut-busting', i.e. running up & down the rugby field – & a prefect shouted at me, 'Kynaston, get a grip,' presumably as I faltered & lost the will to live. I was sort of OK at rugby – mainly full-back, where I was good at kicking, if the most cowardly of tacklers – but my heart was never really in it. And while I was doggedly continuing to follow the Shots (starting an annual scrapbook of cuttings from the *Aldershot News* that lasted almost all through my Wellington years, plus getting quite often to matches, usually with my mother, & with transport supplied by my stepfather, on both of which scores I remain eternally grateful), I gradually came to realise that in my public-school environment rugby was socially acceptable, football was essentially not, or at the most barely tolerated. In 1968 I started, with a couple of friends in my house at Wellington, a magazine called *Soccer Digest*. We had about a hundred subscribers (including A. J. Ayer), John Arlott was among the external contributors, the *Daily Express* ran an article about it ('Not a revolution', ran the caption below the photo of me), & we brought out several issues before I left Wellington at the end of 1969. The flavour of those issues – certainly my contributions – was in retrospect solemn, sententious, almost unbearably priggish. And I had absolutely no doubt that I was occupying the moral high ground.

Then came 'peak football', the first half of the 1970s. Almost the best thing about Oxford was the chance to play proper football again; my friendship with Pete McQuay was predicated on football, though his approach to the game (as to much else) was far more worldly & less naive than mine; my support for the Shots hit a new intensity; after Oxford, I had a couple of full seasons playing for Battersea Park, a Sunday-morning outfit (often playing at Wormwood Scrubs) run by the football journalist John Moynihan, an experience at almost every level feeding into my personal myth; my hero in the football world was undoubtedly Brian Clough; & at some emotional level, the identification was more or less complete between me, football, the working class & socialism – ludicrous, I know, though that now sounds.

The next twenty years, roughly mid-1970s to mid-1990s, were very different & in effect a sort of self-contained continuum, mainly characterised by disenchantment & disengagement. Some obvious 'reasons' – playing football (knees, back, etc.) becoming increasingly fitful and soon non-existent; a rekindled love for cricket; a loss of left-wing certainties; a new seriousness & ambition about my work; marriage & children – are only a part of the story. Although I still followed the Shots – & at moments their fate really mattered to me – I think I came to see football more generally as a kind of swindle, wasting too much of people's time, including my time, & no longer to be taken on its own self-aggrandising terms. It had been building up for a long time – I remember watching (on TV) the 1977 Cup Final between Liverpool & Man U in a completely grumpy, disaffected mood – but the tipping point came in the spring of 1985.

Three events happened in quick succession: the dreadful fire at Bradford; the birth of our first child, our daughter Laurie; & the dreadful events at Heysel.[39] Against that backdrop, I was so pleased that we had had a girl; & I pretty much thought that I was through with football.[40] It helped that not long afterwards I got to know, & became friends with, another historian, Dilwyn Porter. Dil is an exceptionally nice & generous person, a lifelong Leyton Orient supporter & a beacon of decency & hope. If football was still good enough for him, then (I gradually came to realise) it was surely good enough for me. So I didn't quite give up on the game, but still for a long time kept a certain distance.

Since the mid-1990s it's been a process of re-engagement, notwithstanding my increasingly deep & almost irrationally atavistic loathing of certain aspects of the game at the top. First George got

---

[39] Fifty-six spectators died as the result of a fire during Bradford City's match with Lincoln City on Saturday, 11 May; Laurie was born on the 17th; and on the 29th, before the start of the European Cup Final between Liverpool and Juventus at the Heysel Stadium in Brussels, thirty-nine spectators (mainly Juventus fans) died.

[40] As it happened, the Shots on the 17th finished their season by beating Rochdale 5–0 at home. That in retrospect might have been a nice way to go out.

keen, then Michael (six years younger) a bit later; many hours on the touchline at school matches made me feel that I was once again a football person; while supporting the Shots as they steadily if slowly (1992–2008) clambered their way back to Football League status reinvigorated my feeling for the (now re-formed) club. George & Michael both support the Shots, while in the last few years Lucy has started coming with me to matches, which I've really enjoyed. I'm not particularly proud of the fact that football is a significant part of my life – indeed, I quite often feel pangs of envy towards friends for whom the game means nothing, thinking of all the time & mental space that must have freed up – but I accept that it is & value the long-lasting thread. I've always loved the title of that Van Morrison live double album, *It's Too Late to Stop Now*, & that's more or less what I feel. No point wishing it were otherwise, & try to enjoy it – uncensoriously, unpriggishly, with a degree of perspective, even humour – while I still can. Not always so easy if the linesman is blind…

Friday 14 October

A footnote, re Heysel, to yesterday's entry. Eventually that awful evening, after the bodies had been taken away, they played the match. Juventus beat Liverpool 1–0. BBC's coverage ended with a brief studio discussion by the pundits. The very last words came from Terry Venables, saying something like 'the goal was offside'. It struck me at the time that that summed up football's moral bankruptcy. That's how I remember it – I'd love to know how accurately.

This morning, last walk up the hill to San Gimignano – & then for me a long, quite arduous walk around the walls – really enjoyable, with wonderful views of this beautiful, intricate landscape that has been lived in & cultivated for so many centuries.

Bought the *New York Times* while in town. Two things. First, the news that Dylan – my main man, musically, since 1968 – has been awarded the Nobel Prize for Literature. Quite a thrill, though whether 'deserved' is obviously impossible to say. Second, on the Republican/Trump front, the apparent news that they're threatening on polling day to use guns outside polling booths to threaten non-white voters with. Almost unbelievable – & if true, almost unbelievably wicked.

Should be home tomorrow afternoon, perhaps around the time the Shots are at home to Eastbourne United in the fourth qualifying round of the FA Cup. Eastbourne has its associations – T. S. Eliot's ill-fated honeymoon; the aged Archie MacLaren assembling a motley team to defeat the all-conquering Australians in 1921; Kevin Coyne's typically pungent 'Eastbourne Ladies' – but none relating to football. Obviously I'm hoping for a decent Cup run this year, but such is the keenness of my desire that the Shots manage to stick in or around the play-off places through the autumn & winter that I'm a bit less fussed than usual.

Motto for return to England & next phase of this diary: more understanding of the enemies (actual or potential, right or left) of liberalism, & less automatic censorious condemnation. But at the same time it galls me that the words 'liberal' & 'elite' are so automatically linked. After all, if in terms of the print/online media one takes Murdoch + the *Mail*, both essentially *non*-liberal, they have a circulation & influence way beyond that of say the *Guardian* – & it makes no real sense not to call them 'elite'.

Generally, though, LIGHTEN UP.

Monday 17 October

Easier said than done…

Theresa May may be refusing to give or allow a 'running commentary' on Brexit, etc., but this diary is in danger of offering such a commentary.

Starting with the journey home on Saturday, after a week away in which the dominant narrative had clearly been about the ramifications of an apparently clear decision by the government to go for a 'hard' Brexit, i.e. complete control over immigration, even if that means limited or no access to the European single market. The *FT* (bought at Pisa Airport) had, in the context of sterling's dramatic slide, a striking quote by Nicholas Spiro, a macro-economic consultant: 'In the space of a week, Mrs May and her ministers have confirmed the worst fears of those in the markets who not only believed that Brexit meant Brexit, but who sense that the liberal, internationalist Britain perceived by outsiders was turning into a nativist, immigrant-bashing one. Investors, who have wrongly viewed the UK through the narrow prism of cosmopolitan London, are having to come to terms with communitarian, parochial England.' At Clapham Junction I picked up the *Guardian*, where Ian Jack (a favourite writer, on his day approaching the Orwell class & deeply aware of the significance & resonance of local roots) had a piece explaining & analysing the existence of *rival* elites – liberal & non-liberal. And at Waitrose, I speed-read in *The Times* a Matthew Parris piece, claiming that a) the Brexiteer ministers are almost clueless about how to proceed, & b) the biggest British political crisis since Suez is looming.

It's so easy to overestimate the importance of the present, I know. Which made me grateful this morning at the station to bump into a local friend, David Warren, a recently retired diplomat with left-liberal instincts & his finger on several different pulses. I asked him whether we really are living through the moment that will come to be seen as the start of a socially post-liberal era, & he made two helpful points. First, that immigration is a special case, because of its economic dimension, & therefore one can't just take attitudes to immigration & automatically read across socially. Second, that the coming of gay marriage, about which there was little more than rumblings of opposition, shows the extent to which socially liberal assumptions are now entrenched, on the part anyway of the great majority of people born since the war. I should record, though, that we didn't end the conversation on a reassuring note. He was just back from a conference in Japan, where the overriding concern was with North Korea & its nuclear capability – including, on the part of the Japanese, a sense of puzzlement about why the Brits still treat that cruel, capricious & dangerous figure almost as a source of harmless fun.

And the round-ball game? We were back in time to hear commentary on the second half of Shots versus Eastbourne (Borough, not United). Goalless at the interval, with Shots already down to ten after apparently a controversial dismissal. They made a spirited effort, but in the end Eastbourne went through 2–1 with a late winner. A shame, & arguably Waddock over-changed the team from the week before, but maybe, with a small squad & a 46-match league programme, not such a total disaster.

Friday 21 October

I've felt a bit apathetic Shots-wise this week. Not quite sure why. Part of a general gloom, I guess. I can't get rid of this dark feeling that we're heading for something bad. A feeling not helped by watching Trump in the small hours of yesterday morning – the final debate, & generally reckoned to have been won by Clinton, but the abiding impression at the end was of having spent too long in the company of a bully wholly lacking in empathy or sympathy or even basic human decency. He also refused to promise to accept the election result: in its way, a dreadful, historic moment. Fundamentally, he is not a democrat, & believes only in one thing: the promotion of Trump. A bad, bad man – but far from stupid, & systematically exploiting genuine grievances, yes, but also those bad instincts we all have.

Anyway, life goes on in a small corner of an offshore island, & Shots tomorrow are away at Torquay. The scene in 2008 of a memorable winning goal that more or less secured the Shots returning to the Football League. Both clubs have fallen on hard times since, & when I went to Plainmoor in August 2013 to see a meaningless goalless draw against Portsmouth in something like the Freight Trophy, it felt like a decaying sort of set-up. The reason for that visit was a holiday in nearby Greenway – where Agatha Christie lived in the summer & now a National Trust property, including accommodation. A beautiful & serene place, overlooking the Dart Estuary, & I'm not sure I've ever enjoyed a journey more than my first time there, on a late-afternoon boat to Dartmouth from the landing stage below the house. I generally feel fairly Dr Johnsonian on water – given the choice between a ship & a prison, he once said, he'd plump for the latter – but this was completely different, completely inspiriting, with magical light & a magical setting.

One small note for the record. Catching up on last week's *New Statesman*, I've spotted that Will Self refers (in the context of the immediate post-war period) to 'so-called activators', i.e. the term that Lucy invented for *Austerity Britain*... But a long way to go still to the *OED*.

Sunday 23 October

Goalless at Torquay yesterday, though Shots apparently unlucky not to win it – Matt McClure hitting the post just before the end. Down to 7th, & 7 points behind Forest Green, who are steaming away at the top, looking unstoppable. Away on Tuesday to Dagenham & Redbridge (second in the table). Hoping to go, though at the moment feeling a bit under the weather.

Two missing things from Friday's entry. First, the fiftieth anniversary that day of Aberfan. In 1966 it was also a Friday, & because I was laid up (mumps?) in the school Sanatorium I listened all day on the radio as the awful scale of the disaster unfolded.[41] I've a shameful feeling that next day my thoughts were mainly occupied with the Shots, away at Bradford (Park Avenue? City? not sure), & of course therefore the build-up to *Sports Report* at 5 o'clock & the classified results. Just as the stirring theme music was about to play, to my chagrin a visitor walked in – probably my housemaster, 'Mungo' Parkes – & I had to switch the radio off... And I'm sure I then had to wait until 'the latecomers' reading' of the results, at five to 6. Just about worth waiting for: a one-all draw.

---

[41] I missed at the time, and have only recently read, a brilliant and desperately sad article on the BBC News website to mark the fiftieth anniversary. Written by Ceri Jackson, and called 'Aberfan: The mistake that cost a village its children', it includes intensely evocative photographs by David Hurn.

The other missing thing was an article in Friday's *Guardian* by John Foot, a historian of Italy. The headline summed it up – 'We've seen Trump before. His name was Berlusconi' – & of course he's right. No single thing vexed me more about Blair (whom I am far from wholly negative about) than the fact that as Prime Minister he chose to spend *social* time with Berlusconi when he was running Italy. To my mind, the highest duty of a British politician is – apart, I guess, from the defence of the country – to defend & strengthen democracy. (A duty that includes, Gladstone-style, the improved, non-partisan education of that democracy.) Berlusconi was a politician who controlled much of the Italian media – in other words, he was not a democrat. By spending *social* time with him, Blair in effect condoned his existence as a politician – a politician in charge of a Western European country. I don't remember it being a particular issue at the time, but for me that was unforgivable.

Something I missed while I was away but have just caught up with is Timothy Garton Ash's *Guardian* piece of 14 October. I think of Garton Ash as the liberal's liberal, the European's European, & the headline is confessional: 'We liberal internationalists have to own up: we left too many people behind.' In the article itself, noting that 'anti-liberalism is one of the threads that connects Trumpism, the Brexit vote, Poland's nationalist populist government, Putinism and much else', he pins much of the blame on 'free-market, globalized liberal capitalism as it has developed since its historical triumph in 1989', i.e. 'the world we liberal internationalists built – even if we didn't all have our own hands in the bankers' till'. After enumerating some of the misdeeds & excesses of that capitalism, he ends with a neat twist: 'Effectively addressing the cross-border effects of globalized liberal capitalism will actually require more international cooperation, at the very moment when populist nationalists are leading so many countries in the opposite direction. To remedy the unintended consequences of globalization we need more liberal intervention, not less.'

I've never met Garton Ash, but we once talked on the phone. He was writing (for the *New Yorker*?) an article about – of all things & all places – Aldershot, & an old friend of mine, Jeremy Harding, had mentioned me. Sadly, it wasn't a satisfactory conversation. His theme, to which I was sympathetic, was that there was something special & revealing about Aldershot – partly the military character, partly a way of looking at the world (patriotic, Little Englander etc.), partly its rundown feel in an area generally of considerable affluence – but in response I failed to say anything remotely interesting & the conversation ended on a flat note. Of course, the generalisations we agreed upon do get one some of the way, but in the end it is only the poet, the novelist, the travel writer who really gets one to the 'isness' of things, & I'm none of those. Plus for me in that particular conversation there was a whole emotional history & baggage somehow blocking the way. A little bit like when I was doing English A Level & wrote a poor essay on *Howards End* – I'd read it several times, it had decisively shaped my view of things, I loved it – & when it came to it proved quite incapable of doing a clinical 45-minute job on it. Somewhat similar, many years later, when it came to Gissing in the second volume of my City history.[42] One definitely wants a degree of engagement, but not too much.

Quite a lot of this Sunday-morning entry has been written with the cricket on silently in the background. Bangladesh making a spirited attempt to chase 286 & thereby beat England for the first time in a Test. Play ends with them still needing 33, with only two wickets left. If they fall just short tomorrow, will anyone recall the moment yesterday when England got an extra 5 runs because the ball struck the helmet behind the wicketkeeper? Which would make it rather like Melbourne '82, when England won by 3 runs – &, in their second innings, a wild, unnecessary throw at the stumps by Jeff Thomson went for three overthrows.[43]

---

[42] In the late 1970s, increasingly interested in late-Victorian London (and in turn the late-Victorian City of London), I worked my way through George Gissing's considerable output and became very fond of him – despite his undeniably exasperating aspects, self-pity perhaps the chief of them. Few would call him a great novelist; but in the 1880s and 1890s there was no one in Britain who matched him as an urban realist.

[43] That's at least how I remember it (I was there), but I've never seen or heard anyone else mention this surely relevant slice of the action.

Monday 24 October

England won quite comfortably (22 runs). A shame. Almost invariably I support England against Australia or South Africa, but otherwise I find it varies. Depends usually who's the underdog. Is it in fact possible to stay neutral in any sporting contest (at least in a sport one cares about)? I suspect not. Even if one knows nothing about the two sides or individuals, & has no particular feelings towards them, something will tilt one's emotions – even if it's only the name or appearance of a participant that vaguely reminds one of an old favourite.

Yesterday's *Observer* had a notable editorial – 'Britain is becoming mean and narrow-minded' – which, in the context of the recent ugly squall about taking refugees from the 'Jungle' in Calais (now about to be razed by the French government), noted how 'the tabloid vilification of public figures, such as Gary Lineker, who bravely challenge hateful tunes in the debate, has a chilling effect on the voice of the decent majority'. Well done for Lineker. I've always felt a bit so-so – admirably mature perspective on football, but just a little too bloodless, too self-contained – but greatly admire him for speaking out, i.e. to the effect that the 'children' from Calais (belatedly & reluctantly taken in), whether or not they in fact are children, are still *humans*. The editorial itself had some interesting, helpful figures taken from various surveys. Proportion of British population endorsing nakedly racist views: 10%. Population broadly positive about immigration: 38%. Population in favour of only allowing in migrants who help the economy: 60%. 'Tough but pragmatic' is how the paper characterises that third, majority position. And surely that's the position – somewhere between tolerant & intolerant – that's now got to be respected & implemented, for fear of worse, while allowing for a meaningful degree of generosity towards genuine refugees.

Which brings me to Syria: arguably the greatest humanitarian disaster since the war, & so far not mentioned in this diary. Why? No comfortable answers. Because of a lack of imagination? Because of preoccupation with other 'current affairs' issues? (I have a theory that most people, including me, can only really hold in their heads & follow one foreign story at any one time.) Because humankind cannot bear very much reality? Because it's all so complicated & insoluble? I went yesterday afternoon to a poetry reading by my friend David Loffman, & one of the poems was about listening on the radio last year to the latest news from Aleppo & realising that no one, perhaps including himself, was really listening. I suppose at some level, over the last five years, we always assumed that 'they' will sort it out. Given that 'they' include Assad & Putin, two appalling people, it's a doubly, trebly childish, immature attitude. But I'm far from sure that I have the capacity – or perhaps, to be wholly honest, the will – to advance much on it.

The reading was at our local C of E church, Christ Church. Through the 1990s, up to 2003, I was a regular attender. Although I became aware that it was on the evangelical rather than liberal wing of the Church, for years I put aside any nagging doubts & just kind of reckoned that it would all come out OK in the wash of Anglican fudge, mudge & compromise. Three things changed my attitude. First, the end of the twentieth century was a moment to take stock of that unprecedentedly awful century & realise that the only answer was liberalism & tolerance. Second, I began to query (why it took so long, God only knows...) the evangelicals' insistence that *theirs* was the only true way to salvation & that in effect the rest of humanity – approximately 97% of whom enjoyed an appreciably lower standard of living than the congregation of Christ Church, New Malden, Surrey, England – were damned. And third, in 2003, came the Jeffrey John episode, when (Rowan Williams's feeblest hour) his promotion was blocked because of evangelical pressure about the fact he was gay – &, for me the breaking point, our church was part of that pressure... Since when, a kind of spiritual nullity, which I deeply regret but somehow feel incapable of doing anything about. Certainly I have no appetite for any new attachment to a religious institution, though conceivably that might be different if we moved to a new place. But over & above that I just don't seem able to engage any more with religion & faith as such. I don't actively not believe, but I don't believe either. Ultimately, not a happy position. And which I guess is why

I find intensely moving that line from Dylan's 'Not Dark Yet' about not even hearing a murmur of a prayer.

Tuesday 25 October

Sat out the pleasures of the far end of the District Line & stayed at home to listen to the commentary on the Shots at Dagenham. Keenly contested, but a late goal won it 1–0 for the 'Daggers' – & their goalie touched a Charlie Walker shot on to the post in last minute of injury time. 'Scarcely deserved' was BBC website's verdict on the result, so I'm not too despondent, though Shots now slip to 9th. The BBC Surrey commentary featured a series of tweets from Shots fans, of which the most surprising was a reference to how 'a mate is up for tonight's Booker Prize'. In the event, it went for the first time to an American (probably not his mate).[44] For myself, I wish the Booker was strictly confined to British novelists. I never particularly liked the Commonwealth aspect, & now the appeal/resonance seems completely diluted.

I chatted in the BL [British Library] today with Marco Torres, an Italian historian of roughly my age. He lodged with us for a while before getting his own place in Finchley, but he's planning next spring to return to Venice – not least because of Brexit. It's hard not to feel a sense of guilt as well as disquiet. And wouldn't it be nice if the Leavers stopped behaving as victims?

Tomorrow is the thirtieth anniversary of the City's Big Bang. 26 October 1986 was a Monday, & on the Friday before I spent a few minutes in the Visitors' Gallery looking down on the floor of the Stock Exchange – still the scene of face-to-face trading, though that was about to change, along with so much else. Over the last few years I've been gathering material for a short book comparing the old, pre-BB City with the new City.[45] The ubiquitous question

[44]   Paul Beatty, for *The Sellout*.
[45]   In the end, a book destined not to be written, or anyway not by me. I came to feel that I'd done enough on the City. But I did, as a swansong, write some text to accompany Polly Braden's very evocative photographs in *London's Square Mile: A Secret City*, published in February 2019.

now is whether a 'hard' Brexit might result in London losing its place as the dominant international financial centre in the European time-zone. In its way a delicious situation: privileged for so long ('I would rather see finance less proud,' Churchill wistfully observed on the eve of the ill-fated return to gold in 1925), but for obvious reasons increasingly unpopular, the City is now having to fight its corner hard with a government that apparently has rather different priorities, whether social or economic. On the Monday after the Brexit vote, I interviewed Howard Davies for my Bank of England history. We sat on the twelfth floor of RBS's HQ in Bishopsgate & – calmly, judiciously – tried to evaluate the long-term significance, just as RBS's share price was plunging through the floor – & trading for a time having to be suspended. We agreed that financial centres rise, financial centres fall – & that the Referendum might be, rather like the guns of August in 1914, the moment that marked the start of a profound shift in London's fortunes. What do I want? Perhaps for the City to have a nasty scare – & to become less arrogant & to begin doing more for the common weal.

A fortnight to go until the American vote. On any rational basis, it must be Clinton – even by a landslide – but I & many millions won't sleep easily until Trump is history & the Republicans are forced to rethink their whole approach. Of course I realise that Trump himself is in some sense merely the symptom of something bigger, going way beyond party politics. But getting rid of the symptom would at least be a start. We – the West – simply cannot go there. And I don't think I'm being melodramatic when I say that it feels like the single most important moment of my adult political lifetime.

Wednesday 26 October

For B of E purposes, I looked at the BL yesterday at an autobiographical slice, *The Middle Span*, by the Spanish philosopher George Santayana. He lived in London in the late nineteenth century, & although not relevant to the Old Lady I jotted down these sentences: 'I respected and loved the English psyche, and the primacy there of the physical and moral nature over the intellectual. It was the safer order of things, more vital, more manly than the reverse. Man was not made to understand the world, but to live in it.' The English are indeed *au fond* anti-intellectual – & famously, at some distinct level, Brexit was a vote against experts, against know-alls. Obviously, that doesn't make me happy. But yet, there's a lot to be said for just getting on & *living*... I remember a moment in 1973 – Saturday 28 July to be exact. Early that afternoon I was at Crewe station, where in a telephone booth I rang through to the Examination Schools at Oxford & tried to find out what degree I had got (having sat Finals in June). A rather confusing & – at my end – tense conversation ensued, but eventually it transpired that I'd secured the much desired First. I felt a little dazed, hugely relieved & of course happy. About half an hour later I was on a train to Birmingham, & sitting in my compartment were three people (both sexes) of my age – & I looked at them & realised that they were utterly normal, utterly relaxed in each other's company – & that I was never going to be like them. I felt sharp, sharp envy. Unsurprisingly, a favourite novella is Henry James's *The Lesson of the Master*. That lesson is ambiguous – to live for life? to live for the mind? – & of course there is indeed no simple, satisfying answer. But looking back (forty-three years now since 1973), there are moments when I can't but wish the balance somewhat otherwise in my own case.

Thursday 27 October

I got it wrong! *This* is the Big Bang anniversary, i.e. it was 27 October 1986. Homer nods, or something.

Five years ago was of course the twenty-fifth anniversary, more or less coinciding – as it happened – with both the publication of the one-vol abridgement of my gargantuan City history (also coinciding with the 'Occupy' movement encamped outside St Paul's) & the Shots at home to Man U in the League Cup. A hectic, slightly larger-than-life time – & on the former front I did a 'radio' walk around the City with *Today*'s Evan Davis & a couple of comment pieces (*Telegraph* & *Guardian*) calling on the City to reform itself before at some point down the road the politicians took more drastic action. Impact: almost certainly, approximately zero. But fun to do – & one starts to become unhealthily addicted to the sound of one's own opinionated voice.

Friday 28 October

David Loffman brought round yesterday evening the new Leonard Cohen album. It felt unmistakably valedictory – & if that proves to be the case, well, as the title of a review put it rather nicely the other day, 'That's the way to say goodbye'. The sound was dignified, noble, grave – with, crucially as far as I'm concerned, none of that ironic undertone (even overtone) that since *I'm Your Man* in 1988 has given a distinctive & in its way enjoyable flavour to much of his work, but at the same time, at some deeper level, created a barrier between him & the listener (this listener anyway). Last night was different: just him & me – & I might have been listening, in terms of the intensity & intimacy of the experience, to *Songs of Love and Hate* – my all-time favourite Cohen, from back in the early 70s. At the end, I felt almost awestruck: a bit like after, a year or two ago, watching for the first time the opening episode of *Wolf Hall* – everything worked, & I was grateful to have been in the company of the life-enhancing creation. Those moments don't come along all that often.

Blair has argued today that if, over the next year or two, the tide of opinion turns against Brexit – &, specifically, the form that Brexit is taking – then there should be a democratic mechanism for that opinion to be expressed. He's surely right. Cue howls of outrage. But would that mean that the Brexit-mongers were afraid of public opinion? Surely not.

Main news this evening is a new Clinton emails/FBI story – & Trump claiming that this is 'bigger than Watergate'. Apparently, earlier this autumn, a Republican strategist observed that if the election campaign was about Trump, then Clinton would win; but if about Clinton, then Trump would win. So far it's been largely the former, but maybe this gives him the opening for a late upset. And should that happen, 'upset' in the other sense will hardly be the word.

Shots at home tomorrow to bottom-of-table Guiseley, & I'm hoping to go. They're a small club from West Yorkshire & last season pluckily just managed to stay up. They started this season disastrously, but have improved a little (including a 6–1 win over poor old York). For the Shots, slipping down the table & facing a run of four very tough fixtures in the immediate aftermath, it's the proverbial must-win. Not too left-field a prediction, I fear, to expect a rather tense, nervy afternoon.

Sunday 30 October

Well, tense & nervy just about sums it up. No goals in first half, fairly even, but best chance to Guiseley (whose thirty travelling supporters made a huge amount of noise, with variations on the chant 'We are Yorkshire'). Guiseley player sent off earlyish in second half, Shots ramping up pressure, finally the breakthrough in about 73rd minute (neat approach work, Charlie Walker curling into top far corner), then the inevitable tension, with Guiseley missing an excellent chance in injury time. Still, 1–0, & up to 6th, one place outside the play-offs.

The programme editor Victoria Rogers has a nice bit in her notes. After observing that the club's aim – after the financial traumas of 1992 & 2013 – is 'to move forward in a financially prudent way – no boom and bust, but steady progress', she goes on:

> And steady progress is something that takes time, frustrating perhaps when as a supporter you feel that you have been waiting for the sun to come out on your team for a very long time. In Gary [Waddock] though we have a manager who we can already see is moving the team forward. It may not be this season that Aldershot Town finally have their day in the sun, or maybe it will be – I don't have a crystal ball!

What I do know though is that we need to enjoy the journey because sometimes that can be as good a part of the trip as the arrival, all that happens as you travel along the metaphorical road of the football season.

So enjoy the trip and the football, being a Shots fan is fun once more.

Good stuff, good sentiments – although I recognise, of course, that at some level, given the absence of major investment in the club, this is making a virtue out of necessity. But emotionally, yes, I'm with her all the way.

And sort of ties in with Richard Williams's piece in yesterday's *Guardian* – 'Foreign owners chip away at what appeals to clubs' diehard fans' – essentially arguing that the concentration of foreign ownership in the top divisions of English football, an ownership often unaccompanied by any long-term emotional commitment, is proving a significant source of alienation, even cynicism. To which I would add the concentration of foreign coaches & players, though Williams doesn't go there.

I've admired for many years his writing on sport & music. Indeed, when he was at *Melody Maker* in the early 70s, he was really big for me & I used to hang on every word. Some ten years later, in 1982, I sort of met up. He was playing for *The Times*'s cricket team, I was a ringer playing for *Now!*'s team – equipment donated by Sir Jams – & the game was on a bleakish ground at Sudbury.⁴⁶ We batted first – I opened the batting – he opened the bowling (right-arm medium-fast). I did OK, getting to the forties, before he had me leg-before, playing across the line, when he came back for his second spell. At tea we happened to sit opposite each other. Inevitably there was a major potential conversation in my head; equally inevitably, I could see no way into it, & our only exchange was a kind of grin at each other – a mutual recognition of honours even.

---

⁴⁶ 'Sir Jams' was *Private Eye*'s notably adhesive nickname for Sir James Goldsmith (1933–97), businessman, Eurosceptic and long-standing foe of the magazine. *Now!* itself, his short-lived news magazine, had already ceased publication the previous year.

We do have one other link – we both saw what I'm sure we both reckon as the best goal we've ever witnessed. Boxing Day 1971 – City Ground, Nottingham – Williams as a Forest supporter, me because I was staying that Christmas in Nottingham, where my stepsister Zelda & her husband Carl then lived. Big crowd – Alan Ball's debut for Arsenal – & the goal (against Arsenal's then legendarily mean defence) was scored by Forest's Ian Storey-Moore, having run with the ball from near his own penalty area. Sadly no film footage exists, but Williams has lovingly described it in print at least once. Shots aside, that'd be the moment I'd go back to in my football time machine.

Jake rises

Tuesday 1 November

A week to go, & looking ominously tight in the US presidential. Hard – impossible, in fact – not to feel a sense of dread. Elaine Showalter in the *TLS* cites Hardy's *Titanic* poem 'The Convergence of the Twain' & goes on: 'This time, the convergence is between a woman who has dedicated her life to public service and a man who epitomises everything most reprehensible, greedy and selfish in American capitalism.' That perhaps slightly gilds the lily re Clinton, but the contrast remains stark.

I normally don't read it, but some escapist relief from *The Non-League Paper* (which comes out each Sunday). A letter from P. Boggis: 'I was appalled to see a Bowers & Pitsea substitute sneak off at half-time of Saturday's game with Aveley and urinate into the bushes behind the home team dugout! I shan't go there again!' Pages & pages of match reports (including 'Walker Is Saviour as Shots Get Their Dues'). 'Diary of a Ground Hopper' (this week at Odd Down on the outskirts of Bath – 'a couple of ladies in the tea bar inform me there is no hot food tonight'). Lots of tables (Newquay, presumably shorn of its private-school surfers, beached at the foot of the Carlsberg S.W. Peninsula League Premier Division, with one point from fifteen games). And all those seductive-looking fixtures for the week ahead (why wasn't I tonight at Anstey Nomads v Greenwood Meadows in the East Midlands Counties League?). Rather like the book I've got on Swedish progressive music in the 1970s, it's an alternative universe, with all the comfort that that (usually) brings.

Wednesday 2 November

Recent obits of Tom Hayden, invariably with a 70s photo of him & Jane Fonda, have taken me back to August '72 & *Klute*. A cinema in that narrow street [Orange Street] at the back of the National Portrait Gallery/National Gallery – & first time I ever paid a pound to see a film. Jane Fonda of course completely bewitching as the high-class Manhattan call girl Bree Daniels. And the film itself compelling – &, at the end, frightening. I especially loved that incredibly romantic scene when she & the deliberate, slow-talking country-hick-detective played by Donald Sutherland are buying some fruit & veg in a late-afternoon/early-evening street market, & she says something like (or to the effect), 'You've seen me at my worst, & yet you still love me.' It spoke very strongly to the 21-year-old me & somehow made me feel that love was possible. Time-machine-wise, in terms of movies, that one – at that time – would be the one – unless, as its only rival, I could be transported back to watching *101 Dalmatians* for the first time when I was a child... Which I think was at a cinema in Amesbury, Wiltshire – conceivably April '61, the holiday when I discovered, from a butcher's bill pinned on the kitchen notice-board, that the person living with my father was now 'Mrs Kynaston'. We were told so little then as children. That, surely, has been progress.

Friday 4 November

'ENEMIES OF THE PEOPLE' is the front-page headline in today's Ibsen-reading *Mail*. Those enemies are the three High Court judges who ruled yesterday that it requires Parliamentary approval to trigger Article 50 & thus set in motion the process of leaving the EU. Given that the Leavers had at the core of their case the sovereignty of the UK Parliament, the irony would be enjoyable if the prevailing mood was not so thuggish. Does anything matter more than the rule of law & the separation of powers? That is surely what serious, public-minded conservatives believe in just as much as their liberal counterparts do. I know it sounds prissy, but it matters, it really does. *The Times* quotes an interesting reaction from Dominic Cummings, the man who ran Vote Leave during the Referendum campaign & came up with the horribly effective slogan 'Take Back Control'. Apparently he has urged Brexit supporters to accept the judgment because 'at heart it is reasonable', adding that they should take a 'deep breath and stick to important principles of how a serious country works' rather than 'confused whining'. An early election – next spring presumably – now very much on the cards. At some level I dread the prospect – presumably a much enhanced Tory majority, even *before* the boundary changes – but perhaps the end of the Corbyn leadership & a strong pro-Europe showing from the Lib Dems. 2016 has felt like the year when the whole British soul has started to be at stake, & I wish I was more sanguine.

All of which applies in spades to the US (only four days to go). *Newsnight* last night ran a chilling interview with the New York novelist Paul Auster. He argued that 'Make America Great Again' essentially was code for 'Make America White Again'; & reckoned that the country was as divided as it had been at the start of the Civil War – a divide that he can see no way of being healed. Perhaps the sensible thing *is* to divide & no longer be the 'United' States? If it did, presumably into two blocks on a state-by-state basis, each block would still, economically speaking, be sustainably big & powerful. Better that than an actual civil war.

Barely a month after the 0–4 debacle at home, Shots are away at Forest Green tomorrow, & we're planning to go. They're 4 points clear at the top – there's a rich owner (? rivalled in the Vanarama only by Eastleigh) – and I'm dreading another one-sided affair, though hopefully with better decision-making by the officials. I'd almost be happy with a competitive match in which the Shots lost but scored.

Thinking a bit more about films, I *do* have another contender – also early 70s – for the time machine. I was staying outside Taunton with an Oxford friend, Margot Norman – who became for a time (90s?) a regular opinion columnist in *The Times* – & we (I think there was someone else as well) decided one Sunday early evening to go into town to see *Cabaret*. Taunton as we drove in looked utterly drab & uninspiring. But seemingly the next moment we were in our seats, the film was starting & I loved everything about it – the magic of the flickering screen. Over the years I've found it harder to watch – I guess as I've become far more preoccupied with what followed in Berlin & Germany later in the 1930s – & I wonder now if one day there'll be a comparable movie – set in London 2016? Shoreditch perhaps? – about a liberal, international world that was about to disappear. It's not that I actually *love* that world – in many ways I don't, & in some ways I instinctively prefer a more solid, insular, rooted, socially conservative world. But to actually get rid of that liberalism & internationalism? To trash intellectuals & experts because they are 'elitist'? To shamelessly be philistine? What could flow from all that literally does not bear thinking about.

Saturday 5 November

Well, on a bitterly cold afternoon at the top of a hill in semi-rural Gloucestershire, both my minimum requirements were fulfilled. However...

Forest Green predictably the better side in the first half, & one up at the break – felt like a softish goal, but Shots battling hard albeit let down by poor passing. Second half different: Shots attacking the away end (260-odd, raucous throughout, but not including Lucy & me, who watched with Andy in some rather scattered home support) & generally getting to exert a fair degree of control, if seldom threatening actually to score. *Then*, in the 89th minute, the sixteen-year-old Idris Kanu – recent signing from West Ham Youth, & definitely something about him – the principal architect of a fluent move down the centre that led to a well-taken goal (first of the season) by Jake Gallagher, our favourite. A minute or so later, following reasonably judicious celebrations on my part (Lucy by this time had retreated to an indoor vantage point), I turned to Andy & said that, for the first time in the half, I felt nervous... And rightly so, because in about the 92nd minute Forest Green won it with a cross & a fine glancing header into the top corner. A shame, particularly because a draw would probably just about have been fair overall.

After the match, we dropped Andy off in Stroud, drove home (mainly listening to an album of Cohen covers) & on return there was an email from Andy with a Stroud press report attached, saying that the Shots had deserved the equaliser. But of course, in terms of points, no parsnips buttered – & although the Shots stay 6th, that's because virtually no other teams played in the Vanarama today (First Round of the Cup instead). The conclusion has to be that we're a promising side & not at all a bad side, but as yet not quite good enough. Next Saturday it's away at Lincoln, who are about 3rd in the table, so that theory will once again be directly tested.

Meanwhile... I never intended this diary to be also a sort of commonplace book, & I hoped this morning that today's would be a Trump-free entry, but there are a couple of things in the *Guardian* that I feel the need to write down.

First, the final para from a piece ('The shadow he casts') by Oliver Burkeman about the widespread anxiety – among both Americans & non-Americans – about the prospect of a Trump win:

If he loses, it won't mark the end of the problem he represents. But it may nonetheless be a rich source of delight to savour the departure of the toxic uninvited guest who has spent the last year so stubbornly resident in our brains.

If he loses… The second quote is by Jonathan Freedland (whom I rate highly as a commentator). 'We are standing on the brink of the abyss,' begins his article, & towards the end there is this passage:

> Should he win, it would be a victory for a candidate who has lied more than any in history, who is spectacularly unqualified for the job and who stands contrary to the very idea of expertise. (Asked who he consulted on foreign policy, Trump answered, 'I'm speaking with myself, number one, because I have a very good brain, and I've said a lot of things.') It would be a triumph over truth, facts and knowledge. It would be the start of a new age of endarkenment.
>
> It sounds extreme, it sounds far-fetched. But that's because we assume that stability, even the civilised order, is somehow the natural way of things, almost impossible to upend. But that's not how it is. Civilisation is frail. The balances and restraints that hold us in check are delicate: they took many centuries to construct but would take only moments to smash. They rely on goodwill, trust and co-operation more than we realise. Take those things away, and darkness beckons.

Darkness beckons… Hard not to think at this time of the title (sardonic? impossible to say) of the new Leonard Cohen album: *You Want It Darker*.

Monday 7 November

Yesterday evening's dramatic newsflash was that the FBI had found no evidence of criminality in Clinton's latest batch of emails. Enough now to get her over the line? That would be a rational prediction. But reason, alas, seems to have been taking a very long nap.

I'm wrestling today with John Gray's essay, 'The closing of the liberal mind', in the current *New Statesman*. Predictably challenging stuff, but here's a bald summary:

The post-Cold War liberal order fading fast across the world.
Liberals responding by oscillating between 'insistent denial and apocalyptic foreboding'. (Guilty as charged to being in latter camp.)
Liberals, whether coming from right or left, 'can only envision the future as a continuation of the recent past' – a past dominated by what he calls 'market globalisation'.
How is 'a liberal way of life' to be secured? G's answer: stop seeing 'state power' as 'the chief threat to freedom' & instead accept 'the Hobbesian protective role of the state'. (Hobbes! Takes me back to the political thought paper at Oxford in the early 70s. Stupidly, I never imagined he'd be a relevant name in my lifetime. I always liked the story of how his premature birth, occasioned in 1588 by his mother hearing that the Spanish Armada was coming, fundamentally affected his world-view. I've never been to Malmesbury, but on Saturday looked wistfully at a signpost to it.)[47]

Gray then goes on a lengthy excursion into Corbyn's Labour Party. He argues that a) 'the legacy of Marxism is notable for its absence'; that b) 'the consensus-seeking values of core Labour voters are dismissed as symptoms of Labour backwardness'; that c) it has become 'a vehicle for a dedicated fringe of the middle class that finds psychological comfort in belonging to an anti-capitalist protest movement'; & that d) its defining feature 'is not an anachronistic utopian socialism, but a very modern kind of liberal narcissism' – a claim that he seeks to substantiate by pointing to

---

[47] Thomas Hobbes was born at Westport, now part of Malmesbury in Wiltshire, on 5 April 1588. 'My mother gave birth to twins: myself and fear,' he would later reflect. Given that the Armada didn't set sail from Corunna until late May, it was perhaps a false rumour of its imminent coming that precipitated labour.

how this new liberalism, giving overriding importance to rights & identity, is very different to old-style liberalism, which he defines as 'a philosophy that aimed to give a theoretical rationale to a way of life based on the practice of toleration'.

G then goes global again, noting the widespread *dis*connect between the middle class & liberalism, e.g. in Russia & China, as well as the palpable failure (e.g. Iraq, e.g. Libya) to impose human rights 'on societies that have never known them & where most people may not want them'. In short: 'There is no detectable connection between advancing globalisation & the spread of liberal views.' But importantly, returning to Britain, Gray does not see society here as *wholly* intolerant of liberal values. Rather, invoking again the sage of Malmesbury:

> They want what Thomas Hobbes called commodious living – in other words, the amenities of modern economy – without the chronic insecurity that is produced by unfettered market forces. Rather than rejecting market individualism, they are demanding that it be constrained. They would like to inhabit a common culture [what does that mean? a predominantly white culture?] but are happy for it to contain diverse beliefs and lifestyles.

G returns near the end to his notion of the strong state as protector of freedom & toleration – which in economic terms means the state 'delivering prosperity while managing the social disruption that globalisation produces', achievable only, reckons G, by a new type of globalisation – i.e., he suggests, no global free movement of labour across national borders.

Gray's final para is a bit of a scorcher & strikes home:

> Adamant certainty mixed with self-admiring angst has long defined the liberal mind and does so now. Yet beneath this a different mood can be detected. All that really remains of liberalism is fear of the future. Faced with the world they thought they knew fading into air, many liberals may be tempted to retreat into the imaginary worlds envisioned by left-leaning non-governmental organisations, or conjured up in academic

seminars. This amounts to giving up the political struggle, and it may be that, despite themselves, those who embodied the ruling liberalism are coming to realise that their day is done.

Well, there's been plenty of 'self-admiring angst' in this diary, I can't deny it. And I'm fearful of the future. *And* I'm starting to feel old.

But as to the larger arguments... I'm part of an informal group of historians & historical novelists who meet two or three times a year at Sarah Dunant's house for an evening's conversation. Our next gathering is later this month, & indeed we're going to discuss the post-liberal moment & what's to be done.

One other thing. I took part yesterday in an event at Stevenage marking the seventieth anniversary of its designation as the first new town. My fellow-speaker, the planning historian Steve Ward, mentioned two things: that, in 'community' terms, Stevenage had been pretty successful; & that its intake over the years had been relatively narrow (i.e. not much middle class, not many poor people, but instead the in-decent-jobs working class). Presumably there's a connection between these two things – i.e. people on the whole are more comfortable with people like themselves? With the necessary implication that to deny that, to attempt to make it otherwise, goes against the grain of human nature? I sort of made that point during the discussion, but no one really responded to it.

Tuesday 8 November

D-Day in the States. The psephologist Nate Silver – seemingly the go-to man, though always sounds like an Edgar Wallace character – reckons it 70% chance for Clinton, 30% for Trump. Thoughts turn irresistibly to opening scene of Stoppard's *Rosencrantz and Guildenstern...* Well, it *should* be OK, but *might* not be...

Which is a neatish segue to something else about today. Four years ago exactly – an American electoral cycle – I was discharged from St George's in Tooting after three months of in-patient treatment for my lymphoma. Essentially, four intensive cycles of chemotherapy, each lasting just over a fortnight, with a few days off at home between cycles. Lots of memories & conflicted emotions. A deep shudder (including at the nearness to death) – a profound sense of relief & gratitude (sixty-one seemed, rightly or wrongly, very early, though in the dramatic initial stages, after cancer diagnosed but not exactly what sort, I kept thinking of Cohen's wonderful & moving 'If It Be Your Will') – a bit of self-pride, I have to admit, at having got through the treatment without delays or the chemo being diluted in strength – & many specific moments of humour, of frustration, of sadness in the cancer ward generally. Did the whole experience make me a different person? Not really, I suspect. But perhaps a slightly better person – a little more patient, a little more tolerant. At the time, I was grateful for the ten years' training I'd had at boarding school: over forty years later it wasn't, psychologically speaking, that difficult to spend seventy-one nights in hospital. I was happy enough, though, to leave.

A few nights earlier was the night that brought news of Obama's re-election. A good moment – & especially sweet because George was working as an Obama volunteer in Philadelphia & because at about 4am I shared the news with a particularly lovely black nurse from Angola – who had been living in England for quite a while but whose husband was, to her despair, now determined to return to re-engage directly in the political struggle there. Politics, politics… And now, four years on, we have Trump with a 30% chance. Perhaps all we can do is to remember Dionne & say a little prayer.

Wednesday 9 November

Well, someone wasn't listening – or maybe only to the evangelicals…

As I guess for many other millions, a memorably awful night. Trying & failing to sleep (apart from a couple of snatches) – watching it unfold on TV, but finding it unbearable to go on watching – retreating to my study to do a little tinkering with my

B of E draft (the consolations of history) – giving only a glance at what was happening in the first day of the first Test in India.

Of course I'd been deeply anxious about the possibility of Trump winning, but it's undeniably a dreadful shock. Inevitably, plenty of strands of explanation – yet maybe ultimately, as Lucy said to me the other day, it's about a worm turning: the anger of the poorly educated about the condescension/ignoring of them on the part of the well-educated – the latter that self-perpetuating 'meritocracy' that Michael Young warned about. True in the Brexit vote, truer now in spades. And yes, it's also about men hating/fearing women, about whites trying to stem the demographic tide of non-whites, about Trump's TV-honed, TV-established popular appeal to those who don't loathe him: the strong man, even perhaps the father figure, with that inscrutable, tight-lipped smile when he's not frowning or haranguing.

What lies ahead? Perhaps two possible scenarios, & about 50–50 which it turns out to be. One pessimistic, the other optimistic.

Pessimistic: something like the scary Freedland vision – post-truth, post-liberal, even post-democratic – actually coming to pass, plus huge risks in relation to the world at large, notwithstanding his chumminess with Putin.

Optimistic: somehow a recognisably pluralist, democratic structure survives, there is no global blow-up, & the 2016 vote turns out to be the lancing of a very angry boil on the part of people on the wrong/declining side of history. Plus, yes (*pace* Gray), the 'liberal elite' starts taking economic equality seriously, stops going into Wall Street & management consultancy, produces a robust, morally unimpeachable, non-Beltway candidate who knows in his or her bones what life is like on the other side of the tracks.

Altogether, it feels this morning like the biggest political moment of my lifetime – rivalled only (but how sedate & parochial & unthreatening in contrast) by Thatcher in 1979. And it's not just a *political* moment, but something far more existential. Many Americans voted for Trump yesterday *in the knowledge* that he is a self-obsessed bully & a liar (or as Springsteen has said, 'a conman'). I'm certain in my mind that most people aren't wicked, indeed that they are fundamentally decent – & yet they did that. 'You Want It Darker'? Yes, Uncle Leonard, apparently we do. And I'm not sure I'm going to be playing 'Democracy' – inspiriting, 1992 – much in the next few days & weeks.[48]

A final thought. We spent much of yesterday with my mother & stepfather, both ninety-three. I'd guess that the first American President they were aware of was FDR; & the chances are that their last will be Trump.[49] From Roosevelt to Trump in a life-time: surely, surely, we in the West can do better. And if we can't, it's all up.

Friday 11 November

A resonant date, I realise as I write it, but all that feels some-what distant – this particular Armistice Day, this particular year. Though of course it should, given all the instability, all the nation-alism, all the pre-1914 – &, even more so, 1930s – echoes.

I'm sitting in the same café (Bingsoo) as I was almost exactly forty-eight hours ago, & yesterday I'd vaguely assumed that I'd write something more today about the election – though in truth I suspect I'm still in the first stage – denial – with all the other stages (anger/bargaining/grief/acceptance?) still to come. In fact, for today anyway, I'm going to try to park the whole Trump thing.

Over the last few months – in theory every Thursday evening, but in practice with interruptions – David Loffman has been coming to my house & we've been working our way through Leonard Cohen's studio albums. Last night we reached 2001's *Ten New Songs*, one of his very best, & we predictably swooned. First

---

[48] 'I think the irony of America is transcendent in the song,' Cohen said, reflecting on 'Democracy', one of the stand-out tracks on his album *The Future*, released shortly after Bill Clinton had won the 1992 presidential election. In January 2009, my friend Harry saw Cohen perform it in Wellington on the day of Obama's inauguration – a stirring moment.
[49] I should add that from the start they both cordially disliked President Trump. Also that five months earlier they had both voted Remain (the nonagenarian vote holding firm in Farnborough). They, after all, had seen first hand the reality of war in Europe – and accord-ingly valued, perhaps more than younger generations have done, the many years of peace that followed.

thing this morning came the news of Cohen's death. A classic 'not a surprise but a shock' moment, & now, mid-morning, I'm still absorbing that shock. Since 1968 he's been second only to Dylan as the singer-songwriter who speaks most intensely & sympathetically & continuously to me. I've been faithful throughout & love almost everything he's done. As I walked down the High Street to the café, & looked around at the mass of indifferent, bustling humanity, I felt a strong surge of gratitude for all that wonderful, enriching work – which will last & enrich for generations to come. All clichés, I know, but true clichés.

Before starting to scribble this, I've just read through the *New Yorker* profile/interview that appeared last month. Hugely interesting, & now of course especially poignant. I'll jot down a couple of quotes.

One by Suzanne Vega about Cohen's songs, describing them as 'a combination of very real details and a sense of mystery, like prayers or spells'. A simple, straightforward enough analysis, but actually gets one quite a long way. Plus of course the voice & whole feel.

The other by Cohen himself, probably speaking two or three months ago:

In a certain sense I've never had it better... At a certain point, if you still have your marbles and are not faced with serious financial challenges, you have a chance to put your house in order. It's a cliché, but it's underestimated as an analgesic on all levels. Putting your house in order, if you can do it, is one of the most comforting activities, and the benefits of it are incalculable.

Putting your house in order: that's so good, so inspiriting. Materially, spiritually, emotionally. A very conscious process & stage on his part? It seems so. Which he began perhaps in 2014, the year of his eightieth birthday, i.e. after ending his phenomenal world tour of 2008–13 – an astonishing 380 shows. And the article mentions that he finished (in Auckland) with a cover of the Drifters song 'Save the Last Dance for Me'. How I would love to have been there.

Where I won't be tomorrow is Sincil Bank, where the Shots take on second-in-the-table Lincoln City. This is a tough run of fixtures, & it'd be very nice to get at least a point. I'm not confident, but a bit of undeserved good fortune feels – in this of all weeks – overdue.

Saturday 12 November

I'm suitably penitent about that last sentence. Why doesn't a Lincoln-supporting, Trump-regretting, Cohen-mourning person deserve good fortune just as much?

And indeed... I listened this afternoon to BBC Radio Lincolnshire's match commentary. Not exactly one-eyed, but the two commentators barely mentioned an Aldershot player by name, which seemed a bit discourteous. The match itself seems to have been flowing & end to end during the first half, with the Imps 2–1 up at the break, & then much more stop-start, as the Shots scored twice to take a 3–2 lead & sounded reasonably comfortable at the 90. Six minutes of injury time (not unjust after various injuries) – & in the 95th or 96th minute, Lincoln equalised. So 3–3 at the end, & in a sense a good point, but how nice & play-off-affirming it would have been to win. Plus of course very dejà vu after last week. Down to 7th, though still more or less in touch, helped by several of the others above dropping points (but not Forest Green, now a staggering 9 points clear of the field).

Cohen obits & appreciations in today's papers. But somehow, more to collect than to read. Absurd, I realise, but I don't really want to know about *other* people's thoughts & feelings about someone who means so much – & in such a personal, subjective way – to *me*. Plus all the irritating minor factual errors & the recycled, over-familiar stories. Interesting to note, though, that apparently he actually died last *Monday*. Clearly not a sudden, unexpected death (he had cancer, plus had spoken himself in the *New Yorker* interview about its imminence). So did his family take a conscious decision to delay the announcement until the US election was out of the way?

Re that election itself: I think I may have made the transition from denial to anger. Whenever I see a picture of Trump, I just want to scream two words: 'Fuck You'. That's currently my elegant, thoughtful, Socratic contribution to the debate about why it happened & what's to be done.

Tuesday 15 November

A week since the election. This time last week I was allowing myself to believe that somehow it *couldn't* be Trump... Two defining moments over the last few days – one wretched, the other inspiriting. The former was, from a British perspective, undoubtedly the political photograph of the year: Farage as first UK politician to meet President-elect Trump (there – I've written those words), with the two vulgarians grinning together at gilded Trump Tower. Suddenly that seemed the future: an almost unbearable prospect. The other moment was the clip, from American TV, of *Saturday Night Live*'s Kate McKinnon, dressed as Hillary Clinton, sitting at the piano & giving a wonderful, utterly moving performance of Cohen's 'Hallelujah' – a song released in the year she was born & containing some lines that might almost have been written for this historical juncture. At the end, she turned to the camera & said, 'I'm not giving up and neither should you.' Perhaps – perhaps – the moment that will go down as the start of the fightback. I so much hope so, but who knows?

Inevitably I've been reading analysis-cum-prediction after analysis-cum-prediction since last Wednesday. Equally inevitably, the result is a general fuzziness & confusion in my brain. Although I don't want to turn this diary into a history book, the election outcome is *such* an event – the biggest (putting aside terrorism, assassinations etc.) of my lifetime? or second only to fall of Berlin Wall? – that I'm briefly going to set down, as a matter of record, the gist of what six people whom I would normally read or listen to have said. Apologetically, I realise they're all men.

Nick Cohen. 'This year is a revolutionary year for the radical right.' Calls on 'the western left' to 'imagine how it must feel for a worker in Bruce Springsteen's Youngstown to hear college-educated liberals condemn "white privilege" when he has a shit job and a miserable life'. Makes two suggestions for liberals: 'Thinking about class, not instead of but along with gender and race, would be a step forward. Realising that every time you ban an opponent you prove you cannot win an argument would be another.'

Francis Fukuyama. 'We appear to be entering a new age of populist nationalism, in which the dominant liberal order that has been constructed since the 1950s has come under attack from angry and energised democratic majorities.' (Though Clinton did I think win the popular vote – if so, six out of the last seven times for the Democrats.) Refers to Brexit/Le Pen/Putin/Erdogan/ Orban. Notes how the Democratic party became 'the party of identity politics: a coalition of women, African-Americans, Hispanics, environmentalists, and the LGBT community, but lost its focus on economic issues'. Re Trump specifically: 'I find it hard to conceive of a personality less suited to be the leader of the free world. This stems only in part from his substantive policy positions, as much from his extreme vanity and sensitivity to perceived slights.' And the man who brought us the end of history in 1989 – I don't mean to mock, it seemed up to a point a reasonable prediction at the time – now adds: 'The liberal elites that have created the system need to listen to the angry voices outside the gates and think about social equality and identity as top-drawer issues they must address. One way or the other, we are going to be in for a rough ride over the next few years.'

Owen Jones. 'Our crisis is existential,' declares Jones (like McKinnon, born in 1984), asserting that 'centrism, the ideology of self-styled moderates, is in a state of collapse', having 'shrivelled in the face of challenges from the resurgent populist right and new movements of the left'. What about the cultural gulf between the radical left ('often shaped by university-educated young people') & say 'older working-class voters in small town England, France or the US'? J's answer about what the left should therefore do is predictably question-begging, but perhaps unavoidably so: 'It clearly cannot compromise in the fight against racism, misogyny and homophobia but it must urgently work out how to … connect with the unreached… It cannot allow the populist right to portray it as a hater of working-class values.' But what if those values *do* inescapably have a racist/misogynistic/homophobic element or even character? On that, Jones stays understandably if unhelpfully silent.

Ian McEwan. A key predictive passage: 'By inauguration day in January, we'll be mouthing the words "President Trump" without incredulity or mirth. The danger is that it will begin to seem normal, this unique tragedy of national self-harm whereby a suspected con-man (the Trump University case, one of many, comes to trial on 28 November), this narcissistic and cynical vulgarian of limited attention span becomes the most powerful man on earth, ready by his own account to begin his assault on liberal democracy, rational discourse, civil liberties, and all manner of civil decencies, which are known to him as political correctness.' At the end, M raises the possibility that the US 'has elevated to its highest office a fascist by any other name' & concludes: 'At present it looks improbable. But it's going to be terrifying.'

Matthew Parris. The headline sums up P's apparent central thrust: 'Don't panic: Trumpism is just a passing fad'. While as to what to do about it while it lasts (from this voice of liberal Toryism): 'Stuff the windbaggery about engaging with these people [i.e. the electorate responsible for Brexit & Trump]. Stuff the facile columnising about Forgotten Britain. Kick away the condescension and forsake the quest to determine what's *really* worrying voters. These people are just wrong. They don't understand. They're risking self-harm. They could destroy us all. Say so. Have we lost our confidence? We free-market, free-speech, open-society liberals owe the Trumpists and little-Englanders absolutely no duty to understand, sympathise, reach out, or meet them halfway.' Stirring, confident words – but near the end P concedes, crucially, that the two things that 'clinched it for Trump' – namely, 'racism and jingoism' – *might* be so embedded & widespread, with a voice now conclusively found, that Trumpism et al. could turn out after all to be not such a passing fad… He finishes: 'Giving not an inch we must now wait and hope for the storm to blow itself out. Don't panic. Don't reach out. Don't concede.'

Simon Schama. This life-affirming historian, & one of our great public intellectuals, predicts that Trump's bromide-littered inaugural address will amount to 'a bad joke' & that in practice 'the walls of protection and the watchtowers of the security state will rise over the citadel nation', with 'freedom sacrificed to safety'. Can anything stop it? S pins his hopes on 'heterogeneous city culture' – with 'all its disorderly creativity, its flowing tides of newcomers and outgoers' – finding 'unapologetic champions' & making (unlike the Clinton campaign's 'arid menu of policy') 'a full-throated defence of modernity'. In time: 'The decencies of modern life need to be argued with militant passion and broadcast to places where it can be heard by people who don't read broadsheets.'

Well, I think all six say interesting, worthwhile things, & I'm pleased to have done this digest. I have to admit to finding Schama's defence-of-modernity argument personally uncomfortable (given the strong turn-the-clock-back strand to the populist right). The most recent volume of my post-war history is called *Modernity Britain*, covering 1957–62. And in it I argue that there was much about modernity – especially in the sphere of architecture & urban redevelopment – that went *against* the grain of what most people wanted. Moreover, if given a binary, catch-all choice between the 'modern' & the 'traditional', I would certainly pause for a long time before I put my cross in the former box – where, I guess, ultimately I would. So it's complicated.

The most chilling prediction – &, I suspect, horribly plausible – is McEwan's, i.e. that most of us will soon get used to the fact of President Trump. I couldn't face it at the time, but have just caught up with last Wednesday's *Newsnight*, on which Alan Greenspan reckons that Trump is essentially an actor – & that, as an actor, he will play the part of President well. It's back to that father-figure notion. And in 3½ years' time, as America faces real or bogus threats from a malignly depicted outside world, one can imagine – it's not too far a stretch as to be completely absurd – that father figure persuading his people (enough of them anyway) of the security imperative of postponing the next presidential election. Honesty compels me to add that I owe that particular speculation to my elder son George (currently in Houston), but since he mentioned it I've found myself getting quite fixated by it.

One last thing, before I hope this diary resumes more normal service. Which is a cyclical thought – unenthusiastic though I usually am about the cyclical, Toynbee-esque approach to history, implicitly downgrading the role of human agency & indeed chance. Anyway, here goes (with very approx. dates):

Cycle 1. Stage 1. 1850–1900. Internationalism/capitalism/ liberalism/inequality.

Stage 2. 1900–45. Nationalism & world wars.

Stage 3. 1945–80. Tamed capitalism & greater equality.

Cycle 2. Stage 1. 1980–2016. Internationalism/capitalism/ liberalism/inequality.

And now the second cycle to follow the course of the first? Including the dreadful second stage? We can only pray not – &, of course, try to stop it.

Wednesday 16 November

Went yesterday evening with Mike Burns to FA Cup First Round replay between AFC Wimbledon & Bury. Only a quarter of an hour's walk away, but first time I'd been to Kingsmeadow to see AFC since seeing the Shots there about five years ago. In theory I hugely admire the AFC story – & was as incandescent as the next man about the 'MK Dons' manoeuvre (why couldn't Milton Keynes, a sizeable place, organically grow its own football team?) – but in practice harbour jealous thoughts, essentially going back to spring 2013, when AFC & the Shots were two of the teams trying to avoid the drop from the Football League. They met at the Rec in about March – a desperately poor match between two poor teams, with the ball almost permanently in the air – & neither side deserved to win, but AFC did so, 1–0. A month or so later the Shots were down – followed by administration/survival & three for the most part mediocre seasons, while AFC steadily ascended. Anyway, I felt reasonably benign last night, perhaps because things now seem to be going broadly OK with the Shots. Which was as well, because AFC were very impressive, trouncing Bury 5–0 with some fine play, full of quick, slick interchanges on the ground – very different from the old Route One 'Crazy Gang'. An interesting moment, near to us, just before the end. A Bury player running full tilt, & trying to get his cross in before the ball crossed the byline, was charged fairly violently by an AFC player & sent crashing into the barrier, where he lay motionless for several minutes before eventually, a few minutes after the final whistle, being stretchered off. First reaction of home fans was moderately hostile – 'It's a man's game,' someone shouted – but quite soon turned silent & watchful. Then, as he was moved away on the stretcher, a good round of applause. Inevitably I wondered about the reaction if say Bury had been successfully holding on for a 1–0 win against the run of play. Very hard to guess for sure.[50]

This morning at Vauxhall, catching the Victoria line on the way to the British Library, I found myself sitting opposite a young woman with a New College sweatshirt. I thought about leaning over & saying something – maybe 'I was there a lifetime ago,' or perhaps, to prove my credentials, mentioning that the last of my history tutors, Eric Christiansen, had just died ('did you see the obituary in the *Telegraph*?') – but in the end just stayed doggo behind my *TLS*. The issue from the week before last – the last pre-Trump issue. Lucy this morning pointed me to the BBC website & his latest tweet. I reacted irritably – resenting the way he's taking over all our lives – but after she'd left the room did sneak a look. 'Very organized process taking place as I decide on Cabinet and many other positions. I am the only one who knows who the finalists are!' Government as a game show… He seems a man entirely lacking depth. And I'm grateful, as I write this, to be sitting in the BL, having a cup of coffee, looking around

[50] The unavoidable melancholy footnote is that in August 2019, owing to financial problems exacerbated by a period of disastrously unfit and improper ownership, Bury were expelled from the Football League. Echoes of Aldershot in 1992 were also unmistakable.

at civilised people, mulling over the almost infinite learning & wisdom that constitutes the library's purpose, & thinking that perhaps – but only perhaps – the barbarians might not triumph.

Thursday 17 November

Cohen footnote. It seems that he did indeed die on the 7th – in his sleep, shortly after a fall – & then was buried on the 10th in Montreal, next to his parents, at a ceremony attended by family & old friends, i.e. *before* the news of his death went public. Classy.

Friday 18 November

The Shots reaching a critical moment in the season, I suspect. Home to Macclesfield ('the Silkmen') tomorrow & home to Eastleigh ('the Spitfires') on Tuesday. After three away matches against top teams, in which the Shots played well each time but only managed a single point, it feels like a minimum – if demanding – target to get 4 points from the two games.

Interesting letter, from Andrew Purkis, in yesterday's *Guardian*. In essence arguing that New Labour was – in policy terms if not always process terms – broadly on the right lines. 'Blair repeatedly articulated a narrative in contesting both Thatcherism and clause IV socialism: that people do not thrive as atomized individuals, but when they are part of a strong society where people take care of each other and seek the common good. He embraced individual effort, meritocratic competition and people's strong desire for their own families to be successful and secure; but only as part of a society where people could rely on the basics that every person needs if they are to reach their potential.' And Purkis finished by predicting that 'post-Trump, post-Brexit, no narrative that departs too far from that synthesis is likely to attract a winning, progressive coalition in future'. I find that broadly convincing. And what a shame it is that Blair post-2007 has, by his avarice, contributed so much to the needless trashing of New Labour's record & legacy.

I've never met Blair, but have always felt that I know him. Partly because of an Oxford/generational thing (I think he was two years after me), partly because of getting the inside dope on him – non-tribal at a particularly tribal time – back in 1983. In the end, like Clinton, he didn't quite rise to the challenge. And as one of their generation – *that* was our chance, & we kind of blew it – I can't when it comes to it really forgive them. Ultimately a lack of moral stature & purpose on their/our part? The post-war generation that in the crucial formative years knew only soft or softish times? Plus that fatal, look-at-me self-regard. I don't want to exaggerate, to luxuriate in a masochistic beat-up. Our intentions were good – & that matters a lot in any final judgement. (Tolstoy, after all, says so in his foreword to *Resurrection*.) But still, there was something missing. And certainly, during the years of Cameron/Osborne harmony, sick-making in a way though it was, I found it embarrassing & even painful to look back on the starkly contrasting dysfunctional Blair/Brown relationship & the shortfall in character that it symbolised on the part of my generation.

Watched this evening the second half of Brighton/Villa. One all. Brighton featuring Dunk & Bong, but Villa the better side & unlucky not to win. Just a glimpse of their claret & blue always gives me a buzz: a real football club, with long, long traditions – &, of course, consistently underperforming. Now that I can no longer have a soft spot for Man City, I think it may have trans-ferred there.[51]

---

[51] That nascent romance with Villa never really happened. As for City, my old fondness for them (based I think on how their mixture of glorious highs and inglorious lows was somehow richer in human terms than almost any other club) had disappeared instantly once they became a grotesquely well-resourced branch of the Abu Dhabi royal family. But here I must relate my probably all-time favourite football story, told to me (and I suspect to quite a few others) by the distinguished Conrad scholar Keith Carabine. Brought up in Manchester after the war in a house with few books, he was trailing away disconsolately from Maine Road after a home defeat when he heard one old supporter say to another, 'Our goalkeeper's like the ancient mariner: he stoppeth one in three.' This pricked Keith's curiosity, he discovered who the ancient mariner was, and a life in literature ensued.

Sunday 20 November

Brumaire not proving a happy month. Trump, Cohen – & now the Shots sliding down the table. Lost 2–1 to Macclesfield yesterday. Not really firing, though overall perhaps a draw would have been slightly fairer. And on Tuesday it's Eastleigh, well-resourced club & recent Cup victors at Swindon, two leagues above. Shots now lie 10th & in some danger of drifting out of touch with the teams in the play-off places (2nd to 5th). A great shame if the league season fizzles out this early. But it's been a tough run of fixtures, with the prospect of some easier games ahead before long. So I haven't quite given up hope, but another defeat – especially a home defeat – would be a serious blow.

I am afraid I have come to despise (not too strong a word) the self-pitying Mourinho. For a long time I compared him to Brian Clough – both brilliant managers, both massive & incurable egocentrics, both with perhaps just an eighth of a screw missing (rather like Enoch Powell in that respect) – but Clough never felt so pathetically sorry for himself nor had such an automatic default position of blaming others. One way & another, there are currently rather a lot of people out there in the world whom I wouldn't be sorry if they didn't impinge on my consciousness again. Or certainly, in a jaundiced mood, that's how it feels.

Monday 21 November

'Patriotism must no longer be a dirty word' was the headline for a comment piece by Michael Gove in *The Times* the other day. 'Must' because, he argued, the alternative was to leave the field free for 'populist showmen' like Trump to exploit 'deep, powerful and natural human sentiments'.

I've been mulling over whether I'm a 'patriot'. I certainly feel myself to be British/English (the distinction doesn't particularly fuss me), even though I'm half German. Our great national triumphs still essentially thrill me – Agincourt, defeat of the Spanish Armada, 'standing alone' in 1940 – & I value the deep, largely peaceful continuities in our history. Depending on the sport, the opposition & the circumstances, I'm more often than not keen on British teams to win. Deep down, for all my vexation at times about its infantilising effects, I'm pleased we have a monarchy. I do believe there is something essentially different about us from the rest of the world. I love the greenness – & sometimes the intimacy – of our countryside. But does all of this make me a 'patriot'? I'm not sure. What I do know is that I loathe & fear nationalism – & that it is the apparently irresistible rise of nationalism that is turning 2016 into the worst year (in a public as opposed to private sense) of my life. Perhaps patriotism *is* possible without nationalism. Perhaps 'progressive patriotism' is even possible. I simply don't know. The 'salon' meets on Wednesday to discuss our emerging post-liberal age, & I'm hoping to read before then the Billy Bragg book.[52]

Of course, much turns on values, which I'm sure will be Bragg's thrust. And, although it suddenly feels so long ago, there was that wonderful '2012' moment: the Olympics opening ceremony, celebrating a Britain-at-its-best mixture of energy, of inclusiveness, of practical compassion. Utterly different from narrow-mindedness, from demonisation (& worse) of 'the other'. Something though that doesn't get much said is that *all* this identity stuff, if exclusively & dogmatically pursued, is fundamentally *boring* (including following a football team). I should be honest here. Although my first book, *King Labour*, had William Morris as its hero, & although I do still essentially admire & utterly respect him, the truth is that I find him – or anyway his vision – *boring*. I don't dispute that England would be merrier if the worker was less alienated from his work, if everything was either useful or beautiful, if society was somehow 'whole' & 'organic' – yet as a utopian vision (perhaps like any utopian vision?) it just doesn't do it for me. Life can only retain its savour if it is – at least to a significant degree – messy,

[52] *The Progressive Patriot: A Search for Belonging*, presciently enough published in 2006, a full decade before the culture war of the Referendum and beyond.

complicated & full of conflicting/conflicted motives. Or in the classic definition of a novel, 'a beginning, a muddle & an end' – & it's the muddle that really counts. Which in another sphere is why, in the great debate about urban planning, I probably come down on the side of Jane Jacobs & Ian Nairn, who back in the 60s argued against the functional 'zoning' of cities & in favour, in any one part of the city, of mixed purpose, mixed social composition & a generally light touch from the planners. Where life is *real* – philosophically, I appreciate, an absurd distinction – & where there is always a visual spectacle for one's eyes to feast on.

So why have I lived in a fairly undistinguished London suburb (though not without its charms) for almost the last third of a century? I'm tempted to answer, 'Who knows?' – as the elderly Shots supporter replied at half-time on Saturday when asked by another aged supporter how the Shots had managed to score three at Lincoln the previous week – but apart from inertia & perhaps geographical convenience, the truthful answer is that a) it's seemed a good – anyway, a possible – place to bring up a family, & b) as I've got older, I think I've lost the nerve to return to the inner city. Maybe I could still do it during daytime, but no longer at night.

I'm writing this at a Starbucks (one of my unfavourite franchises) in Canary Wharf (one of my unfavourite places). Surrounded by plenty of citizens of the world… Arriving at Canary Wharf during the morning rush hour – as I quite often did when doing HSBC's history – has always reminded me of Fritz Lang's *Metropolis* (the *very* opposite of the Jacobs/Nairn city), & there is something deeply & even chillingly inhuman about the place, as efficiently enough – I guess – it fulfils its role as the physical nerve-centre of international finance. The global, the modern, a smooth-looking glide-path from present to future, no sense (Jamesian or otherwise) of the past: at such moments, as I look around & struggle to see anyone older than barely half my age, I feel grateful for those things – even if they close down other things – that help to provide *my* identity.

Tuesday 22 November

Just checking out this morning the Shots website – as I do most days – & there's an announcement re three new directors, 'bringing decades of expertise [all three have a business background] and increased investment into the Club'. Who on the face of it could quarrel with that? But my personal alarm bells start ringing at one point. One of the three, called Lewis Scard – currently a management consultant, after thirty years in management at BA, & described as 'a Shots supporter since watching Aldershot thrash Gateshead 8–1 in September 1958' (so no quarrel there) – says: 'I see enormous potential in a club that sits in a huge and wealthy area of population, but it needs a product and a facility suited to 21st century needs and that will be something I'll focus on.' Which I think can be loosely translated as prawn sandwiches & a new ground – the very thing I dread, but fear is on its way.

I'm not especially looking forward to this evening. Shots on a poor & rather fraught run – the fans starting to express discontent – Eastleigh themselves obviously a very capable outfit who now need a run of wins to get into the play-offs zone. The signs, to my inveterately pessimistic mind, all point in one ominous direction.

I've a short letter in today's *Guardian* – always gives a bit of a buzz. It started as a correction to yesterday's editorial about C. P. Snow & 'The Two Cultures', pointing out that it was in Oct 1956, not Nov, that he first wrote about it. That in the event went into the paper's 'Corrections' corner, but they printed the rest of it as a letter: how the actual first publication date, 6 October 1956, coincided not only with Bobby Charlton's debut for Man U but also the day Lucy was born. And the letter finished with my assertion that in the 'Two Cultures' debate I'm firmly on the Leavis side: science (by which I really meant scientists) can learn far more from the humanities than the other way round. I wasn't just trying to be provocative – I strongly believe that. Assuming some external guidance is required (which I concede may not be), it's only the humanities that can possibly teach one how to live – as a human being in relation to other human beings. Which surely is *the* most important thing.

The function I went to at Canary Wharf yesterday evening was at Barclays' gleaming steel-&-glass HQ. Thirtieth floor, & predictably amazing to look out at lit-up London spread before one. Just for that few seconds I felt a master of the universe. So how can those who work there – the top people anyway, on the top floors – fail to feel it too?[53]

Wednesday 23 November

I forgot to mention about Monday evening. After Starbucks (part of the shopping complex by the tube) I took the long escalator that takes one up & out into much wanted fresh air (even if Canary Wharf fresh air). At the foot of the escalator was a young busker playing – admittedly not very well – Cohen's 'Suzanne'. Cheering somehow. I've often wondered whether the Victorian phrase 'all Lombard Street to a China orange' (meaning a near certainty) was conceivably somewhere in Cohen's mind. Unlikely, I admit.

Yesterday afternoon, at about 4, I had the revolutionary thought, 'Try & enjoy the match, whatever the result.' Which I duly tried to do – & as well I did, because the Shots duly went down by the only goal. Actually played much better than on Saturday & unlucky not to get at least a point, with Waddock justifiably not too downhearted in his post-match interview on 'Shots TV'. So yes, the slide continues – down now to 11th in the table – but a decent chance that things will turn. One way & another, I'll be happy enough when November ends.

Except that December will be the penultimate month of Obama's presidency. Trump fought his campaign on dishonest

[53] Three years on, it feels unnecessarily coy not to have mentioned that the function itself was the Wadsworth Prize for a business history book, awarded that year to *The Lion Wakes*, the history of HSBC that I'd co-written with Richard Roberts. A bittersweet memory, because it was the last time I saw Dick, who died just over a year later. We'd worked closely together on three books, enjoyed each other's company, and (for all our political differences) barely had a cross word.

promises & is now just as dishonestly (except in a different way) distancing himself from some of those promises. He is a man without shame – the most dangerous sort.

Thursday 24 November

Yesterday early evening I was on the Northern Line, heading for the north London 'salon' & starting to dip into the Bragg book. At Embankment, someone sat next to me – a middle-aged man, & I sensed he was curious to see what I was reading. After a bit he started reading himself, & I sneaked a look. It was – I'm not making this up – a photocopy of the Statutes of New College, Oxford, mainly in Latin but with a little English in the margins. Again, the dilemma of whether to say something; & again – the carriage getting too crowded? because he sat down on my deaf side? – I once again stayed shtum. My guess is that he was a lawyer, who'd come one stop from Temple, & was preparing for a case (to do with land?) involving the college.

Talking of colleges… I see that Clinton is now some two million – a packed Wembley Stadium times at least 20 – ahead on the popular vote. It beggars belief how Trump would have reacted if the situation had been the other way around.

I won't say much about the salon. They're private occasions, in which we all feel relaxed & can speak freely. It was predictably congenial & stimulating. After one of us had cited Hannah Arendt – about how the decline of the extended family, leading to atomisation & loneliness, can be one of the facilitating conditions for totalitarianism – I found myself saying something about how I increasingly felt that Michael Young had the right of it: not just about kinship, etc., but also his dystopian warning about the danger of a self-perpetuating meritocracy. More generally, we all seemed to feel that these are seriously dark days; & although of course our analyses & predictions varied considerably, it was undeniably good for morale (my morale anyway) to have been there. I appreciate that this may sound all too like whistling (or even pissing) in the wind.

Meanwhile, here fairly briefly are some voices/views etc. I've come across in the last week or so. (Putting this stuff down on paper – being 'the historian' – as therapy?)

Rowan Williams. 'Naught for our comfort; but at least an opportunity to ask how politics can be set free from the deadly polarity between empty theatrics and corrupt, complacent plutocracy. What will it take to reacquaint people with control over their communities, shared and realistic values, patience with difference, and confidence in their capacity for intelligent negotiation? It's the opposite of what Trump has appealed to. The question is whether the appalling clarity of this opposition can wake us up to work harder for the authentic and humane politics that seems in such short supply.' The Incredible String Band fan writing here in the *New Statesman* – where recently criticised for his overly dense & opaque prose style, but surely not applicable in this case.

Laurie Penny. 'The bullies have won, but they will not win for ever, unless we let them into our hearts as well as our governments.' Indeed (as Flop might say to Bing Bunny).[54]

Mike Harding (taking his cue from the revelation that 'the *Chicago Tribune*, the Midwest's biggest newspaper, doesn't even have a Midwestern beat any more and seldom sends reporters outside the Chicago metro area'). 'The (ex-*Manchester*) *Guardian* and other major media voices need to build a northern (and a Welsh, a Scots and a Midlands) presence. They need writers who understand the lives of the people that they are among. Otherwise we will end up in a J. G. Ballard world where shadowy figures stumble round a decayed hinterland while, smug in their southern citadels, the higher orders sleep safe.' I've never really listened to his songs, but that last sentence makes me want to. And of course he's right: the media has become ludicrously London-centric – a major contributor to anti-London feeling.

---

[54] In the animated children's TV series *Bing*, the calm and judicious voice of Bing Bunny's minder, Flop, belongs to Mark Rylance. A personal theory – not contradicted by the chronology – is that this worked as a dry run for his Thomas Cromwell in *Wolf Hall*.

NB: As I was writing down the Harding quote, the train slowed for St Albans City & just before the station went past a lovely, old-fashioned signal box on the left. Philip Hammond in his Autumn Statement yesterday apparently announced a centralising communications revolution for railway signalling, which will lead to the redundancy & presumably destruction of all 500 of Britain's surviving signal boxes. I'd guess the box in Wales where Raymond Williams's father worked is already no longer there.[55]

Steve Kropper (letter to the *Economist* from Lexington, Massachusetts) – *in toto*: 'Mr Trump's election transfers joy, hope and optimism away from us coastal liberals to America's geographic and economic middle. Therapists and serotonin boosts will flourish in this new depression. But we progressives pledge to rediscover the common man. We will buy at Walmart, not Amazon, get coffee at McDonald's, not Starbucks, shop at Piggly Wiggly, not Whole Foods, listen to AM radio, not NPR. Soon we will become reacquainted with our fellow Americans.' Ironic or not? I guess it has to be but I'm still not absolutely sure after several readings. (The first, on the train to Aldershot on Tues, was followed soon afterwards by having something to eat at Burger King, so that seemed appropriate.) The letter irresistibly reminds me of the *Frasier* episode when, somewhere miles from Seattle at a roadside diner, Frasier likewise decides to reacquaint himself with his fellow Americans. Suffice to say that it doesn't end well.

Zadie Smith: 'Trump is a little petty narcissistic fool, there's one in every school... But he is President, so his arena for that sin is suddenly monumental.'

Sarah Sands (*Evening Standard* editor): 'Those who fundamentally oppose the world of Trump – its Vegas, reckless, bullying, hyper-masculine nature – need to find a strategy. I'm afraid merely

---

[55] Presumably not, given that Pandy station (on the Marches Line between Hereford and Abergavenny) closed in 1958. That signal box loomed extraordinarily large in Williams's world-view as well as personal mythology. See D. L. LeMahieu, *Lost Fathers: Raymond Williams and the Signal Box at Pandy* (Lake Forest College Publications, 2014), available online at https://publications.lakeforest.edu/cgi/viewcontent.cgi?article=1007&context=history_pubs.

making fun of Melania Trump's pout isn't it. The Breitbart brigade are at the top of their game, sharpened by confrontation, and they have an unnerving combination of rigour, belligerence and bursts of politeness as weaponry. Because some are gay, Jewish or female they can dismiss accusations of hostility to these groups. They are impressive in argument, and in a psychopathic way they are good company.' An uncomfortable observation, not often enough made. But what's the 'strategy'? Perhaps no alternative but to fight fire with fire? No more Mr Nice Guys... Yet given the degradation of public discourse already, it's a hateful thought.

Paul Mason points out how the psychologist Erich Fromm located the origins of inter-war fascism in a fear of freedom & specifically how he attributed the centre-left's failure to resist Hitler to 'a state of inner tiredness and resignation' (Fromm's words). And Mason concludes: 'Only one thing can make this most educated and liberated generation [referring to the under-forties, where according to YouGov's UK polling evidence liberal globalists outnumber the ultra-right by two to one] succumb to tiredness and resignation: if the centrist middle classes and the liberal media give up on freedom.' Giving up on freedom... It's almost thirty years since I read it, but I often think of a passage in Jocelyn Brooke's *The Orchid Trilogy*, when the central character decides at the end of the war *not* to come out of the Army – because it's only when he doesn't have freedom that he actually has freedom.

Giles Fraser cites & endorses *The Trouble with Diversity*, written in 2006 by 'the socialist academic Walter Benn Michaels' (I hadn't heard of him). The thrust is that affluent western liberals privilege the evils of sexism & racism in order to avoid focusing on economic inequality. To which one might add the accompanying focus on inequality of opportunity as opposed to inequality of outcome.[56] 'Rich western liberals, Michaels argues, don't want to challenge the economic structures that produce inequality

---

[56] Not that, when it comes to the private school issue, that focus on inequality of opportunity is nearly relentless enough (in Britain anyway).

because that might seriously impact on their own standing and wealth.' Sounds convincing to me.

And finally, quite closely connected, the *Observer* had a piece about how Richard Rorty – American, Old Left, now dead – predicted in 1997 how disastrous would be the left's increasing preference for 'cultural politics' over 'real politics' – disastrous because, as economic conditions/anxieties worsened as much for the middle as for the working class, then they would 'start looking around for a strongman to vote for – someone willing to assure them that, once he is elected, the smug bureaucrats, tricky lawyers, overpaid bond salesmen and postmodernist professors will no longer be calling the shots'. 1997 ... Blair & Clinton ... Third Way... Impossible, at this moment of intense foreboding in November 2016, not to tip one's hat to Rorty.

Friday 25 November

Coleridge apparently (according to Martin Kettle in today's *Guardian*) described history as the lantern on the stern of a ship ploughing forward across the sea through pitch darkness. A wonderfully compelling image. And as I write this down, with Barnsley v Notts Forest on silently in the background, Nicklas Bendtner comes on as a late sub for the visitors. A good man to have on your side when you're 4–2 up against ten men.

Shots away tomorrow at Sutton United. Only a 213 bus ride away, but we've got Wolfie for the weekend so won't be able to go. I've only been once before to Gander Green Lane & was disappointed by how far away from the pitch I was standing. Sutton got promoted last season & are doing quite well, especially at home. But on their artificial pitch, I rather fancy the Shots – badly due for a win.

I have a degree of fondness for Sutton the place, because both our sons went to the grammar school there. Not an inspiring education perhaps, but a generally good, cohesive atmosphere & producing generations of very solid, decent citizens, often on the science/medical side. I'm certainly not knocking it. But the place itself ... well, it's a huge shame: probably a lot going for it up to the 60s/70s, but then almost catastrophic redevelopment, destroying the character/individuality & slicing through with particularly brutalising one-way traffic systems. I remember a Saturday morning I spent there in around November 2005, sitting in a café reading obits of George Best but mainly walking around while Michael was taking his dreaded 11-plus exam at the school. By the end I was in a cold fury about that redevelopment thirty or forty years earlier. So unimaginative, so unnecessary, so stupid. And of course it was repeated in many, many places – all part of a 'modernity' zeitgeist that now on the whole looks tawdry, as well as being largely malign in its social consequences.

Saturday 26 November

To think that at one point this season I was slightly anxious that the Shots might have *too* successful a season, thereby making this diary unrepresentative of my Shots-supporting experience. It didn't sound great at Sutton today. Jake Gallagher sent off – unluckily? – on the stroke of half-time, & Sutton taking the spoils with two second-half goals. On balance, happy enough to have missed that one. Still in 11th place, but the prospect of a play-off spot starting to fade away into the distance. One point from November's five games. Certainly some misfortune, but hardly enough to account for 14 lost points.

Monday 28 November

'It's legitimate to lose sleep on account of a private worry, but not on account of a public worry,' Gladstone once said (or words to that effect). I don't think I've been losing sleep over Trump, etc., etc., but truly – & not to strike a rhetorical pose – I feel as pessimistic about things as I suspect I've felt in my adult lifetime – & apologies if I'm tediously repeating myself. 'Bleatings of a liberal wimp' is shaping up to be the subtitle of this diary, but I can't do anything about it. Our Labour leader praised the recently dead Castro for seeing off a succession of American Presidents – to which Jacqui Smith neatly responds, 'That's because they have elections in America.' The President-elect reacts with his usual destructive, undemocratic coarseness to attempts to make sure that the voting & counting were correct in the key swing states. UKIP elects a leader who will target – probably successfully – the traditionally Labour-voting 'patriotic working class'. The choice in France next spring is likely to be between Le Pen & a socially conservative Thatcherite. And Ed Balls – dancing while Rome burns – is finally voted off *Strictly*.

Tuesday 29 November

My rather hazy impression of Paul Nuttall, the new UKIP leader, was of a bruising skinhead northerner. Today I read that he used to be a history lecturer – which came as a complete surprise. So on the *Daily Politics* (to which I'm unhealthily addicted) I caught up with the interview they had with him yesterday. For most of it I found myself not wholly disliking him: not my kind of guy, but seemed reasonably straightforward, not a fanatic, & less self-serving than Farage. Until near the end, when he said the words, 'If you're a Remainer, we're coming for you.' We're coming for you… What would I have felt if that had been said the other way round, e.g. by Tim Farron? Presumably I'd have found it at best distasteful. As it was, I found it chilling & even frightening.

The Times today has a clever, revealing item – namely, a Premiership league table based on the cost (in transfer fees) of each point won so far this season by each club. The top four are WBA (£2.94 million per point), Bournemouth (£3.01 million), Watford (£3.09 million) & Burnley (£3.39 million). The bottom four of this 'value table' are Arsenal (£8.74 million), Chelsea (£11.59 million), Man City (£12.64 million) &, almost tailed off, Man Utd (£18.06 million). Presumably the 'efficient markets' hypothesis should have more or less parity of cost per point? But as 2008 conclusively showed, markets are not efficient.

Wednesday 30 November

Bitterly cold today, & my thumb & fingers are struggling to write even though I'm sitting on a train.

On the *Daily Politics*, the shadow Education Secretary, Angela Rayner, was asked about a) whether Blair deliberately misled Parliament in the run-up to the Iraq War (there's an Alex Salmond-inspired motion about it today), & b) Castro's reputation & the left. Both of them interesting questions, but in neither case did she show the slightest interest in giving any sort of answer. (After all, as she observed, she wasn't even alive when Castro came to power.) The shadow *Education* Secretary... I'm really trying in this diary to avoid grumpy-old-man stuff – not least because it's generally the old who are screwing the young these days – but I thought this was desperately poor, as well as revealing about Corbynistas & history.[57]

On the second question, I guess I would have wanted her to say, as a Labour spokesperson, that, yes, there had been something noble & even heroic about Castro's resistance to malign American intentions & his prioritisation of welfare; but that ultimately that was outweighed by the mixture of human rights abuses & political dictatorship – the mixture that has been the Achilles heel of the left for most of the last century. Either liberty, democracy & pluralism are inalienable givens, or they aren't. And in Cuba – like China post-1949, Russia pre-1989 – they're not. I appreciate the obvious charge that this is very much a western, first-world perspective; but actually, I do believe in universal values – & certainly in our modern, interconnected world. I could, I know, well be mistaken. I've always, & I'm not remotely defending this, been far more interested in the developed world than the developing world – & never, even as an adolescent, got off on Fidel & Che. Probably a lack of imagination – never my strongest suit. But maybe also an impatience/irritation – at root

---

[57] Subsequently I've come much more to respect Rayner (who didn't vote for Corbyn in 2015). Albeit late to recognise the importance of the private school issue, she seems to me more generally to be made of the right stuff.

puritanical – jealous? – with those on the British left keener on fighting glamorous battles in distant places elsewhere than getting their hands dirty here. Not of course that I've ever particularly got my hands dirty here either.

Bernard and Kundai: stars together

Friday 2 December

The fightback starts in New Malden: six words I never thought I'd write. To be precise, the part of New Malden north of the railway line (I live to the south of it). The general expectation was that [Zac] Goldsmith would hold on at the Richmond Park by-election held yesterday – a by-election triggered by him over the issue of Heathrow's third runway, but in practice fought predominantly over Brexit. The successful Lib Dem candidate, Sarah Olney, only got into politics as a reaction after last year's general election & made a strongly pro-tolerance, pro-Europe pitch. (Obviously a good egg, because there was a photo last week of her standing at home in front of bookshelves that included a

copy of *Austerity Britain*.)[58] It's clearly not a representative constituency – Richmond itself is a seriously wealthy place – but I'm
still thrilled. The Tories have now in effect defined themselves
as the party of Brexit, & that leaves plenty of space – *if* the left-
of-centre, which now potentially includes the moderate-just-
right-of-centre, can get their act together. A big 'if'. Labour now
seem strangely irrelevant – but at some point they're going to
have to resolve things. Owen Jones yesterday argued strongly &
cogently that the party needed to find voices capable of speaking
to the working class in the North, the Midlands, South Wales,
etc. But he was unable to bring himself to the logical conclusion: that Corbyn & the Corbynistas are – with few exceptions –
incapable of being those voices. Admittedly, his argument begs
the question of whether those Labour voices should to any significant degree jettison middle-class social liberalism. That's
a tough one. I think where I am is, yes, greater controls over
immigration, e.g. no one able to come from Europe without a job
lined up. But at the same time, adamantine re core liberal values
of tolerance, inclusiveness, pluralism & accountability (including
of the media). Ultimately, it could well be that, like in the States,
there are two cultures that can no longer find sufficient to agree
about. In which case London, with outposts in Oxbridge & a few
other places, declares UDI?

Vanarama matters. Shots, at halfway point (twenty-three
games) through the season, are now 12th, so barely in top
half. (Up in the stratosphere, Lincoln have clawed back Forest
Green's seemingly unassailable lead & even gone ahead.)
Tomorrow it's home to Boreham Wood. It almost feels that the
point of no return (in terms of a play-off place) has already
passed, but just possibly not. But another defeat tomorrow, &
I'll start looking anxiously at the gap between the Shots & the
bottom four.

---

[58] What I didn't realise was that her father Ian and my stepfather Bill had been for
many years good friends as fellow-members in Farnborough of the local Railway
Enthusiasts' Club.

Sunday 4 December

Some other words I didn't expect to write: the Shots won yesterday. Mind you, it's all relative: I went with Dil Porter – seriously committed watcher of lower-division & non-league football – whose own team, Leyton Orient, have now lost eight on the trot at home, apparently approaching Newport County's all-time league record. It was a decent, hard-working, disciplined performance, if a little ponderous at times. Nice opening goal midway through the first half – a run down the left from Bernard Mensah, low cross, crisply (& expertly) turned in at the near post by Scott Rendell – eventually followed about a quarter of an hour from the end by a special moment. Long, searching ball by Matt McClure out to Idris Kanu on the right. 'Cross it, cross it,' Dil & I kept saying, but he held on to the ball, beat his man & fired home between keeper & post. The 'disappointing' – though not to me – Boreham Wood (lying just outside the play-offs) hadn't threatened all that much, & they didn't really before the final whistle. Shots move up to 9th – albeit somewhat flattering, with most other teams having played fewer games. Still, hugely welcome, & perhaps a turning-point. Though sadly, like A. J. P. Taylor on the 1848 revolutions, a football season is full of turning-points that fail to turn. And incidentally, up at the top, it's Tranmere who have regained the lead.

Today is the other fiftieth anniversary that I had in mind when I started this diary. Sunday 4 December 1966 was the day the *Observer* published 'The Agony of an Aldershot Fan' by 'David Kynaston, Wellington College, Berks'. I'd sent the piece in wholly on spec, & I couldn't quite believe it when I saw it in print. (I'd spent the night before on a ghastly CCF – Combined Cadet Force – exercise, trudging around some bleak countryside before finally having to pitch tent in the school grounds. My enforced companion was one of those unhappy, bullied boys whom everyone despised – the pack hunting together. We sort of got on OK, just about, but no, not a happy night.) Next day, being taught about Bismarck's Germany by our young, charismatic history teacher

Dave (as we all called him) Ward, he mentioned Potsdam – & then, looking briefly but meaningfully at me, called it the German equivalent of Aldershot. I did get paid for the piece – £5, or was it guineas? – & spent the money on two LPs: by Glenn Miller & Django Reinhardt (the latter mainly because of the name).

And reading it now? Embarrassment of course – & an acute sense of what a strange fifteen-year-old I must have been. It mainly focuses on the club's history & recent travails, plus also about my own history as a Shots supporter: high points, low points, etc. After noting that the Shots had won only six out of their previous fifty-six away league matches, it ends: 'A strong masochistic streak is needed, I feel, to be a fanatical football supporter, especially if one follows a side like Aldershot. But I suppose that you have to be a masochist to be a monk or a nun.' Well, words rather fail me to comment on that. Except perhaps to reflect that, half a century on, I'm pleased still to be a Shots supporter; but also pleased that I'm not quite a 'fanatical' one, or I hope not anyway.

I think I should add something – it feels dishonest not to. About a week & a half ago I posted a print-out of my 'Agony' piece to Aldershot's programme editor, mentioning in an accompanying note that I'd be perfectly happy for her to reprint any or all of it in the prog for the Boreham Wood match. No acknowledgement, & nothing in actual prog yesterday – though, to be fair, it did have two pages on a rather more significant Shots anniversary, namely ninetieth of the formation of the club in December 1926. Undeniably a pang of disappointment, though I'd been ambivalent about whether to send it in the first place. One's adult relationship with the football club that loomed so large in one's childhood & (protracted) adolescence: a weird & rather edgy business.

Monday 5 December

On the train from Wimbledon to St Albans. Early afternoon, just stopped at Herne Hill. I used to go to the dentist there,

c. 1957. No local anaesthetics then to make one's mouth numb, so during a filling he'd try to distract me from the pain by putting a couple of bits of cotton wool on the string (or whatever it was) that was attached to his drill & would whizz round. I don't think I've set foot there since, but the hill itself always looks rather alluring.

Thinking about the match on Saturday, I reckon it exemplified the maxim that Eamon Dunphy formulated in his terrific & pioneering mid-1970s diary, *Only a Game?* – namely, that in a contest between two fairly equally equipped teams, the winners will almost invariably be the team that most wants to win.[59] I suspect that on the day the Shots wanted it just a little bit more – & at one point a Boreham Wood supporter got as near as he could to the touchline &, shaking his fist, fiercely upbraided one of his players for lack of commitment. That said, 'the Wood' did in fact keep going, & near the end Dil remarked that one of the things he admired about professional sportsmen is that they never give anything to their opponents – that everything has to be earned. It reminded me of a moment in the late 1990s when I took George, about ten, to a Shots match. It was injury time at the end, the Shots were losing 2–0, it was inconceivable they were going to get back, & the ball came to me. A Shots throw-in, but because I thought he'd be thrilled to have a touch, I gave the ball to George to throw back. The Aldershot player by the touchline was highly impatient & wanted the ball back as quickly as possible – in other words, as a real footballer, that was how he was programmed, *whatever* the circumstances. Which brings me neatly to AFC Wimbledon's latest exploit. Yesterday, three down in the Cup away to lowly

---

[59] The nadir of Dunphy's season (1973–4) came in November when he was dropped to the reserves. 'As we don't have a match tomorrow, we got extra training when the first team had finished,' he wrote on a Friday. 'We have to do weights. I don't believe in weight-training anyway. But it means that by the time you get in, the bath is cold and full of slime, someone has used your towel, and everyone has left already, and it really gets to you. You think "What am I doing here?" All you have got to look forward to is Aldershot reserves away next Wednesday.' A literary reference beaten only by the moment when, in Peter Terson's exuberant if nihilist 1967 play *Zigger Zagger* about football fans, Zigger rhetorically asks his friend Harry who has tried unsuccessfully to join up, 'Who would you have supported in the army? Bloody Aldershot?'

Curzon Ashton with only 10 minutes to go, they came back to win 4–3. I can't deny it, there's something special about them. (And in the first match at Bury, before the replay, they were two down at half-time.)

Yesterday's *Observer* revealed that that very day was the paper's 225th birthday. Which meant that my 'Agony' article must have appeared on its 175th birthday. Back in the mid-twentieth century...

Tuesday 6 December

The current *New Statesman* has a full-page ad for RADICALTEATOWEL.com – 'Tea towels, aprons, cards, fridge magnets, mugs, coasters and other gifts inspired by history's radical thinkers'. Sixteen of those thinkers feature in the ad, each with a portrait (in some cases iconic). Ten men, six women. The men are on the whole predictable enough: Aneurin Bevan, Nelson Mandela, Karl Marx, Mahatma Gandhi, George Orwell, Keir Hardie, Tony Benn, Che Guevara. Two perhaps more surprising: George Washington (but I'm so ignorant about American history – 'a world-indoor record for ignorance', as I once heard John Peel say about himself & classical music – that I don't have any clear idea of how 'radical' he was) & Oscar Wilde. Radical? Yes of course in one sense – *De Profundis*, Reading Gaol, etc. – but he also wrote that sceptical essay on 'The Soul of Man under Socialism'. I once heard the story – true or not I don't know – of how Raphael Samuel became a socialist. Apparently when he was nine or ten, he read somewhere in Wilde (? one of his stories) about black clouds 'lowering' over the East End – & in a moment of epiphany, he wondered to himself why black clouds didn't lower over the West End. Anyway, turning to the six women: Sylvia & Emmeline Pankhurst, Maya Angelou, Rosa Parks & Virginia Woolf would be on many such lists. But surely not the sixth – Jane Austen. There is a new book out arguing for her as a radical writer, but still a bit of a stretch. The only one of the sixteen that I've personally encountered is Benn. First at a Hatchards

'Authors of the Year' party c. 1995, where I asked him something to do with the Attlee government's nationalisation of the Bank of England, & he was pretty brusque & *de haut en bas*. Still, better than our phone conversation about eleven years later. I'd sent him some draft pages from my *Austerity Britain* that included passages from his diary. He was distinctly unfriendly, taking exception to an interlinking passage by me that related to him, & at one stage the temperature dipped further when I had to point out that he was confusing Bevin & Bevan. I found myself shaking when I put down the phone. Since then, partly following his death, some fondness for him has gradually returned, & I've also got to know a little – & like very much – his daughter Melissa. In the end, putting aside personal pique, my criticism of Benn would be that he never took the trouble really to get to know 'middle England' & that he, like so many upper-middle-class progressives, retained an almost ludicrously sentimental view of the working class. But still in his way, when all said & done, a great figure. And also, not the least of his qualities (certainly legacies), a terrific political diarist.[60]

Thursday 8 December

A month since Trump won. A month & a day since Cohen died. David & I listened yesterday evening to his penultimate album – *Popular Problems*, in my case first time for quite a long time. Predictably inspiriting. But in relation to the world at large I remain depressed & fearful, only marginally alleviated by last Sunday's Austrian presidential result – where, after all, some 47% voted for an extreme right-wing candidate.[61] A possible strategy of course is just to treat Trump as a comic figure – as someone so preposterously self-regarding deserves to be. And maybe that's what it'll have to come to, though I'm not quite there yet.

[60] Also of course, like Michael Foot, a great orator. How we miss those figures on the left now.
[61] The actual figures were 46.2% for Norbert Hofer and, fortunately, 53.8% for the much more moderate Alexander Van der Bellen. Austrian politics generally, however, remain on the dark side.

We – the 'metropolitan liberal elite', etc. – are constantly told it's our fault. We ignored the white working class; we patronised the white working class; we privileged everyone but the white working class. And now that white working class has voted for the illiberal, nationalistic right – & looks like going on doing so.

Do I feel guilty? Sort of. In a partial defence, I'd say that I have a somewhat greater awareness of the 'left-behind' than some anyway of my friends (predominantly, like me, privately educated + Oxbridge) – an awareness, in as much as it exists, largely derived from background research for my post-war pro-ject, e.g. in Sheffield a few years ago making a point of visiting a grim (utterly grim) 1960s concrete shopping centre celebrated by Owen Hatherley for its brutalist brutalism – a place where the middle-class footfall must be infinitesimal. And of course I also go to football matches. But that's about it. I don't watch soaps, I don't read the tabloids, I barely have a working-class acquaint-ance let alone friend, I don't think I've ever set foot inside a factory, I mouth platitudes about the need for greater equality but have no intention of making significant voluntary financial sacrifices. In practice, I'm on my planet, they're on theirs, & never the twain... So given that 'my sort' have largely had it our own way for a very long time – certainly in terms of pushing & even imposing social liberalism – isn't it time they had their turn? That in essence is the argument of Charles Moore (Thatcher's biographer) in the current *Spectator*, i.e. 'the people' trump 'the elite', especially as the latter have in some fateful ways, e.g. the banking system, made such a mess of things. Yet in the end, no. Not when 'the people' themselves embody values I can under-stand but not accept – & above all not when malign political-cum-media manipulators try to exclude from their definition of 'the people' all those people (like the 48%) who inconveni-ently see things differently. So yes, we certainly need a tougher-minded, more self-critical, less hypocritical liberalism. And if that involves being a member of 'the elite', unashamedly warning against the dangers of 'populism' – with its invariable whiff of mob rule – well, so be it. (Incidentally, some years ago on *Newsnight*, I warned against the dangers of populist politicians

& was briskly put in my place by Janet Daley, who in effect said 'populist' = 'popular' = no problem.)

I'm scribbling all this on the train to Oxford – a day out, to see a couple of friends. I hope I live long enough to go on the envisaged Oxford-to-Cambridge rail line – in my day as a student, it was a tortuous three-hour journey, via Luton, on a Percival's coach. They're trying to avoid the obvious name – calling it the East–West (or is it the West–East?) line – but I'll be amazed if it doesn't finish up being known as the Oxbridge line. And with any luck servicing an Oxbridge that is more open & inclusive than it is now.

Friday 9 December

Shots away in the Trophy tomorrow to East Thurrock United – deep in the heart of Brexit country (Thurrock voted 72% Leave, fourth-highest in the UK). I'd been intending to go, but a mixture of tight schedule for doing the BoE references + discouraging weather forecast + general fatigue means that I'm going to sit it out. Which makes me feel a bit pathetic diary-wise, but there it is. As for the FA Trophy itself (for the higher echelons of non-league clubs), it strikes me as not wholly wishful thinking that this could be the year, although of course it never has been in the past. I suspect that Waddock is particularly keen to have at least a decent run, whereas more genuine promotion contenders than the Shots might perhaps be rather more ambivalent. East Thurrock themselves are on a good run, & although a division below it could well be a tricky one. Idris Kanu, incidentally, was seventeen last Monday & signed his first professional contract. He's given a potentially exciting extra dimension to this season. A few weeks younger, & he'd have been the first Shots player to have been born this century.

Monday 12 December

Listened to the BBC Radio Surrey commentary on Saturday – with suspended Jake Gallagher fulfilling the 'expert analysis' role. Best moment came when they were discussing how referees this season are supposed to be clamping down on manhandling in the penalty area, e.g. at corner kicks. 'You've just got to keep your arms down,' said Jake, before adding, 'or make sure you don't get caught.' Definitely a back-row rather than front-row member of the class.

The match itself a slight disappointment. Shots mainly on top, but unable to take their chances, & in the end a 1–1 draw, with Bernard Mensah scoring in the first half after Kanu had powered down the left. The rain belting down by just after the final whistle, which made me grateful not to be finding my way back in the dark to the nearest station – apparently about a mile from the East Thurrock ground, though with the ominous rider, 'as the crow flies'. Replay tonight & I'm hoping to get there, though rather a lot depends on the trains between now (early afternoon) & then – am taking the tapes of my references to my transcriber, Mandy Howard, who lives near Maidstone.

Today's *Guardian* has an obit of the *Sunday Times* columnist A. A. Gill. It's by Stuart Jeffries & includes the sentence: 'If contempt and hatred were virtues, Gill was the most virtuous of men.' I never much read him, but that chimes with my impression. It also chimes with my growing sense of – & distaste for – the current arrogance/triumphalism of the right. Take a couple of recent moments. Louise Mensch was on the panel of last week's *Question Time*, & the topic was briefly that of socialism. The rather uninspiring Labour guy made a decentish stab (including invoking the NHS as the prime example of socialism in practice), while she was caught by the camera making thumbs-down signs at the audience. The other was a recent Sky clip of Douglas Murray (from the rising generation of public intellectuals) trashing Richard Gott (from the fading generation) in the context of Castro's death. Repeatedly, Murray insisted that Gott, with his one-time links to the KGB according to Murray, was on 'the wrong side of history'. Of course, in an obvious & important sense he's right. But a) the New Left was in non-Stalinist, pluralist existence for a third of a century before the fall of the Berlin Wall, & b) are Murray & the rest of the right quite so sure that they're now on the 'right' side of history, given what seems to be their relative complaisance about the fast-rising forces of populist-cum-authoritarian nationalism? I suspect that when (if?) the history comes to be written of this dark period we're now entering, they're the ones who will come to be seen as the useful idiots.

Tuesday 13 December

Trains all good (despite Southern's woes), & a memorable evening at the Rec. The crowd fairly sparse – inevitable for early stages of Trophy, plus season-ticket holders having to pay at the gate – & the south side (where we usually sit, & where I sat the first time I came to the ground) was closed off. Shots started well on top & took the lead (cross from Anthony Straker on left, firm header from Matt McClure) after about 25 mins. Then the turn-round. Smartly taken equaliser – Jack Saville then sent off (last defender, etc.) for the Shots – & East Thurrock scored from the free kick. The second half saw a storming performance from the ten in red & blue. A fine early equaliser came from Charlie Walker after a brilliant bit of play from Bernard Mensah down the left, & Shots then very unlucky not to take the lead – before East Thurrock regained it with a good set-piece in about the 80th. But never say die, & the Shots pulled it back (Mensah) in injury time. Extra time. The palpably flagging ten tried to get it to penalties, but the visitors scored early in the second period & it finished 3–4, though not before Shots came desperately close right at the death. Michael & I thought it a really gutsy effort, so disappointing to get home & watch Waddock's post-match interview. No acknowledgement of that, but instead sustained finger-pointing at 'mental weakness' & talk of how a promising start to the season was turning into a very average season. Perhaps a bit unfair (& unimaginative) in terms of last night, but in essence I suspect he's right – as those cruel late goals last month at Forest Green & Lincoln probably testified. And bottom line, the fact is that in both cups this season the Shots have fallen at the first hurdle – in both cases at home to lower-league opposition, though of course each time involving a debatable first-half red card. Déjà vu again.

Today's date brings into focus that long-ago epoch when the Shots & the Biscuitmen (aka Reading) were big local rivals, in the eyes of the Shots anyway. The key year was 1967, with two vividly contrasting FA Cup matches.

First up was midweek in mid-Jan, at the Rec after a postponement. It coincided with the final episode of a three-part adaptation of Evelyn Waugh's *Sword of Honour* trilogy – the one with Apthorpe & his thunderbox, plus with a detail about his unsuccessful efforts in goal for his prep-school team. I dearly wanted to watch it, but naturally the Shots took priority – this, after all, was *the* big one. No video recorders then, & in the event I would never get to watch the episode, almost certainly wiped. The match itself, in front of a packed crowd, completely compelling – & indeed a man died of a heart attack. The decisive moment came midway through the second half. Peter Kearns, a small, clever inside forward for the Shots (? equivalent of Blackie Gray, probably grammar-school educated, for Melchester Rovers), played a perfectly weighted through ball that got Jack Howarth in – one on one on the keeper. Big & lumbering, he was never the greatest finisher on the ground, though wonderful in the air. I couldn't believe he was going to score, but he did, lashing it home, in front of the East Bank, for the only goal. In my all-time top three Shots moments, no question. And at the end of the match, over on the tannoy came the current single by the Who – 'Happy Jack'.

Eleven months later, on 13 December, came another midweek postponed Cup encounter, this time at Elm Park. It was still term-time at Wellington, so with official permission almost certainly out of the question I had no alternative but to take a chance. After dinner (or whatever we called the early-evening meal), I found a nicely concealed part of the back drive, where I was picked up by my very game mother & stepfather (who already lived in Farnborough, about seven miles away). We drove to Reading, & I went to the match with my mother (definitely not Bill's scene). A nightmare unfolded. 5–0 to Reading at half-time, including a free kick from the touchline that floated over or past our agile but small keeper, Tony Godfrey. A better second half irrelevant, & it finished 6–2. We'd crumbled before the Biscuitmen. Afterwards, Bill – what had he been doing during the match? in my self-/Shots-absorption I'm fairly sure I never thought to ask – drove us back to Wellington. I think I was back in the Stanley [my house] just before lights out at 10 (in those days a 7.30 kick-off, not 7.45, & only 10 mins for half-time), & fortunately my absence hadn't been noticed.

The rivalry fitfully continued through to about the mid-80s, but nothing again quite so momentous or technicolored. It must have been in the 1983/4 season that I took Lucy to her first two Aldershot matches – a total of one goal scored, & that by Reading. It was a long time before she went to another – & even longer before she saw the Shots score.

Then, as the Shots steadily sank & Reading steadily rose, I became in the course of time (during the 90s? no, more like the new century) more or less indifferent to the gulf. Unless there's a freakish change of circumstances, I doubt I'll ever see the two play each other again – & for local, demonised rivals I have to make do with Woking, which somehow doesn't quite cut it.

Thursday 15 December

Today's *Guardian*. Top of front page: photo of Le Pen ('The Le Pen insurgency: The rise of the far right'). Inside: a measured but infinitely depressing & damning editorial ('Donald Trump's team shows this is not a normal administration'). And on the obituaries page: an obit of E. R. Braithwaite, author of *To Sir, With Love* & a hugely dignified figure, who was born before the Great War & has just died at the age of 104. About ten years ago I wrote to him asking for permission to quote a passage & was thrilled to receive his wholly courteous reply.

The Trump appointment that has really got to me – amidst stiff competition – was the one the other day of the pro-Putin oil mogul Rex Tillerson as Secretary of State. It was the appointment of an amoral power worshipper by an amoral power worshipper. It is hard to see how the situation could be worse or more dangerous. That Clinton received 2.8 million more votes, & that Putin's hacking smoothed Trump's path to power, merely adds salt to the gaping wound. I long ago (around 1974?) lost my love of *Rolling Stone*, viewing it as increasingly corporate & complacent, but its current warning that the conditions are horribly ripe for the making of an American tyrant seems entirely plausible to me. Whatever the failings of the 'liberal elite', nothing but nothing makes defence or endorsement of Trump justifiable. The man is a monster.

All of which – in this fragile, neurotic place that liberals like me find ourselves in – makes it doubly important not to exaggerate. I don't believe the above para does, but I think I did exaggerate about A. A. Gill. It is clear from stuff I read later on Monday that he was a real & rounded person – &, specifically, that he wrote powerfully & sympathetically about the Calais migrant camp, as well as more generally about refugees. So, apologies there.

One utterly reliable balm over the last six or seven weeks has been Trollope's *Framley Parsonage*. A chapter a night since late Oct, finishing it on Tues. Few outstanding passages, unlike Dickens; but also, unlike Dickens, he really understood human nature – how everyone is a mixture of good & bad, how our motives are always mixed. And maybe I should try harder to hold on to that. Perhaps it's stupid to call Trump a 'monster'. Perhaps, he genuinely wants for his country what he sees as the best. Perhaps he'll be a servant of the people...

Friday 16 December

Discussed Trollope with David Warren this morning. He said that T, unlike (or anyway more than) any other novelist he knew, had characters who evolved from day to day, even minute to minute – & he also said something about T's unsentimental realism: even in the good times, life is never *that* good. My less insightful contribution to the conversation was to mention the chapter in his *Autobiography* where he discusses other Victorian novelists – & specifically, how he places Thackeray way above Dickens: not so much on purely literary grounds, but more because Thackeray is a far more *moral* novelist, who thereby teaches his readers to lead better lives. Which of course reads strangely to modern eyes, but I'm not wholly unsympathetic.

Sticking with the world of letters, the first two letters in the current *New Statesman* both come from Tunbridge Wells: surely a record – & hard not to wonder what Kingsley Martin or even John Freeman would have thought.[62]

Have just watched on TV the second half of Norwich v Huddersfield – 2–1 to the visitors, with probably the highlight being the chant of the disgruntled home supporters, 'Sort it out, Delia'. The closing minutes not quite as irritating to the neutral as they often are. I've come intensely to dislike the almost invariable tactics of the winning team: the keeping of the ball in the corner (pioneered by Revie in the late 60s), the take-the-heat-out late substitutions (featuring a barely jog-trot departure from the field of play), the goalie making a simple save & then diving forward to lie motionless on the ground for several seconds, the general anti-life, anti-sport time-wasting. I'd like refs to be completely draconian: an instant red card for any hint of time-wasting. But it's barely even talked about as an issue – all under the acceptable guise of 'professionalism'.

The Shots tomorrow away at Chester, just above them in the table. It's a place (like Harrogate) that I have quite a deep instinctive dislike of, & not just because of the 8–2 mauling last season. In both cases, probably *au fond* because they're so far removed from my notion of what a northern town or city 'ought' to be like. In Chester's case, my prejudice has even affected my research: at the Mass-Observation Archive, I came across its study of shopping habits soon after the war at Chester's department store, Browns – &, on the ludicrous grounds that I didn't want a place like Chester in my book, barely glanced at the survey. As for Harrogate (at one time, & maybe still, the last postcode in Britain not to have a Tesco), I've long associated its arch-gentility with Pete McQuay,

---

[62] They were successive editors from 1930 to 1965, when the magazine's influence was at its greatest. And traditionally, letters from Tunbridge Wells tend to be to the *Daily Telegraph*, ideally from retired colonels.

who in the mid-70s was fined for having a pee in the public gardens after he was caught short.

I won't be listening to the Shots commentary, because my plan for tomorrow is to meet Nick Humphrey at Dulwich Picture Gallery – where I haven't been for a long time but which now has a particular extra interest because it was built by John Soane, who also built the B of E (before it was more or less destroyed between the wars by Herbert Baker). The idea is to have a look round, have a bite & then head to Dulwich Hamlet, home tomorrow to Tonbridge Angels. Apparently there's quite a cult developing about DH, & it'll be interesting to see the phenomenon close-up. Nice also to watch a match where I can feel entirely relaxed about the outcome.

Saturday 17 December

The Shots slumping to an entirely predictable 2–0 defeat – Waddock a malcontent bunny in the post-match interviews – but still an enjoyable day. The Picture Gallery a thoroughly civilised experience (with the odd 'wow' moment, such as the Rembrandts) & interesting to get a glimpse of Dulwich Village (not many 'left-behinds' there). The football (2–1 to the Angels) was fun: fast, pretty skilful, with enough blood & thunder to satisfy my old-fashioned tastes. And yes, something definitely going on. Attendances are double those of anyone else in the Ryman League; lots of young spectators (both children as such & young adults); while socio-economically, though a mixed crowd, the fact of a Thai food stall spoke eloquently. However, like Aldershot, the ground had a somewhat rundown feel – &, also like Aldershot, there's apparently talk of moving. Inevitably I find myself thinking about Aldershot's future, & my guess is that it's going to happen within the next few years: not just because of maintenance/ upgrade costs, but just as much if not more because of a fundamental repositioning strategy, i.e. a new ground somewhere in the Aldershot region that will have the requisite upmarket facilities & ambience to appeal to the residents of that highly prosperous area that lies around impoverished, working-class Aldershot itself. Almost certainly, in business terms, it makes sense as a strategy. For myself, I can't bear the prospect; but that's my prediction.[63]

From 'Editor's Notes' in today's match programme, this sentence about Hamlet's match (a 2–2 draw) against Royston Town last Saturday in the Trophy: 'It was a most interesting game, between two sides who had never met before, but sadly it was marred in the dying minutes by an unsightly melee, which resulted in two players being red-carded and both managers sent to the stands.' As written by Sir Alf ... except perhaps that he'd have had 'regrettably' for 'sadly'. And though I'm sort of poking fun, there's something (the dignity?) about the tone that I really like.

Thursday 22 December

A bit of a diary hiatus. Partly the usual pre-Christmas stuff. Partly through giving a higher priority to helping to edit the memoir of an ill friend & fellow-historian, Juliet Gardiner.[64] Partly an overwhelming sense of fatalism & enervation in the face of Trump et al. (Why, I've been wondering almost ever since, did I write those absurd, Trollope-influenced words? He's a bad man, & no good can come of this turn of events.) Partly because my optimism about the Shots – seldom abundant – is running almost on empty. And also, football-wise, because I am finding the Premiership virtually a complete turn-off this season. The top six comprise exactly the top six almost everyone would have predicted in August – the two Manchesters, the three big London clubs, Liverpool – & as to what precise order they finish in I feel more or less indifferent. Foreign players – foreign management – foreign (big) money.

[63] A faulty prediction, mercifully enough, to judge by the June 2019 news that Rushmoor Borough Council had agreed to grant the Shots a new 118-year lease at a reduced rent to help the club with its redevelopment plans – plans which, we are assured, will modernise the ground without losing its essential character.
[64] *Joining the Dots*, which enjoyed a justifiably warm critical reception on publication in August 2017.

Who the fuck cares? Except of course that a lot of people still seem to, but I'm not one of them.

It's high time that something was done to level things up. Perhaps a handicap system (e.g. Burnley start the season on zero points, Man U start it minus 30). Or something like American football, where the smaller clubs get the first pick of new players. My own pet solution – ideally to be enforced globally – is that professional footballers can only play for the professional club nearest to their place of birth. Not great in terms of freedom of labour, I fully concede, but could be wonderfully capricious & egalitarian. I've yet to broach it to anyone without them thinking it's barking.

I might as well set down here the other related & long-term bee in my bonnet. Essentially it's a desire-cum-plan for the World Cup (& maybe the Euros also) to be played out on a genuinely 'cup' basis. In short (re the World Cup finals): 128 countries to proceed on a seeded, knock-out basis à la Wimbledon tennis championships, though in this case lasting a bit longer, perhaps three weeks. Every match would matter – & we'd no longer have to endure the interminable group stages. A cup is a cup is a cup... It's never going to happen, I know, but again, what larks (which in the end is what sport is about) if it did.

Christmas Day

Have just been with Lucy to the 8am service at St John the Baptist in Old Malden – a really lovely & very old church, which could easily be in a picturesque 'olde' village but in fact lies barely a stone's throw from the dispiritingly impoverished & thoroughly modern (in a dilapidated, mid-twentieth-century sort of way) immediate surrounds of Malden Manor station. The benign & inclusive Kevin taking the service, beautifully subdued lighting, a congregation of ten (Lucy at sixty close to the youngest), & an unshowy, quietly nourishing feel to it all. I'm pleased to have gone, though my 'belief' remains in a strangely semi-detached state of limbo: wanting to, yes, but somehow unwilling to retake the plunge. Alan Bennett, in an endearing (? valedictory) documentary about him on TV last night, talked of how he remains deeply moved by the hymns of his childhood, but has lost all faith – & now has no one to say 'thank you' to at moments of blessing or deliverance. I suspect that upsets & worries him more than he publicly acknowledges, though generally he seems in a calm place, looking back on a fortunate life. On that tranquil note was *almost* how the programme ended – but not quite. Instead, he read out his diary entry for the day after the Referendum vote, comparing the Leavers to the self-serving, self-deceiving supporters of Munich & appeasement in 1938. A strong, salutary, non-saccharine coda – & good on the BBC for including it in a seasonal tribute to a national treasure.

Catching up with a recent *TLS*, I've been struck by this by Kate Webb (new name to me) reviewing a short-story omnibus, *The Visiting Privilege*, by the American writer Joy Williams (a newer name to me than it should be): 'Written over the past forty years, these unconsoling tales ("There is no happy ending," one character warns) lay bare the disturbed psyche of America. Cumulatively they seem to forewarn of the derangement we are witnessing in the age of Donald Trump, the loss of proportion and propriety, and a vast carelessness, even about the truth. Beginning in ordinary circumstances, her stories often lurch into something more sinister or perverse, presenting solipsistic individuals, environmental degradation, cruelty to animals, and an uncertain sense of what constitutes reality.' Wow (if that's not itself disproportionate)... And touches brilliantly on the sort of pervasive fear/anxiety 'we' now all have about this horrible turn of events, as e.g. expressed these last few weeks in many Christmas card messages between friends.

On the Shots front, it's a double-header against Woking over the next week – home tomorrow, away on New Year's Day, & in both cases early kick-offs. Am confident, irrationally perhaps, that the Shots will take at least four points from these two local derbies, maybe re-energising their season. I've always enjoyed going to a Boxing Day match: a robust spectacle in the fresh air, human nature not always at its best, a necessary counterpoint to those elevated but not wholly realistic sentiments of Christmas. I'm fairly sure that it was on Boxing Day forty years ago that I saw the Shots beat Crystal Palace 1–0 at home in the old Third Division (a briefish stay there). Now four divisions separate the clubs, & Palace have just appointed Allardyce as manager – the specialist in percentage football & avoiding relegation. I hope they do stay up – I like the idea of that vast swathe of suburban south London having a club in the top league. The first time I went to Selhurst Park was on a midweek evening in around March 1970, mainly to see Jimmy Greaves (only time I watched him in the flesh, alas), then at West Ham & past his prime. A goalless draw. And afterwards, trying to find my way to the station, I got completely lost in a maze of hilly, anonymous streets near the ground – the first time I realised viscerally how huge & mysterious London was, as I started running in a panicky, sweaty way – & eventually returned that night to Shenfield (where, post-school, pre-univ, I was working in a children's home) very, very late.

Tuesday 27 December

'I think the Shots will win comfortably,' I said to Michael yesterday as we approached the Rec, & so for once it proved – a thumping 4–0 win, with all the goals in the first half, including a Scott Rendell hat-trick (the first helped by a wretched piece of goalkeeping as the Woking man flapped at a cross). All very gratifying, though not nearly competitive enough to be a truly memorable derby. A good crowd (home support of about 2,800), & not *completely* impossible that this could be the start of a surge towards the play-offs (Shots currently in 8th, but quite a gap to 5th), with eight of the next nine games being against teams lower in the table (though on the whole not much lower).

Two Christmas deaths have reminded me of my judgemental, Leavisite streak. Status Quo (Rick Parfitt) sometimes seemed single-handedly, as it were, to take the imaginative possibilities out of the counter-culture moment & its immediate, 1970s legacy. Denim, 'catchy' choruses, loud & plodding guitars, male & proud of it. Industrial music for what was then still an industrial age. My critique has of course a significant element of class-cum-cultural snobbishness, I realise that, but that's just how it is. The other death has been George Michael (coincidentally, I think, the names of our two sons, in that order). When we moved to New Malden in Nov 1985, the music that soon after started to come ceaselessly through the thin walls, being played at max volume by the teenage boy next door, was that 'wake me up before you go-go' song – I came to loathe it with an almost unrivalled intensity. Thereafter, I'm not sure I heard him much, but instinctively my associations are with showbiz & tabloids & the ratcheting up of overblown personal emotion, with little or nothing to 'say' about the world at large, or even connection with it. I could of course be completely unfair, & obviously he had something, but that's my feeling – as, I'm afraid, it also is in the end about Elton John: potentially wonderful (I especially loved 'Rocket Man'), but seduced by glam, & despite honourable, well-meaning efforts could never quite get back.

Thursday 29 December

Another 'Gill' moment. Have been reading in last day or two about George Michael as gay icon/activist + lavish (secret) philanthropist + backer of striking miners in mid-80s + free concert for NHS nurses... I think that next time round I'll pause before scribbling down my crabby reaction.

A Labour MP for a north-west constituency (Whitehaven the largest town) resigned just before Christmas – tricky test for Corbyn. The MP was quoted the other day about how both government & Labour needed to stop neglecting areas like Copeland (rather artificial name of the constituency). A cliché of course, especially since June, but I'm struck by one particular sentence, surrounded by the usual stuff. Here's the quote by Jamie Reed: 'Remotely accessible peripheral areas are ignored by the centre of government and that has to change. And I passionately believe that the sense of grievance is one of the principal factors which fuelled Brexit. I've talked about our lower league towns, our rugby league towns, it's true. It's true vast swathes of people in our country feel ignored...' Yes, indeed, & how refreshing as well as helpful it would be if the *Guardian*, for instance, stopped in its football coverage so obsessively & unimaginatively focusing almost exclusively on the big-city clubs. Reed himself goes on: 'And that means they are unsure about their sense of worth as a community. That's not a good place to be.' Seems a shame he's leaving politics.

Michael very thoughtfully gave me for Christmas the pro-gramme of the Man U match in 1970. Just the 16 pages, & what is really striking (& struck Michael) is the plethora of small ads for small local businesses. V. J. & V. H. W. Truss ('Home Cooked Hams Our Speciality') of 82 Church Road, Aldershot. Balmoral Grill ('Grills, Sandwiches, Ice Cream, etc. Moderate Charges') of Station Road, Aldershot. W. Knott (Tyres) Ltd ('Personal Service while you do your shopping') of 3a Arthur Street (Nr. G.P.O.), Aldershot. While in the notes on the visitors, this about their Belfast-born winger: 'A colourfully modern character who has business interests outside football'.

Friday 30 December

We're about halfway through *The Crown*, the recent drama series about the early years of the Queen's reign. Utterly compelling as drama, treating the royals as 3D, entirely fallible human beings. And at times brilliantly conceived, e.g. treating the Coronation largely through the wistful eyes of the Duke of Windsor. But as history? Weirdly enough – certainly for me as a viewer – Andrew O'Hagan in his *LRB* review of the series characterises its period settings as being like 'an implosion of David Kynaston'. Well, perhaps, but really, quite apart from the apples-&-pears aspect of any book/TV comparison, the terrain & preoccupations of 'my' kind of history are very different from this: altogether more common & commoners. While as far as I can tell, which isn't all that much, the series is pretty cavalier with the historical record (e.g. its treatment of the relationship between the young Queen & her aged PM, Churchill) – though of course what we *truly* know, historically speaking, about the modern royals is very limited. I noticed in the series credits – as usual, rolling past far too quickly, in the current discourteous (to participants) & inconsiderate (to viewers) idiom – that there didn't seem to be a historical adviser. Which made me feel better – only a minor pique, but even so – about not being asked. Though really, for this, it should have been Peter Hennessy anyway.

Saturday 31 December

For the last few weeks I've imagined that my New Year's Eve entry would be a penetrating & magisterial overview of the unlamented year about to slip away. But now when it comes to it...

On my way here (Bingsoo, mid-morning) I saw a couple of front-page headlines, both in their different ways profoundly depressing. *Times*: 'TRUMP SIDES WITH PUTIN' – or was it the other way round? We're in *Animal Farm*/*1984* territory here, as the thugs & bullies become interchangeable. *Mail*: 'ARISE, SIR FOREIGN AID' – about a New Year's honour for a mandarin in charge of dispensing foreign aid, expenditure now the target of intense venom – & comprising 0.7% of our annual budget.

All in all, it's starting to feel like that once-in-a-generation moment. This morning the odds feel stacked in the wrong direction; but yesterday afternoon, walking across the footbridge linking Northumberland Avenue and the South Bank, just as the sky darkened & the fog closed in, I found myself gazing along the Thames & succumbing to a sudden burst of optimism – something to do with London the global city, where the possibility exists of tolerance & acceptance, of live & let live, even of a generosity of spirit. I don't for a moment forget the economic aspect. Poverty, lack of work, badly paid work, demeaning work: all these things can easily – & forgivably – curdle the spirit. My gripe is with the adequately (or better) well-off, with the decently educated, who parrot all the crap about the evils of 'political correctness' & do not care about democracy, about pluralism, about the dignity & importance of the public-cum-civic dimension.

While as for the Shots... It's away at Woking tomorrow, & in theory Lucy, Michael & I are going. But the weather forecast is for heavy rain, we'd be standing on an uncovered terrace & I'm starting to think there might be a case for – feeble though it sounds – ducking out. Amidst all too many signs of mortality (David Miller, of my agents Rogers, Coleridge & White, & whom I've known since he came in the early 1990s as an assistant to Deborah Rogers, died yesterday – just fifty), I'm not sure I want to start 2017 with a bout of pneumonia. As with so much else, we'll see.

P.S. Since writing that, & back home, have read Tim Lott's 'family' column (which more often than not I like very much – especially its realism & streak of the curmudgeonly) in today's *Guardian*. He notes that the most popular New Year resolutions are (according to a YouGov poll): '1. Lose weight. 2. Get fitter. 3. Eat more healthily. 4. Take more care of my appearance. 5. See more of friends and family.' Salutary, because the top three – aptly categorised by Lott as 'purely individualistic and somewhat narcissistic determinations' – are precisely what I've been resolving for myself. And quite apart from the relatively lowly place of resolution no. 5, he observes that 'notably non-prioritised are resolutions to be kinder, to try to help the poor, read more and better books or stop watching junk TV'. So what to do? His own resolutions (to be adapted 'in a gentle, non-gritted-teeth kind of way') are 1) to 'embrace' one's family 'as a kind of precious and achievable closeness' (as opposed to seeing one's family as 'a burden or an irrelevance obstructing larger goals within the thick of daily and professional life'), 2) 'not to spend any more money on our house unless it was absolutely necessary', but instead to spend the money on 'holidays and days out', & 3) to 'stop trying too hard to be a better parent or spouse' – 'Don't resolve to do better. Resolve to do what you can. That way lies not perfection, but sanity.' Not perfection... The crack where the light gets in... Thank you, Tim... And above all, final thought of 2016, thank you, Leonard.

Rens celebrating, Will and Callum on their way

Sunday 1 January 2017

Well, I manned up – but, like Lucy, was grateful to be able to find a seat in the covered stand (while Michael truly manned up, standing with a friend on the rainswept terrace – much closer to the heart of the action). Not a great game, played on a poor pitch in difficult conditions, & indeed at half-time (with the score 0–0) I thought that the bulk of this entry might be about a couple of moments during the interval. First, 'Days' coming over the loud-speaker – always a magical song, & making Ray Davies's just-announced knighthood feel completely appropriate. And then, queuing for the Gents, an overheard snatch of conversation between two middle-aged Shots supporters – apparently about Europe, with one challenging the other, 'Give me one directive that isn't controlled by trade.' To which came the hopeful rather than confident reply, 'Immigration,' but I heard no more.

The second half had its drama. A fine cross from Anthony Straker followed by a fine header from Scott Rendell giving the

Shots the lead in around the 63rd minute. Woking almost immediately equalising & then pressing quite hard for the winner –
before, just at the start of injury time, a rare fluent move by the
Shots ended with Jake Gallagher apparently throwing himself at
the ball (it was a long way away, down the other end) & managing to squeeze it over the line. So, 2–1 to the Shots, the double
completed over local rivals, & up to 7th in the table. Quite suddenly, a sniff at the play-offs seems a realistic possibility, though
only if there's a consistent run of good results over the next month
or two. Anything – anything – rather than the season petering out
with three months still to go.

Today's encounter had its echoes of April 2014 at the same
ground. The Shots, newly relegated from the Football League,
had gone into administration the previous summer & accordingly
had started the season on minus 10 points. Easter Monday at
Woking was the penultimate match, & a win would in effect keep
the Shots up. The pattern was almost exactly like today: 0–0 at
half-time, Shots taking the lead, Woking equalising, a late winner
for the Shots, though not quite so late as today. The winner was
a speculative strike from distance by Mark Molesley that got a
fortuitous deflection. At which point he hared down the touchline past the away support on the long terrace – & a photo that
would be evocative anyway caught the applauding supporters
behind him – including an ecstatic Michael & a more measured
George plus Laurie's husband Graham. As for me, I'm almost
completely hidden by Molesley, apart from a small corner of my
cloth cap. And by a coincidence that I can't deny bugs me, the
comparable photo that we have – from back in 1996, of a Diadora
Cup Final against Kingstonian – shows after an Aldershot goal a
cheering George (aged seven), a startled Laurie (aged ten) looking
up from her book, & me entirely concealed by a vexed-looking
Kingstonian player (it had been a goalie howler). The second time
round, it did make me feel a bit of an unperson – & reminded me
of that virtuoso start to a Kundera novel (*The Book of Laughter
and Forgetting*?) about someone high up disappearing from the
photographic record, presumably as a result of the Communist

takeover of Czechoslovakia soon after the war.[65] Still, one of the lesser agonies of this particular Aldershot fan.

Tuesday 3 January

Two overheards this morning at Center Parc, Woburn, in both cases a mother to a child of about five or six. 'If you stop sucking your thumb & complaining...' I lost the rest, but presumably some reward. And: 'It's not just about you, it's about everyone.' The first said unpleasantly, the second rather less so. A struggle during the day to get hold of the *Guardian*, but managed it eventually. News in it of the death of John Berger (presumably an obit tomorrow). A major figure, & to my regret I've never watched or read *Ways of Seeing*. My friend Micky Sheringham (who died almost a year ago & whom I miss badly) told me once how in 1972, the morning after Berger had won the Booker with *G* (also never read, less to my regret) & had announced he was donating half the prize money to the Black Panthers, he saw Berger on an escalator in the Underground – I half think Camden Town station, but not sure. Perhaps Micky's equivalent – albeit more thrilling – of how I, also in the early 70s, walked past A. L. Rowse, outside the Bodleian, the morning after his *Times* 'discovery' article about Shakespeare's *Sonnets* – 'the Dark Lady' & all that?[66] It's silly really, but nice every now & then to catch those moments.

The Times today in its football section noted that, of the eighty-seven Premiership matches so far this season between the

[65] Yes, that's the novel (1982); and the high-up was Vladimír Clementis, who had helped lead the coup but was later purged. Immediate airbrushing out of history followed. In 1978 I lived for some months in Rennes in the same high-rise modernist block of flats (Les Horizons) as the exiled Kundera and his wife Vera. That Easter they went for the first time to England, the country of their dreams. Oxford was high on the wish list, so in advance I gave detailed advice about what to look at. On their return it transpired that something about the dreaming spires had turned them off and that instead they'd headed to Leamington Spa, which they'd absolutely loved and where they'd stayed for several days.

[66] Rowse's lengthy letter (not an article), headed 'The Dark Lady, nature of historical proof' and based on his research in the Bodleian into the papers of Simon Forman (a contemporary of Shakespeare), appeared in *The Times* on Tuesday 20 February 1973. Sadly, his claim that he had identified the 'real' Dark Lady of the *Sonnets* was soon widely disputed.

top six & everyone else, that privileged sextet had lost only five. As I write, Michael & Graham just back from the Center Parc Sports Café & the second half of Bournemouth v Arsenal, with the visitors recovering from three down to get a point. So still only five.

Wednesday 4 January

A big date from my childhood. Saturday 4 January 1964 – school holidays, staying with my mother & stepfather in their Headley Down house ('Stonehaven') – Third Round of the Cup – the Shots (Division Four) away to Aston Villa (Division One) – waiting for the teleprinter – 'Aston Villa (stutter, stutter) 0 (stutter, stutter) Aldershot (stutter, stutter) 0'. Aldershot's best-ever away result (it still is). Next morning, my mother & I queued for 2½ hours – outside the ground, up Redan Hill – to get tickets for the replay the next Wednesday (no week-long delays those days). An amazing evening for this twelve-year-old. No goals at half-time – Shots going two up (Jim Towers direct from a free kick, Chris Palethorpe direct from a corner), before Tony Hateley (not yet the object of Michael Parkinson's 'Tony Lovely' satire) pulling one back almost at the death. 2–1 to the Shots, & Villa's manager, Joe Mercer, very gracious in defeat. The Shots' all-time best result, & over the years I've felt very grateful I was there.

Two and a half weeks later, it was home to Swindon Town in the Fourth Round. Kick-off moved to 2.15 because Swindon unhappy about the Recreation Ground floodlights. I was back at boarding school (Prestfelde in Shrewsbury), & went to a master's house (Mr Milne, who owned an Alvis car) to wait for the result on *Grandstand*. Too early (all the other kick-offs being at 3) for the teleprinter, so when it came through at about 4 or soon after, just read out – very matter of factly – by David Coleman between other items. 'Aldershot 1 Swindon Town 2'. Could hardly have been a flatter, more anti-climactic feeling.

This seems the moment in the calendar to set down briefly a trio of other Third Round memories. So here goes.

1) January 1961. Shots drawing 1–1 at home to Shrewsbury Town, then 2–2 at the Gay Meadow. I think both matches – certainly the first – took place while my mother & I were staying with Opa & Omi in Bonn, & it was a case of waiting a day or two to find the result in an English paper. The second replay was at Villa Park, & by then I was with my other grandparents (in Wem), just before going back to Prestfelde. I went to bed, perhaps even to sleep, before my grandma (whom I loved very much, but who got on badly with my father, who never stopped believing that somehow she had always tried to frustrate him) came in to tell me that she had heard (on the TV regional news?) the result – 2–0 to the Shots... (In the Fourth Round it was two goalless draws against Stoke City – my father's team when he was a boy in the 30s & Stoke had the young Stanley Matthews – of the Second Division, before the Shots lost 3–0 in the second replay, at Molyneux. In goal for the Shots those days was Chic Brodie, an early favourite – & famous/infamous post-Shots for being bitten by a dog during a match.)[67]

2) January 1970. I'd just left Wellington, about to start work in children's home.[68] Shots away at Huddersfield, top of Div 2 & with Frank Worthington in his prime. Outside the railway station, before the match, I walked past Aldershot's general manager Dave Smith – very much old-school – & wished the team luck, eliciting a taciturn, non-committal response. I stood on a terrace along one side of the ground, close to the action, & watched the Shots get a thoroughly deserved 1–1 draw, with the goal coming (via a deflection?) from left-back Len Walker. By the replay, nine days later, I was ensconced at Hutton Poplars & missed the Shots winning 3–1 – Melia's finest hour at the Rec. I also missed the Fourth Round. 2–2 away at Div 2's Carlisle United (though I did that afternoon watch Rodney Marsh at the Valley give a virtuoso

---

[67] The unfortunate Brodie was playing for Brentford, away at Colchester United, and the injury effectively ended his professional career. A graphic 28-second clip on YouTube reveals the dog as a box-to-box performer.

[68] It was called Hutton Poplars: on the outskirts of Shenfield in Essex but administered by the London Borough of Hackney, where most of the children came from. I went there through a Community Service Volunteers (CSV) placement.

display to pull it round for QPR, & on the way to the station heard one disgruntled Charlton supporter complain to another about how their side couldn't be more like Aldershot), & then being crushed 4–1 in the replay in front of the Rec's all-time record attendance (almost 20,000 – inconceivable now, when the max allowed is about 7,000).

3) January 1971. The Shots – player-manager Jimmy Melia, an old Anfield favourite – drawn away at Bill Shankly's Liverpool. On a misty afternoon, I watched it sitting high up in a stand, & it all seemed rather remote. Dennis Brown for the Shots had an early half-chance, Liverpool won it with a single goal (following a Melia mistake), & altogether it remains just about the most one-sided 1–0 I have ever witnessed. A creditable result, of course, but definitely the proverbial whimper rather than bang.[69] That evening I went with Pete McQuay – whose Blackburn Rovers had just lost 2–0 at Everton, the other side of Stanley Park – to see *Hair*, at I would guess the Liverpool Empire, & that in its way seemed an equally remote experience. The Age of Aquarius never really dawned for me.

Actually, on reflection & trying to avoid the sins of completism, I think I need to add two others.

First, January 1986, home to Oxford United. Oxford then in the First Division, but only briefly & always seemed imposters, so I found it pleasing rather than thrilling when the Shots more or less cruised to a 3–0 win, helped by a seemingly uninterested performance from Oxford's ace striker John Aldridge, about to move to Liverpool. So although in theory I suppose it has to rank above the win over Villa, in my book it doesn't. And anyway, everything seems larger than life when young... (Fourth Round, missing both, it was 1–1 at home to Barnsley, followed – with an away tie at Arsenal tantalisingly on offer – by a 3–0 defeat.)

Second, January 2013. Home to Rotherham United (managed by the abrasive Steve Evans & a division above the Shots), my visit to the Rec my first following lymphoma & convalescence, so pretty emotional. A terrific afternoon, Shots winning 3–0

---

[69]   Or perhaps TS Eliot (in *The Hollow Men*) made it proverbial.

with a Danny Hylton hat-trick, before he got sent off. After the final whistle, he came on the pitch & approached the ref. For a recriminatory word or two, we assumed – but in fact to ask for the match ball... (Fourth Round: away to Middlesbrough, top or near-top of the Championship. Listened on the radio. Danny equalising shortly before the 90, but Shots going down to a late, late winner – just like Forest Green a couple of months ago.)

Generally, the late 60s & early 70s were my zenith as a Shots supporter, & today's *Times* has Danny Finkelstein in his column exploring those years – the partial triumph of the Nixon-coined 'silent majority' over counter-culture liberalism – to draw a parallel with the present: a less frightening parallel, he rightly reflects, than with the 30s. Or as he puts it in his final para:

> The 1930s ended in war. The parallel with the 1960s is a more optimistic one. It suggests instead a prolonged, bruising but ultimately successful struggle to achieve reconciliation between the idealism of the young and the attachment to traditional identity of older people. A balance between liberty and order.

Well, I can see the virtues of such a balance. But how much liberty, how much pluralism, has to be conceded before it is reached? And after all, this is not (as Finkelstein concedes) Platonic, seminar-room stuff. As it all gets played out over the coming months & years, it will instead involve brutish power, stupid & visceral prejudices & huge vested interests. Is it really conceivable that the rise of nationalism can have a happy ending? I don't believe it can.

Two obits of Berger today – moderately unfriendly in the *Guardian* (Michael McNay), distinctly unfriendly in *The Times* – & I haven't even seen the *Telegraph*'s, but presumably still more barbed. Various charges: that he concealed his middle-class background; that he sentimentalised the working class; that as a Marxist critic he placed political considerations above artistic integrity; &, gravest charge of all, that he was humourless. In addition, the *Times* obit approvingly quotes Auberon Waugh's wholly negative assessment of Berger as a novelist. I have to admit that when, for research purposes, I read his *New Statesman* pieces of the 50s & early 60s, I found them fairly unreadable & strangely difficult to quote from. Also, in his great stand-off with Lord Clark of *Civilisation*, I likewise admit to a sneaking preference for the latter, appalling man though he was.[70] (A preference based on admiration for his sheer knowledge, discrimination & authority – however much delivered *de haut en bas*.) Yet rather like some other controversial Marxist intellectuals – supremely, I guess, Eric Hobsbawm – there remained an essential greatness about him, a deep seriousness of purpose, that should be recognised better than these two somewhat mean-minded obits do. Marxism may have 'lost', but that's no excuse – quite the reverse – for putting in the boot gratuitously.

Walked down this evening to Center Parc's Sports Café to watch the second half of Spurs at home to runaway leaders Chelsea. Huge screen, which had the slightly offputting effect of making the players seem too tall for the pitch, so that they moved around it in a strangely gingerly fashion. Spurs won 2–0, comfortably enough, but Chelsea still well clear at the top. Even so, the result keeps Spurs (my pre-season tip) just about in contention. And as far as I could tell, a popular enough outcome among my fellow-inmates.

Saturday 7 January

Outside Waitrose this morning (back in New Malden), I asked the sweet-voiced, gentle-mannered young Romanian guy who sells the *Big Issue* whether he'd had a good Christmas. He said he had, & added, 'Christmas Day is a happy day even for the poor.'

Shots at home to Southport this afternoon – a 'must win' if serious about the play-offs. A nice video message on the club's website from Mark Butler, record goalscorer of the post-1992

---

[70] John Berger's influential TV series and book, *Ways of Seeing* (1972), was at one level a vigorous Marxist-feminist repudiation of Kenneth Clark's much more old-fashioned approach to art history. Clark's own hugely acclaimed series, *Civilisation*, had appeared three years earlier.

reformed club, urging supporters & lapsed supporters to build on this season's sense of revival – to come together & banish the 'dark times'.

Clark v Berger. I suppose I want it both ways. Cultural hierarchies *and* a questioning of those hierarchies, with all their often deeply privileged socio-economic baggage... It's a questioning, though, that can easily – not of course in Berger's case – slip into a kind of philistinism (& indeed one I often feel myself slipping into, e.g. with my anti-opera prejudice). And in the early 70s at Oxford, I was one of the philistines who stormed into the TV room at the New College JCR at about 10.30 one weekday evening & successfully demanded that the handful of people watching a BBC adaptation of *Howards End* switch the set over to the football highlights on ITV... Even though I wasn't the leader of the stormtroopers, a completely shameful memory. And, of all places, at Oxford.

Sunday 8 January

A relatively comfortable 2–1 win yesterday (Southport's goal coming only a minute or so before the final whistle). The Shots played some fluent passing football, seldom resorting to aimless long balls, & quite suddenly there's the sense of a young team – almost half its players twenty-two or under – coming together in a potentially very auspicious way. Still in 7th place, & a shame that the next fixture's not until the 21st, at Gateshead, where perhaps a rude northern shock awaits. I hope not – it feels like this up-&-down season still has some exciting possibilities.

I realised about halfway through the second half that, during a winter match on a Saturday afternoon, I'm still thrilled during those moments that the sky darkens behind & above the trees, the floodlights are fully on & those footballers in their red & blue (a combination that I'm ridiculously pleased are the Shots' colours) strive their utmost. It sounds absurd, but there's not much I'd swap those moments for. When Nabokov was more or less on his deathbed in 1977, & his son noticed tears in his eyes, he asked him why. 'Because I will never go butterfly-collecting again,' said

Nabokov (or words to that effect), & I think I can begin to understand where, given my equivalent, he was coming from.

'Waterloo Sunset', incidentally, over the tannoy at half-time yesterday. Even better than 'Days'.

Monday 9 January

I've felt fairly detached from the Third Round of the Cup, which as usual in recent times has been strung out from Friday to Monday, dissipating the traditional intensity. Entirely predictably, I hate the way that the big clubs take the competition only semi-seriously & field seriously weakened teams. I especially dislike the practice because it cheapens the potential achievement of small clubs playing against them, e.g. Plymouth's battling draw yesterday at Anfield (where man of the match was Argyle's central defender Sonny Bradley, a big Shots favourite a few years ago). And of course the TV coverage is almost relentlessly of the big clubs, much to the chagrin on Saturday of Sutton United & AFC Wimbledon, who played out a draw.

Wednesday 11 January

Nine days until Inauguration. Put another way, Donald Trump will be President of the United States before the Shots play again. I imagine like many people, I find myself viewing the prospect of a Trump presidency almost as a personal affront. His coarseness, his bullying, his materialism – I still can't quite believe it's happening. But it is, & of course there are all too many precedents. I read the other evening the preface by 'Q' to his *From a Cornish Window*, & he writes of the loathsome rise of the 'Superman' philosophy.[71] And that was in 1906! Long before the arrival on the scene of

[71] 'Q' was Sir Arthur Quiller-Couch: Cornishman, Cambridge don, well-known literary figure of the day, now almost completely forgotten. His anthology, *The Oxford Book of English Verse*, was a particular favourite of John Mortimer's Horace Rumpole, now presumably also well on his way to being forgotten.

some very fateful supermen, responsible for millions & millions of deaths. Does all this mean I want Trump to fail badly as President, even if that failure impacts harshly on many people's lives? Reluctantly, I think it has to. Trump, & the appalling bunch of people around him, is different. Somehow he & they have to be expunged from public life, certainly any position of power. I'm far from confident this is going to happen. The tragedy is that if he fails as comprehensively as I hope he does, the people who suffer will be mainly those who – stupidly but sincerely – voted for him.

Thursday 12 January

More on Trump (who was his disgusting, brutal self at yesterday's press conference, his first for six months). Something by Stephen Bush from last week's *New Statesman* just before it hits the recycling bin. He wants an end in 2017 to 'the easy comparison' between Trump & the Brexit vote, rightly arguing that there is a difference in kind between the two & their possible outcomes. 'The superficial attraction of the comparison has moved from irritating to dangerous: it is blinding large parts of the British establishment to the dangers of Trump.' Absolutely right.

Sad news of Graham Turner's death. The better sort of footballing person – essentially decent & non-vainglorious. The last England manager whom I felt any real sense of warmth towards. And unfairly crucified by the *Sun*.

I heard a good – well, terrible – story today from Stephen Bates, former *Guardian* journalist who I'm hoping will write a *real* history of Oxford (the university) since the war. As a young, Reading-based journalist in 1976, he interviewed the very poor parents (living locally) of the West Indian cricketer Gordon Greenidge, as he made his first big impact on the cricket scene. The parents didn't want the piece published without their son's go-ahead, so Stephen one afternoon waited in his paper's newsroom for a phone call to come through from a cricket pavilion somewhere. The communal phone rang – a hardboiled news editor picked it up – &, giving the phone to Stephen, said, 'Here's your nigger.' Unsurprisingly, permission was not granted.

Saturday 14 January

It's Saturday morning, & there's no Shots match this afternoon – a slightly empty feeling, & of course my secret worry is that the players are going to go off the boil, having rather nicely come to it.

A ranking issue on yesterday evening's BBC radio news. The death of Lord Snowdon above or below the resignation of the Labour MP Tristram Hunt (in order to become director of the V&A)? They prioritised Hunt, but in the sense that the news is a reflection of the ever-rolling pageant of national life, I'd have given the nod to Snowdon. 'But how many younger listeners would even have heard of Snowdon?' pointed out Lucy. Fair enough – but how many, come to that, would have heard of Hunt?

I had an accidental run-in – or that's how it felt – with Tristram almost three years ago. The *New Statesman* published a lengthy piece by George & me about private schools, including the failure of Labour over the years to do anything effective about them. Tristram at the time was shadow Education Secretary. We didn't criticise him specifically, but the *Statesman*, for understandable journalistic reasons, made our piece the vehicle for a sharp campaign against him over the next few weeks, which I found a little uncomfortable but also quite exciting. I actually got to meet Tristram for the first time only last autumn – at Broadcasting House, as I contributed to an *Archive Hour* programme on Asa Briggs that he was presenting. All perfectly friendly, & at the end, just before I left the studio, he asked after George (whom in the interim he'd had some communication with). I replied he wasn't quite sure what he was going to do next, to which Tristram said something like 'Aren't we all?' The question now of course is whether, as a prominent Labour moderate, he's justified in jumping ship. It's easy to see why he's doing it – the current feeling of frustration & impotence must be intense, & he's a real historian who could do something big at the V&A. But I still think it's the wrong decision. He's a bright guy, with some real intellectual heft, & should be pulling his weight when Labour rows back towards the centre. That has to happen. 'Wanted: A Credible Labour Leader Who Takes Equality Seriously' are the words (my words) that have been on my mind in the last day or two, & though I don't think Hunt would ever have become the leader (one way & another, too much baggage, not least his unfortunate first name), he could have been crucial to the process. And my hunch is that that process – that filling of a huge vacuum, unless just left to the Lib Dems – could be under way sooner than most people expect.

As for Snowdon, the lengthy obit in today's *Guardian* is, as it happens, by Stephen Bates. A terrific piece, generally unfavourable, but not unduly so, & written with understanding, e.g. of his neglected childhood. Includes a wonderful detail about Princess Margaret wolfing down her food – not just greed, but as a way of ensuring that all eyes were fixed on her, given no one at the dinner table was allowed to start eating before her – or continue eating after she'd finished. The Edward St Aubyn 1990s novel (in her lifetime), depicting her as the utterly selfish guest at a country-house weekend party, is unforgettable – &, I'd guess, essentially accurate.[72]

An email a few minutes ago is a piquant coda to the obit. It comes from a historian friend, Adrian Smith, whose only child, Adam, died of cancer just before Christmas, aged thirty-two. Adrian & his wife Mary have written a short obit for the *Guardian*'s 'Other Lives' section of the obit pages, & today it would have appeared in the paper's print version (& hopefully still will) but for Snowdon's death. However, it's online (attachment to the email), & combines warmth & dignity. He was obviously a determined, creative guy (born in Aldershot as it happens), & I find it a helpful reminder – because of course any parent fears this more than anything – that in even such a cruelly brief lifespan it is possible to have really done something with one's life. But

---

[72] *Some Hope* (1994).

poor Adrian, poor Mary – it's still a truly awful thing, & presumably life will never be the same again.

Sunday 15 January

Corbyn on the Andrew Marr show this morning. He came over as reasonable, principled & not without a sense of humour. The only interesting moment was when Marr pressed him on levels of immigration – specifically, whether he shares concerns about communities & their sense of identity. 'Of course identity matters,' he replied, but then said, 'Communities change,' before going on to praise the contribution of immigrants. It's obvious enough, from a left-of-centre perspective, that there's a balance to be struck; but Corbyn is as yet unwilling – pigheadedly? – to strike it. And it seems likely (or at the very least possible) that that will do for him.

A family gathering yesterday afternoon/evening, & perhaps inevitably some fairly agitated discussion about the prospect of Trump. Some of us clinging to the desperate hope that something extraordinary will happen before next Friday to prevent him taking office. In the context of so much being so strange & so unpredictable, that's perhaps not a wholly irrational hope. But presumably, with only five days to go, not really going to happen.

The *New Yorker*'s 'Daily Comment' piece on its website had on Friday a fine piece ('The Music Donald Trump Can't Hear') by Adam Gopnik. Partly about Trump's inability to attract musicians (representing the country's 'best shared traditions') to his Inauguration, partly about the importance, from an oppositional point of view, of making a clear distinction between on the one hand policies (however rebarbative) that are legitimate for a Republican President to pursue & on the other hand policies/ procedures that are illegitimate & democracy-threatening. 'At that terrifying first press conference of Trump's on Wednesday,' he reflects, 'we saw the looming face of pure authoritarianism.' So what exactly have we to fear?

Assaults on free speech; the imprisoning of critics and dissidents; attempts, on the Russian model, likely to begin soon, to intimidate critics of the regime with fake charges and conjured-up allegations; the intimidation and intolerance of even mild dissidence (that 'Apologize!' tweet directed at members of the *Hamilton* cast who dared to politely petition Mike Pence); not to mention mass deportations or attempts at discrimination by religion – all things that Trump and his cohorts have openly contemplated or even promised – are not part of the normal oscillations of power and policy.

It is – still shocking though it is to admit it – a plausible stab. And Gopnik finishes by calling for 'calm but consistent opposition shared by a broad front of committed and constitutionally minded protestors' in order 'to save the beautiful music of American democracy'.

Finally for today (actually, it's only just gone midday, but probably 'finally'), something from history. The *TLS* before the current one has a review by Janet Todd of a study of Madame de Staël's contemporary analysis of what went wrong in France during the decade after the 1789 revolution:

> By the end of the revolutionary decade she had to conclude that the French public had been simply too uneducated and badly informed to assume political responsibility. The press and opinion-makers had bombarded people with half-baked ideas which they had neither the time nor the ability to question. Fatigued by slogans, they had become blasé and confused and in the end had not even bothered to vote in elections. A culture of social envy had grown up, while shared standards of moral and aesthetic judgement collapsed. There was a disjunction between political elite and people. Public opinion could hardly be known and certainly not trusted.

Well, the parallels are obvious enough. And of course, out of France in the 1790s (including the Terror) came Napoleon – whose claims for greatness were surely forever crushed by

Tolstoy's damning verdict. (*War and Peace* also has that amazing scene – a stunning premonition of the horrors of the twentieth century – where, as the French occupy Moscow, a demagogue on a balcony manipulates the emotions of the crowd below.) So, trust the people? If democracy is its own worst enemy? I find Todd's phrase about the collapse of 'shared standards of moral and aesthetic judgement' especially resonant.

Monday 16 January

Trump has a pop today at Angela Merkel – for her 'catastrophic mistake' in 'taking all of these illegals' – i.e. the refugees fleeing from Syria. He is also full of praise for Brexit Britain. I suddenly find myself feeling proud to be half-German.

The context is an interview in *The Times* with Michael Gove, who in his piece refers to how no previous President 'has come to office facing anything like the level of scorn and condescension from British politicians and commentators as Mr Trump'. Undeniably there's been plenty of scorn & condescension. But the emotions that Gove fails to note are those of fear & loathing – a famous combination of course, & far more powerful. He also fails to ask Trump anything about democracy & about pluralism. Instead, apart from a fair amount of geo-political stuff, the thrust of the piece is as much as anything an implicit endorsement of Trump, in effect arguing that he deserves to be trusted because 'much of his world view' springs 'from his experience as a businessman rather than any ideological preoccupation', & that he has an essentially 'transactional approach to politics'. Gove at one point almost echoes those progressives in the 1930s, who met Stalin & then conferred superhuman qualities: 'When you meet him you realise there is nothing, absolutely nothing, small-scale or low-wattage about America's President-elect.' The interview itself took place in Trump Tower ('his glitzy, golden man cave'), & the accompanying photo shows Trump at a rather chaotic-looking desk surrounded by gold-framed photos & mementoes of himself.

As I write all this, I realise I hate the way that this diary is getting dominated by this thin-skinned egotist. And though obviously I can't ignore him, I feel somehow demeaned & besmirched, prissy though that sounds & even though the citizen-(of-the-world)-cum-historian in me knows the folly of pretending it's not happening. So yes, it has to remain a strand, but a less obsessive one. I'm aware that I've made this resolution before. This time, I'll try to stick to it better. And over the coming weeks & months, it'll be interesting to see how everyone's coping strategies turn out. I suspect/fear, including quite likely on my part, a fairly rapid process of normalisation & semi-indifference. Let's hope not.

Wednesday 18 January

A day of triumph for Lincolnshire yesterday: first, Theresa May's announcement of an uncompromisingly 'hard' Brexit (control over borders = no membership of European single market); then, Lincoln in injury time scoring a brilliantly executed breakaway goal to knock Ipswich out of the Cup.[73] In fact, a gratifyingly good Vanarama evening, as Sutton in their replay went to AFC Wimbledon & won 3–1 (to, I admit, my schadenfreude). On the Brexit front, it's undoubtedly a moment, with the *Mail* hailing May as the Iron Lady redux. And if those slippery Continentals don't play ball in the forthcoming negotiations? Well, Hammond threatens to reboot the UK economic model into Singapore- or Hong Kong- or indeed US-style low tax/low welfare. It's a prospect that I find 20% invigorating, 80% dismal & even dangerous. In essence, we're looking at an attempt to return to the nineteenth century, to make Britain once again the 'switchboard' (Eric Hobsbawm's apt term) of the world – an ironic putative destination, given that the Leave vote was at one level a *cri de coeur* against globalisation… I've belatedly come to the conclusion, incidentally, that (quite apart from the blatant

---

[73] All seven districts of Lincolnshire voted Leave in June 2016, with percentages ranging from 56.9% (Lincoln itself) to 75.6% (Boston, the highest Leave percentage in Britain).

press bias) the Referendum vote was essentially unfair. Yes, each side told a massive scaremongering lie (the collapse of the economy, the hordes of invaders). But the Leave side *also* told – & kept on repeating, even when definitively exposed – that huge lie about the £350 million a week being able post-Europe to go to the NHS. Futile gesture department, I know, but I've therefore decided in my mind that the outcome was illegitimate & that I can emotionally remain a Remainer without either being a remoaner or holding democracy in contempt. Good – that at least is sorted.

Thursday 19 January

On the Aldershot website there's currently a supporters' survey. One of the questions asks, 'How important are the following to your enjoyment of a match day?' Here are my answers, with 5 as the highest possible.

Atmosphere – 4
Quality of football – 3
Catering – 2
Facilities – 3 (would once have been 2 or even 1, but I'm getting old)
Other entertainment – 1
Comfort – 2

The factors, of course, that would get my 5 are continuity of ground & of colours – but they weren't on offer.

A friendly & apologetic email from the programme editor, Victoria Rogers, pinged through today. It transpires that she doesn't work at the ground & only discovered my November letter enclosing my 1966 *Observer* article this week. That makes me feel a little better, because I'd felt undeniably a little hurt by the complete lack of response. Rather like the Woody Allen joke – 'It's worse than dog eats dog. It's dog doesn't return dog's phone calls.'

Last full day today of Obama's presidency. Flawed of course – in particular, I'd like him to have gone for Wall Street while he had the chance – but also something inspiritingly noble & dignified about it. 'He's going to be missed' is usually just a semi-meaningless platitude, but sure is true this time.

Friday 20 January

Today's the day (I'm writing this in the morning). There doesn't seem much point in another rant or cry of despair. 'Enjoy the grotesque spectacle,' 'Relish the black humour,' seems to be advice of many, but I don't think I can go along. I'm just too apprehensive. We're going to have a spectacularly ill-qualified US President beating the nationalist drum in a world succumbing to the virus of nationalism. All that quite apart from his continuing & presumably intensifying assault on American democracy, pluralism & accountability. Of course I hope the satirists & others sharpen & twist the knife – good for them. But I feel myself rendered inert, almost paralysed, by sheer fear & pessimism.

I've just watched Trump's inauguration speech. Crude & nationalistic – at times, tinpot-dictator stuff. But no less frightening for that. It's not the sole motivation – far from it – but this diary is being written with the thought that someday others might be interested in reading it. At that point, I really hope that I will be seen to have been deeply & unnecessarily neurotic. Well, time will show the wiser – an old favourite of a song title (& indeed song), from the first Fairport Convention album.

I'm intending this evening to read Gideon Haigh's new book about the Australian batting genius Victor Trumper. (In 1983 I walked some five miles from Pulborough station in order to interview Captain A. C. Wilkinson, who as a boy in Sydney had bought a bat from Trumper's sports shop & had shaken his hand. Which meant that I shook the hand that... Trumper himself died in 1915, the same year as WG, so that was quite a thrill.) I hadn't particularly planned it this way – I'm steadily, as a judge, working my way through the long list for the cricket book prize administered by the Cricket Society and MCC – but at this moment it feels like a good idea. Art trumps life; Trumper trumps Trump.

And tomorrow the Shots are at last back in action, at Gateshead, lying just below in the table & also in good form. A tough one, with a draw a reasonable result. Certainly important not to lose, if that putative 'surge' to the play-offs isn't going to be castles in the air.

Later in the evening (with Dover, in 5th place, handily having lost at top-placed Lincoln), two final things. First, I've been surprised that apparently no one has picked up on Dylan's 'Union Sundown Blues' (an unfavourite song, from 1983's *Infidels*) as an early post-industrial sign pointing towards protectionism. (I should add that, on the same album, Dylan quoted Dr Johnson re patriotism as the last refuge of the scoundrel.) And second, this from today's 'Loose Canon' column by Giles Fraser, quoting Trump's reply when asked what God was to him: 'Well, I say God is the ultimate. You know you look at this... here we are on the Pacific Ocean. How did I ever own this? I bought it 15 years ago. I made one of the great deals they say ever. I have no more mortgage on it as I will certify and represent to you. And I was able to buy this and make a great deal. That's what I do for the country. Make great deals.'

Actually, one final thing. Trump's speech: essentially it was bombastic & second rate. I'm relieved, because I'm more susceptible to rhetoric than I should be & had feared that it just might make me think or imagine that he could be good news. Now I know for sure that the Boss is right: he's a conman, a snake-oil salesman. An enemy to be taken seriously – very seriously – but in no way to be admired.

Sunday 22 January

Listened to most of the Shots match yesterday. 1–1 draw – both goals in the first half – sounded fair enough – & Shots still in 7th place, with other results on the whole quite helpful.

Major anti-Trump women's marches (but also involving men) around the world yesterday. Laurie & George went to the one in London, while Lucy & I looked after Wolfie. Up to 100,000 people there, while the one in Washington itself absolutely huge – far more people than at the Inauguration, as plainly & unequivocally made clear by the visual evidence, albeit stoutly denied by Trump's press officer, following on from his master's affirmation that the media had lied about the size of the crowd on Friday. They're a tacky, tacky bunch. Did I write that Trump was 'in no way to be admired'? Well, that certainly. But also in no way to be respected.

None of which lessens my feeling of apprehension. I woke up this morning around 5 &, finding it difficult to get back to sleep, started in my head what seemed like an entirely plausible scenario about the US now being on the road to civil war – except that this time it would be a war won by the bad guys, the guys with the guns, backed by the military, the police, the big corporations, the surveillance people. Can such a scenario, I wonder as I scribble these words in the middle of the day (cold but sunny New Malden, life going on much as usual), really be possible? Actually, I'm afraid, I think it could.

What specifically got my mind racing was a stray remark heard on TV last night, when I wasn't really watching. (Perhaps a discussion on Sky News?) Someone, I don't know who, observed that Trump in his Inauguration speech had gone out of his way to emphasise that it was a *movement* – according to him the greatest ever – that had brought him to power (despite, Trump didn't add, losing the popular vote); & the TV speaker then observed that what twentieth-century history told us was that when movements, as opposed to conventional political parties, attained power, the consequences could be deeply unfortunate. That's all too true, of course. And two days into the new era, it's looking like two huge movements potentially emerging to confront each other – a kind of expanded, more militant, more deadly version of America's long-standing culture wars. Which is why, at the very least half seriously, I return to my autumn suggestion: time to split... And just conceivably that's also true here, where in the current issue of the *Big Issue* John Bird writes perceptively of the post-Referendum divide & the refusal of either side to even attempt to engage or listen to the other, instead staying in their self-righteous bubble. True about me, I accept, & I'm sure many millions of others.

Tuesday 24 January

Already, less than 100 hours (as I write) since those two dread words 'President Trump' became a reality, I find myself slipping into a kind of passive acceptance – or at least, no longer twitchily clicking on the BBC website to see what the latest is... Life inevitably goes on, & I've just done the first serious day's work on a potential cricket book (about John Arlott & E. W. Swanton) that I'm hoping to write with Stephen Fay. But actually, of course, the fundamentals remain in what is a profoundly *abnormal* situation: an authoritarian demagogue (complete with thumbs-up signs during the ceremony) becoming President of the leading country in the West – & there can't be any compromise with the hatefulness of that. Sunday's *Observer*, in its leader on the Inauguration ('Bullying, aggressive, nationalist Trump sets out his stall'), put it well in a couple of sentences: 'His contempt for "Washington DC" and all its works, including the elected Congress and the federal bureaucracy, was as startling as it was undeserved. It was, at bottom, profoundly anti-democratic.' And from earlier in the editorial, this passage: 'Trump is as bullishly self-confident as he is ignorant. He will not be easily deflected or denied. And the crass, know-nothing nationalism that lay at the heart of Friday's speech is a powerful force. Like America's new leader, it appeals to the darker side of human nature, bolstering the insidious claims of jealousy, envy, greed and hubris. It thrives on fear, chauvinism, discrimination and not always subliminal notions of ethnic, racial and moral superiority. It is a product of our times.' So it is, so it is... Human nature surely doesn't fundamentally change – the good on the whole outweighing the bad? – but the prevailing culture does. And there are some significant ways (the three obvious ones, straight off, being the entwined growths of materialism + celebrity + immediate techno fixes) in which our culture has become rotten.

To continue analysis of the ills. Have just read a letter in the current *Economist* from Peter Haydon of Croydon, giving a list of mid-1980s Thatcherite chickens that would ultimately come home to roost. Viz: 'The shift from manufacturing to services; the indifference of central government towards the regions; the transfer of wealth from poor to rich; the creation of an unemployable underclass that generates demand for a resented immigrant workforce to fill the skills gap; the failure of education to consider how knowledge advances in the wider world; the neglect of obvious housing needs; the unaddressed problem of low productivity and the accompanying tendency of Britain to become an *ancien régime* rentier economy.' I find that a wholly convincing sevenfold charge-sheet, although obviously these negatives have a pre-history & post-history, i.e. not *just* the product of the mid-80s. Haydon adds, his killer point, that 'thoughtful Conservatives' know that 'not one of these issues has a root cause in Britain's membership of the EU.' We really have done – above all at this Trump moment – a very stupid act of self-harm.

The *Observer* also had a long piece by Daniel Taylor about London's football grounds, in the context of the probability that by 2021 almost all of the capital's clubs will have, since 2006, either have moved ground or so fundamentally redeveloped the existing ground that it is essentially unrecognisable. Crystal Palace & Fulham, according to Taylor, likely to be the honourable exceptions. He concludes, inevitably, with a remark about football 'losing some of its soul'. 'Some'... (And, incidentally, the grim effects of moving to a new ground confirmed by watching the highlights yesterday of the Shots at Gateshead: tiny crowd in an athletics stadium – far from the pitch – & the whole effect dismally antiseptic...)

Friday 27 January

Wedding anniversary yesterday, & we treated ourselves to a double-header in Wimbledon. Lunch out in a café – I foolishly went for an oversize mixed grill (tempted by the liver): perfectly tasty (Hoggart's word about the key criterion of the Hunslet working class),[74] but I vowed afterwards it was the last time I ate a crammed-full big plate of food – followed by a film. *Manchester by the Sea*: an impressive drama, & beautifully filmed, but spoiled by over-emphatic, emotionally controlling music, plus perhaps handicapped by the central character's lengthy periods of silence & non-communication, with just the odd punch thrown at a stranger at a bar to express his inner anger. But we were pleased we saw it – & always nice, just slightly decadent, to be snug in a cinema on a cold weekday afternoon.

Comparing him to an attention-seeking three-year-old, Jenni Russell (a favourite columnist) has a priceless detail in yesterday's *Times*. Trump not only wants the Queen to invite him to Balmoral (traditionally it'd be Buckingham Palace or Windsor for a visiting Pres), but insists that the Queen watches him play golf on Balmoral's private course.

But seriously… (Though of course, in an indicative way, that detail is all too serious.) I've just come across this from 1876 by the American poet and critic James Russell Lowell: 'What fills me with doubt and dismay is the degradation of the moral tone. Is it or is it not a result of democracy? Is ours a "government of the people by the people for the people," or a kakistocracy rather, for the benefit of knaves at the cost of fools?' It turns out that 'kakistocracy' – new to me – translates from the Greek literally as government by the worst people. All this comes from a recent *New Statesman* piece by Mehdi Hasan, who then goes on clinically to anatomise the people around Trump, a truly appalling crew, calling them 'a bizarre mélange of the unqualified

---

[74] ' "Something tasty" is the key-phrase in feeding: something solid, preferably meaty, and with a well-defined flavour. The tastiness is increased by a liberal use of sauces and pickles, notably tomato sauce and piccalilli.' (Richard Hoggart, *The Uses of Literacy*, 1957.)

and the unhinged'. That relates specifically to his cabinet ('the richest, whitest, most male cabinet in living memory') – but as for some of the others, e.g. the Bannon/Breitbart person...

Meanwhile, I've been mulling over this by Richard Davenport-Hines (old friend, as well as enviably gifted historian-cum-biographer), reviewing latest tranche of Roy Strong's diaries: 'There are many reasons to keep a diary: to mitigate loneliness; for introspective self-abasement; as an *aide-mémoire*; as a historical record of interesting times or places; as a safety valve when exasperated; as a repository of doubtful gossip; to drop names; as a money-spinner in old age; and as a way to perfect an artful myth-image of one's character and accomplishments.' So, nine motives, & Richard reckons that Strong has been motivated by all but the first two. Above all, he thinks Strong's diaries are an exercise in what John Cowper Powys called 'life-illusion' – that is, 'that secret dramatic way of regarding himself which makes [a man] feel to himself a remarkable, singular, unusual, exciting individual' (JCP's words).

And my motives? In terms of Richard's categories, I think it goes:

1 – No.

2 – Yes, a bit.

3 – I suppose so, but not for an especially functional purpose.

4 – Yes, & increasingly as I've been keeping it.

5 – Not a motive, but at odd moments has definitely made me feel better.

6 – Not really, but am certainly not above gossip.

7 – I'd have to admit it comes into it. (Not that I have that many names to drop – albeit a self-referential time-waster is to look at the birthdays list in the paper & see if I can find someone whom I could go up to at a drinks party & more or less legitimately call by their first name.)

8 – Somewhere at the back of my mind? But not a prime motive – & anyway, unrealistic.

9 – Ah, now – & with the Cowper Powys, we're getting somewhere near the heart of the matter... Though

who, when it comes to it, is wholly immune from self-dramatising? Well, perhaps just the odd person.

Somewhere also near the heart, but not the very heart. I think what has *really* motivated me – in addition to particular football-oriented motives – has been the desire to use the diary as some kind of tool for a process of self-exploration. Not perhaps in a hugely introspective way – that would be a different kind of diary, & not one I could ever imagine I would want to show to a stranger – but more to do with my relationship to the world, to try to work out what I think & feel about various things. In those terms I'm doubtful if I've got all that far – but some way possibly, & of course it's a work in progress.

Watched the last half-hour this evening of Leicester's cup tie at Derby. Leicester 2–1 down for most of that time, & although I'd normally support the underdog I found myself rooting for Leicester (who indeed got a late equaliser). I guess because I'm still emotionally engaged with them after last season's extraordinary triumph & don't want them to start thinking it was just a fortuitous fluke (they're currently struggling in the Premiership, though are still in the Champions League). And, like presumably almost everyone, I'm fond of Ranieri.

The Shots at home to York tomorrow. They're bottom, but last Sat got a late winner against Barrow, who in turn on Tuesday beat the leaders Lincoln – so could well be a real contest. I'm probably forgetting something, but the last time I remember seeing this fixture at the Rec was around the mid-60s, when I persuaded my stepmother Vivienne to come with me, almost certainly the only football match of her life – &, unfortunately, the dullest of goalless draws. As for tomorrow itself, I'm not massively confident, but have to believe the Shots can do it. Either way, I'm looking forward to it a lot.

Saturday 28 January

(Morning) Reading the reports about Theresa May's meeting yesterday in DC with the pro-wall, anti-refugee, anti-abortion, anti-media Pres. It all feels a bit undignified, & in practice is unlikely to subdue his desire to cut The Big Deal with Putin, but it's easy to see why she felt she had to do it – especially given our act of self-mutilation vis-à-vis Europe. As for Trump's hand-holding of her, Lucy's theory is that as a boy he was never allowed to hold his mother's hand, & it was the act of an emotionally inse-cure man (manchild?) finding himself for the first time truly on the world stage.

Two quotes about Trump that neatly encapsulate the problem for me or people like me. First, Philip Roth's description of him as 'ignorant of government, of history, of science, of philosophy, of art, incapable of recognizing or expressing subtlety or nuance, des-titute of all decency, and wielding a vocabulary of 77 words that is better called Jerkish than English'. All probably true, & of course deeply depressing. But second, this from the latest assessment by the *New Yorker*'s Adam Gopnik: 'There is no political cost for Trump in being seen to be incompetent, impulsive, shallow, inconsistent, and contemptuous of truth and reason. Those *are* his politics. This is how he achieved power. His base loves crazi-ness, incompetence, and contempt for reason because sanity, com-petence, and the patient accumulation of evidence are the things that allow educated people to pretend that they are superior. Resentment comes before reason.' So yes, it does all come down to the back-row kids against the front-row kids. And perhaps – perhaps – it's only fair if the back-row kids every now & then have their turn? Especially if this makes the front-row kids belatedly stop being so pleased with themselves. To that extent I'm torn. Yet I only have to look at Trump, above all to hear his voice, to know that something bad & cynical & exploitative is happening.

Enjoyable game – good atmosphere – lots of end-to-end play & close-run things – but ultimately no goals. Just about fair, though York (a much reinvigorated team) probably shaded it. That said, Fenelon & Gallagher missed gilt-edged chances for the Shots. Pantomime villain of the afternoon was the man-mountain of a striker that is Jon Parkin, whom I last saw playing for Forest Green against the Shots. Midway through the second half he had an expertly despatched goal narrowly ruled offside; & then towards the end he had his name taken twice, the second time committing such a blatant foul that he was seemingly down the nearby tunnel before the ref had time to get out his cards. Arguably a point gained as much as 2 points lost – that anyway was the Wadfather line in his post-match interview. The Shots stay 7th, though it's deceptive (on the high side, sadly) in terms of games played. Still, just about hanging in there in the play-off mix.

Cup news of the day is that Lincoln, 3–1 winners over Brighton, are through to the Fifth Round (while Sutton play at home to Leeds tomorrow). Pleasure & jealousy just about evenly matched. Though given that it's apparently their furthest progress for over a century, it'd be poor to be too green-eyed.

May, questioned today about Trump's virtual ban on Muslim refugees (& indeed many non-refugees), refuses to condemn it. Ineluctably, we're being dragged over to the side of the bully.

Sunday 29 January

Footnote to yesterday. The 'match ball sponsor' is usually a local engineering firm, or something like that, but this time it was Oriental Belly Dance Performers ('Hire the perfect entertainment for parties, corporate events, weddings and restaurants!'). The accompanying photo in the programme shows two fairly homely-looking girls, wearing just skirts & bras, against a vaguely Japanese-garden backdrop.

Two deaths: John Hurt & Alexander Chancellor. Hurt for me earned some sort of immortality with his 1970s TV portrait of Quentin Crisp – utterly compelling at the time, & one of those great liberating, fresh-air moments. As for Chancellor, who in his prime was clearly a great editor of the *Spectator*, the only time I met him was at an *Oldie* lunch a few years ago &, though he was perfectly benign, we didn't quite fire, in large part because it was a noisy room & he was sitting on my deaf side. I was a speaker that day, & the other two were Terry Wogan & Brian Sewell, both also now dead. ('My, that's a mighty tome,' remarked

Wogan when he glanced at my book during the pre-lunch signing session – during which Sewell & I just about managed to look serene & indifferent as the queue steadily lengthened for the great man, & I tried to get Sewell to tell me about his time in Aldershot doing National Service.) The current issue of the *Spec* features Chancellor's regular column – a good thing on the whole to die in harness? Cohen would certainly have said so – in which he asserts about Trump that 'irrespective of whatever he does in government, even if some of it proves to be beneficial, he is unworthy to be president'. Essentially, argues Chancellor, because 'he is a liar on a Hitlerian scale, fomenting distrust and hatred of groups that bear no blame for the popular grievances that brought him to power'. The piece as a whole is a strong but dignified attack by a dignified, old-style Conservative/conservative – as far from the obnoxious & sinister 'alt right' as it is possible to imagine. But sadly – no, more than sadly, tragically – it's the vicious certainties of the alt right that now have the head of steam, epitomised by Bannon's demand that the dissenting media shut their mouths. And at this point, for the record, I should follow Chancellor & quote Trump's recent description of journalists as being 'among the most dishonest human beings on earth'. How on earth, it's impossible not to wonder almost obsessively, is it going to play out? At this particular January moment, eighty-four years on from another January moment, I'm just waiting for the equivalent of the Reichstag fire.

Monday 30 January

Today actually is the eighty-fourth anniversary of Hitler coming to power. (Also my half-birthday – not much celebrated these days, though the odd friend may remember that treasure hunt in Oxford's Botanical Gardens in January 1972.) And in the course of yesterday, the row over Trump's anti-Muslim banning order really gathering a head of steam, amidst chaotic-cum-angry/ emotional scenes in American airports. Theresa May herself half changing tack. It feels potentially like a decisive episode. Does the West seriously try to go down the nativist road? Which is certainly what many of Trump's white supporters want for America. Or do we accept that, even allowing for a measure of immigration control, we live in a global & interconnected world? And for Trump himself, giving to many the impression of a blundering, impulsive & ill-qualified rookie, is this the moment that, only ten days in, credibility begins significantly to drain away from his presidency? It's possible. But, like that equally rookie Chancellor in 1933, he's not – absolutely not – to be underestimated.

Sutton beat Leeds yesterday (1–0 at home) & join Lincoln in the Fifth Round. Remarkable of course, but Leeds fielded such a weakened team that it didn't feel such a huge surprise. So two non-league clubs in the last sixteen. Envy, inevitably, continues to jostle with nobler sentiments.

Tuesday 31 January

The familiar view this morning from New Malden station, Platform 1. The second-ugliest car park in the world (the ugliest is just across the nearby roundabout); two ugly high-rise office blocks that create a ferocious wind tunnel (positively dangerous to the frail elderly, at times literally unable to move & struggling not to be knocked down); a rather pitiful thing that was envisaged as some kind of civic 'banqueting hall' & now, as far as I can tell, lies derelict. All of this concrete blight happened in or around the 1960s – a full half-century ago, but still with us. Instinctively I dislike demolition, but not in this case – time surely for a new start.

Lucy Mangan – talented, perverse, simultaneously endearing but not wholly likeable – had a nice column yesterday about the micro-comforts to hold on to in dark times. Not all chimed with me (e.g. green light for a new *Sex and the City* film), but a trio did:

1. Kindle sales flat for second year in a row = survival of the physical book.

2. Tweet by Dan Guterman (ex-*Onion* writer): '@ barackobama when do u get back from vacation no reason everything is good just curious'.
3. A recent day spent in London (tubes, buses, shops, streets), revealing 'nothing but a million little courtesies and kindnesses out there'. (Something that my often impatient urban self should be more mindful of.)

'Ears of wheat to be gathered,' she ends her piece, 'ahead of a long winter.'

Trump himself meanwhile still dominates almost everything – hearteningly big anti-ban protests last night in London & other British cities; the petition against his state visit here having over 1½ million signatories by this morning; our inglorious Foreign Sec [Johnson] stoutly denying the validity of any Hitler analogy; middle opinion I suspect no longer giving him the benefit of the doubt; & in the US itself, big corporations like Starbucks & Amazon remembering the first word of 'liberal capitalism' – but somewhat overshadowed, MPs shortly to vote on triggering Article 50. Polly Toynbee today calls on Labour MPs to defy 'Corbyn's three-line whip' (a phrase itself to savour & roll around the tongue), on the basis that self-preserving 'respect' for the Leave views of their Midlands & northern constituents should be secondary to their judgement that we are walking into a historic disaster. It's hard not to have some sympathy with both positions. But in the end I go with her: MPs should vote for the outcome that they believe is right – & what higher court is there than the court of conscience? And surely this is even more the case given last summer's deeply flawed exercise in democracy? I also think – because of Trump, quite apart from anything else – that an in/out vote held tomorrow would see a victory for Remain, around 54–46. But of course, who knows?

Nick takes the plaudits

Thursday 2 February

'LIFT-OFF!' is the jubilant *Mail* headline this morning, after an overwhelming Commons vote to trigger Article 50. And a sub-headline: '114 MPs Defy the Will of the People'. Of course, there's a half-truth there. But if the situation had been the other way round, how brave & principled those rebels would have been.

To return, as usual, to Trump. I haven't had the heart to follow & analyse it assiduously, but what has struck me since the autumn has been the apparently intense reluctance of the *mainstream* right to ring the alarm bells about the threat to western democracy. We're now almost a fortnight into the administration – a fortnight which has shown on the administration's part almost no respect for democratic or pluralist norms – but when I looked this morning at the latest issue of the *Spectator*, it seemed an almost entirely qualm-free zone. Understandably, the magazine was full of tribute to Chancellor; but unwilling even to consider, let alone agree with, his valedictory message.

But before I get too high on my horse about entrenched, evidence-free positions, I should note something else. The other day *The Times* ran a fairly typical piece by Melanie Phillips, trenchantly defending Trump's banning executive order. I read the first third & last third of her column, but glazed over – & essentially was unwilling to engage with – the middle third, in which she cited various pre-Trump examples showing that the substance of the ban was not especially out of line with precedent. In other words, I had *my* position – one of moral outrage – & instinctively (I realised afterwards) did not want to countenance any 'alternative facts' (however reputable those facts might have been) which might have challenged or undermined that position. Or as George said when I mentioned this to him yesterday evening, the problem is one of inability to accept or embrace 'cognitive dissonance'. It's a poor look-out, I have to reflect, when someone who calls himself a historian can't handle that. (What the *Spec* did have, I should add, was a piece by Matthew Parris offering a deal to strident – but deep-down insecure – Brexiteers: he was prepared to accept he *might* be wrong about the outcome, & asked if they would be willing to do the same.)

In his *Times* column today, David Aaronovitch – the centrist's centrist, after his long journey from the far left – defends the anti-Trump protesters against the charges of childish hysteria & argues that he *is* a truly dangerous man, not at all funny. In passing he notes that Bannon recently arranged a showing for White House staff of Leni Riefenstahl's *Triumph of the Will* – in its way, almost *the* most startling piece of information to emerge during the last fortnight.[75] Similarly startling was when, a year or so ago, my mother mentioned, without apparently any recognition of the bombshell nature of what she was saying, that as a child in Berlin in the 1930s she had had a relative who was friendly with Riefenstahl – & that occasionally she used to meet her at tea. I was so taken aback that I failed to press her & get further particulars, & now somehow I don't feel (perhaps feebly) that it's something I can do. And talking of those Nazis... The

[75] *Triumph of the Will* (1935), directed, produced, edited and co-written by Riefenstahl, with music by Richard Wagner, was the infamous Nazi propaganda film about Hitler and the 1934 Nuremberg Rally. 'Brilliant, tedious and irredeemably evil' is the crisp verdict of the American film critic J. Hoberman.

Goebbels secretary in the 1945 Führerbunker, Brunhilde Pomsel, died last week at the age of 106. In a late interview, she said she was 'not an evil Nazi' & claimed – far from implausibly – that most people would have done as she did. 'These people nowadays who say they would have stood up against the Nazis – I believe they are sincere in meaning that. But, believe me, most of them wouldn't have.' I tend to have an AJP-style scepticism for 'lessons of history' stuff, but not this time.[76]

Friday 3 February

Actually, Aaronovitch was ambiguous about the White House film screening – it might well have been Bannon (an acknowledged Riefenstahl fan), but it might have been Gordon Liddy (Nixon's henchman, who used to take his children to see the film) back in the 70s. Either way...

Sometimes I feel quite hopeful that, in the medium to long term, things are going to work out all right – that what the West is going through is an ugly but counterable blip. I don't feel that this morning. Martin Kettle in the *Guardian* writes today about the *Daily Mail* & its tightening grip over our political discourse & outcomes. He depicts the *Mail*'s world-view as essentially three-fold: hostility to foreigners; hostility to any whiff of socialism (to which he might have added that it is none too keen on liberalism either); and an unremitting proclamation of Britain's unique capacity for greatness. It's a journalistic product assembled, he also might have added, with consummate professionalism & ruthlessness. For the future historian of early twenty-first-century Britain, it will undoubtedly be *the* prime press source. (Whereas the *Sun* will be for the 1980s & 1990s – & I see that David Hockney, having done a one-off redesign of that paper's masthead, has apparently proclaimed himself a lifelong *Sun* fan...) So,

[76] A. J. P. Taylor, by some way the most prominent British historian when I was growing up and getting interested in history, always took the line that the only lesson of history was that it taught no lessons.

coming back to that mix of nationalism plus anti-foreigners plus anti-socialism/liberalism, it's a formula ultimately just too viscerally powerful, I feel this gloomy (actually, quite sunny) morning, to be overcome. Crucially, it is a mix aimed at the heart not just of Middle England – mainly comprising thoroughly decent people in terms of the conduct of their day-to-day lives – but also, more obliquely but no less insidiously, even self-defining liberals & progressives who, somewhere irreducible inside them, are *also* susceptible to those messages. Put another way, I know I am.

Incidentally, for the record, that *Mail* headline yesterday was 'MOMENTOUS DAY FOR BRITAIN – WE HAVE LIFT-OFF!' – & also on the front page, an image of Churchill, plus just the three union jacks. All that, actually, I do think I find 100% resistible (& risible?), consciously or unconsciously.

Trump-wise, a salutary moment out of my bubble yesterday morning. Lunch at Lord's, after a meeting of the Arts and Library Committee I'm on, & inevitably he hoved into view as a subject for conversation. Opposite me a man I rather like. His line was that a) Washington badly needs a shake-up, & Trump can provide it; & b) there are people around him who will restrain & modify his worst excesses. To my question of whether he believed Trump to be a democrat, he didn't really give an answer.

While I think of it, something I've been meaning to jot down since the autumn. Even though Woody Guthrie once wrote a song about the callousness of 'old man Trump' (i.e. Trump's Rachmanite father), I never really thought that Dylan would come out & say something during the election, much though I hoped he would. And of course he didn't. Almost certainly it wouldn't have made a significant difference, but he still should have.

Finally, & these strange days it always does seem to be finally, a quick football update. Up in the stratosphere, Mourinho has been highly critical of Hull's time-wasting during a goalless draw at Old Trafford. It reminded me of a moment a couple of years ago – that cruel afternoon at Anfield when Gerrard made his fateful slip & Mourinho's Chelsea, mainly camped in their own half, effectively deprived Liverpool of the title. The moment was during the first half: a throw-in to Chelsea – the ball thrown to the Chelsea player taking it – easily within catching distance – & he just let it sail past – i.e. utterly blatant, cynical time-wasting. Meanwhile, down among the journeymen (or what Philip Marlowe might call the grafters), the Shots away to Maidstone tomorrow on their artificial pitch. Not going, but hoping to listen to some of the commentary. Maidstone somewhat on the slide, & if the Shots are going to start winning more of their away matches, which they really have to, this has to be one of them. My prediction is a reasonably comfortable 2–0 victory.

Sunday 5 February

I truly did write that final sentence on Friday, not yesterday... 2–0 to the Shots indeed it was, though to judge by the commentary the emphasis was on 'reasonably' rather than 'comfortable', with the Shots getting a fair battering before Jake G sealed it near the end. Michael was there, with a bunch of Warwick friends, & gives high marks to the sub Johnny Giles, bringing not only a 2:1 in Physics from Durham but also some twinkling toes on the left. The result pushes the Shots up to 6th, though as usual it's somewhat deceptive because of games played. Realistically, it looks highly likely that Lincoln, Dagenham, Forest Green & Tranmere will carve up the top four places between them, leaving perhaps four other teams (Barrow, Dover & Macclesfield as well as the Shots) as the likeliest contenders for that remaining play-off spot. Shots at home to Barrow next Saturday, so that's a big one. My gut feeling is that we're not quite good enough – & tellingly, the current good run (14 points from six matches) has been almost entirely against low-placed teams. But back in early Aug, I'd certainly have settled for 6th in early Feb.

Talking of Johnny Giles... I found myself the other evening, during a rather aimless YouTube session, watching for the first time the 1974 Yorkshire TV programme in which Austin Mitchell (not so long after his book about the Whigs in opposition) interviewed Brian Clough & Don Revie, sitting awkwardly next to each other, on the day that Leeds sacked Clough. An acted-out version is in *The Damned United* film, but this was the real, full-length thing. The sparks at times flew sideways rather than upwards, but it was still compelling stuff. Underlying the conversation, & not ever remotely questioned, was the assumption that football really *matters*. Which of course it sort of does, but only sort of.

The Premiership forty-three years on turning into a procession, probably the cue (now that the cricket's over in India) for very belatedly giving up the Sky subscription.[77] That in itself a cue yesterday for watching Chelsea v Arsenal, i.e. while still possible. A wonderful solo goal by Hazard (best against Arsenal since that Storey-Moore one in '71?), spoilt only by a shot immediately afterwards of the exultant Russian. Hazard himself something very special, & I love the fact he's slightly built & not tall – instead, balance, speed, imagination, intelligence.

Across the herring pond, Trump at war with the judiciary & Bannon doing his level best to provoke a global war against Islam. That man (not Trump) thinks big, thinks long. And in terms of the US itself, things now seem to be moving swiftly towards a full-blown constitutional crisis. Much of yesterday spent waiting for the Trump Twitter response to the Seattle judge's ruling against his banning executive order. Impossible to avert one's eyes & attention, but it's already proving wearying & enervating – not least because of the sure knowledge that when that response comes it will inevitably be childish & blustering, with nothing remotely dignified or uplifting. From the President of the USA... Occupying the White House... The heir of George Washington... It's a desperate situation, & I was pleased by the tough, anti-Trump line being taken by most of the European leaders (but not of course ours) at their Malta summit on Friday. Remarkable to realise that there's still a fortnight & a day to go before the administration is one month old – at which point we'll be precisely 1/48th of the way through the (first?) term of office. The sun I know will keep rising each morning, but still...

---

[77] Chelsea eventually won it with 93 points, followed by Tottenham (86) and Manchester City (78).

I sense a lot of people trying to locate the imaginative literature that seems fit for the moment. I've turned to Nabokov's 'political' novel, *Bend Sinister*, set in a tyrannical state & which I haven't read since about the 1980s. All done through his familiar incorrigibly lofty/patrician prism, but quite apart from the power & emotional tug of the narrative, there's something moving & inspiriting about the highly varnished prose style, the necessary reminder of art's capacity to transcend life. (Will it ever be possible again happily to use 'trump' as a verb?)

An irony, incidentally, that the judge is from Seattle, given that the real-life Frasier – the actor Kelsey Grammer – announced last year, before the election, 'I'm a Trump man.' I'd like to think he's starting to have his doubts.

Monday 6 February

'This is not a place with a name in the tourist world, yet, standing high on a bracing common, among scenery which, though denounced as monotonous, has charms of its own, and abounding, as it does, in lively martial sights and sounds, it is one many would like to visit.' So starts the entry on Aldershot in a 1913 guide to Hampshire that I came across over the weekend, as Lucy & I were sorting through books.

Wednesday 8 February

It's so depressingly obvious what Trump & his gang are trying to do. Ramp up the fear of Islamic terror, ramp up anti-immigrant bans, condemn all liberal/constitutional/fair-minded opposition to those bans, blame that opposition when – at some point down the line – the next terrorist act happens. These people are not democrats, they are not pluralists, & – quite apart from their intellectually one-dimensional view of the world, which of course does not preclude a low cunning – they are bad, bad people, with whom there can be no accommodation. I'm pleased that Bercow is not willing to have Trump address the Commons, citing his racism, his sexism & – crucially – his disdain for the independence of the judiciary. Particularly threatening at the moment is the sight of Trump cosying up to the military. I can't see how this is going to end well – I really can't. Joan Baez talked the other day about the importance of setting an *example* of courage, & how that example can quickly spread. She's surely right. Would I be among those setting an example if I was American? Perhaps, but at best only perhaps.

Friday 10 February

I've felt reluctant over these last few weeks to quote Trump himself all that much – just too demoralising, even degrading. But this from the other day is him in a formal address to a conference in Washington of law-enforcement officials, i.e. it's not even a tweet. The passage comes after he quoted the portion of the immigration law that, according to him, gives him the power to enact the travel ban (on seven Muslim-majority countries):

> I watched [the appeals court] last night in amazement and I heard things that I couldn't believe, things that really had nothing to do with what I just read. I don't ever want to call a court biased, so I won't call it biased, and we haven't had a decision yet [it's since gone against him], but courts seem to be so political and it would be so great for our justice system if they would be able to read a statement and do what's right, and that has to do with the security of our country, which is so important.
>
> I was a good student, I understand things, I comprehend very well, OK. Better than, I think, almost anybody. And I want to tell you that I listened to a bunch of stuff last night on television that was disgraceful, it was disgraceful, because what I just read to you is what we have and it just can't be written any plainer or better.

Irrespective of any legal arguments (& I have no faith at all in Trump's respect for the law), it's that mixture of childishness &

ludicrous vanity that really gets to me – the sheer lack of dignity – & the grotesque disparity between all that & the utterly serious, utterly solemn position that he now (God help us) holds.

Perhaps anyway it's now all going to be OK? That is now Aaronovitch's new, more reassuring line, in relation to here & Europe at least, where he argues that recent events – above all the coming of Trump to power – have 'changed the mood among usually phlegmatic centrist voters', i.e. toughened it up, as evidenced e.g. by a majority poll in favour of delaying or cancelling his state visit, & in France the possibility of Macron this spring defeating Le Pen. He ends: 'If it reinvigorates itself, the centre can hold. I think that's what most people want.' Well, let's hope so. It's a pretty big 'if' – & as to exactly *how* that reinvigoration happens, or of *what* it comprises... Here, for what it's worth, my guess is this. Labour loses both by-elections (including Stoke-on-Trent) the week after next. Corbyn has to go, but Labour elects an equally left-wing & less than credible leader. At which point, either there's a terrific spike in Lib Dem support & many moderate Labour MPs cross over, or (perhaps more plausible?) those MPs form the core of a new party. *Something* has to happen soon. The existing vacuum – across much of the 'centre' – is just too big. And if *nothing* happens? Well, that's game over.

Talking of which, it's the Shots tomorrow, & hopefully not play-off hopes over. A win against Barrow would signify that we're *really* in the mix, & on balance – though without any great confidence – that's my prediction. What we do know is that it's going to be horribly cold, probably in a damp sort of way, with for this 65-year-old intimations in his chilled bones of real old age. That said, I'm much looking forward to it, as much as any home game since Tranmere in Sept – & who knows, perhaps it'll be something like that.

Alan Simpson died this week (his obit in *The Times* appearing on the flip side of Tara Palmer-Tomkinson). It always amazed me how he & Galton went on living for so long after Tony Hancock was dead, Sid James was dead, Harry H. Corbett was dead, Wilfrid Brambell was dead. There was a time in the early 60s when Hancock meant almost everything to me – shaping how I talked, how I saw the world. Perhaps ultimately that was limiting & even unhelpful (in terms of something quite core that lasted into adulthood), but the news still gave me a pang. And I liked the fact that he had devoted so much of his time (and presumably money) to a non-league football club, Hampton. Back in 1968, incidentally, my actor friend Stanley Page used the same dressing room in Sydney that Hancock had used a week earlier, when he took a fatal overdose.[78] While as a possible quiz question, it's nice to know who Hancock's political hero was. Answer: Michael Foot.

Sunday 12 February

Waitrose in New Malden yesterday morning. I was buying eggs, & waited to the side as a middle-aged man bent down & investigated various boxes. He took eggs out of one box & put them in another one, & vice versa. Finally, once he had a box of eggs to his satisfaction, he went off with it. At first I assumed he was a member of staff, but eventually realised he wasn't. One-quarter impressed & three-quarters appalled (the apotheosis of individualism?), I didn't say anything to him. I remember my friend Micky saying to me years ago, in Canterbury in the late 70s, that in terms of greengrocers, he didn't like the recent move to selecting one's own fruit & veg – with all the attendant anxiety – & preferred the old system of accepting what you were given. But yesterday I felt it wasn't anxiety that characterised the man, but calm, focused purpose – with the focus of course being entirely on what was best for him.

Well, & so to the football. (Bitterly cold, as expected, but my six layers just about did their job.) Barrow a big, physical team, but Shots played them off the park in the first half, gaining a deserved

---

[78] Not quite right. Hancock had been in the dressing room (rehearsing an episode for an Australian TV series) just before going back to his flat, where he committed suicide with a mixture of vodka and barbiturates. 'Things seemed to go wrong too many times,' said a suicide note. The scriptwriter for the series was Michael Wale, not very rugged left-back for Battersea Park when I was playing for them (equally unruggedly) in the mid-70s.

two-goal lead – McClure with a very early opportunistic strike, Evans with a thumping header from a corner. As for the second half, here's the bare chronology (approx timings):

73 mins. Barrow pull one back, with one of their players running from deep with the ball & scoring, probably via a deflection.
82 mins. Barrow player sent off.
90 mins. Another Barrow player sent off.
95 mins. Barrow equalise with a superbly struck free kick from some thirty yards out.

Or put another way, the Shots failed to see it out against a nine-man team… Essentially, a loss of composure, a loss of nerve. Poor indeed, & what was all too apparent during those first five minutes of injury time, as Barrow for all their numerical shortfall pressed hard, was that this was a team, with quite a high proportion of very young players, not at all good at closing out a game. The four of us (Lucy, Michael & me as well as Nick Humphrey) all I think felt numb at the end – & it certainly felt very hard to continue to view the Shots as serious play-off contenders. Actually, the other results didn't go too badly (Dover & Macclesfield both drawing, Shots still 6th), but the blow to collective morale (supporters as well as players) is perhaps incalculable. All that said, it was a compelling, dramatic, high-octane spectacle – which in the bigger picture (what bigger picture exactly?) is surely worth something.

An interview yesterday with Mel Brooks, now in his nineties. 'Trump doesn't scare me,' he says. 'He's a song-and-dance man. Pence and Bannon, those guys make me nervous.' He adds: 'We are not talking about Athenian democracy here.'

Monday 13 February

I watched yesterday afternoon the extended highlights of the Barrow match. Foul after foul – I don't think I'd quite realised at the time what a dirty side they were. They probably did 'deserve' their point: two fine goals, plus remarkable fight (of the better sort) when reduced to nine. But still left a slightly sour taste.

The *Observer* included an admiring review by Peter Conrad of A. A. Gill's collected journalism. The final para puts in further shameful (i.e. for me) perspective my glib reaction to the news of his death:

> Near the end of the book, an eloquent defence of the EU and a scathing anatomy of the 'angry losers' who voted for Trump made me wonder if Gill might not be better off dead: at least he won't have to endure our new era of big-mouthed, small-minded demagoguery, with its borders that snap shut like a mastiff's jaws. But he would never have succumbed to defeatism. Instead his essays – so delicate in their connoisseurship of nature and culture, so tender in their sketches of family, friends and anonymous strangers in refugee camps, so brightly witty and yet so unexpectedly profound – affirm the manifold pleasures of being alive, which is why they enrich the life of anyone who reads them, and in Gill's absence will go on doing so.

An obstinate/perverse bit of me wonders if this isn't just a little over-egging the pudding. Even so…

I've never met Conrad but admire him, especially his early book *The Victorian Treasure House* (title taken from James's semi-damning verdict on *Middlemarch*).[79] I got to know it in 1974 when I was writing a book on Victorian taste (never published – it was for a series that, soon after I'd finished it, got dumped by Methuen). And if I was to write it now? Perhaps I'd be more sceptical of those great, thundering male prophets – Pugin, Carlyle, Ruskin, Morris. Perhaps I'd be more tolerant of prosperous, middle-class culture (those elderly Forsytes on the Bayswater Road). Above all, I wouldn't patronise the epoch as a benighted prelude to the triumph of modernism. If I could live anywhere at any time, with roughly the same socio-economic background,

---

[79] '*Middlemarch* is a treasure-house of detail, but it is an indifferent whole' (Henry James, surely on the whole unfairly, in 1873).

it would be Victorian England. Essentially for the seriousness, the moral worth of the individual life lived well, the sheer *heaviness* of being. And I've always imagined that my final phase as a historian would be getting deeply immersed in Victorian letters, diaries, etc. Though now, trying to be realistic, I'm far from sure that that's going to happen.

Friday 17 February

Just back with Lucy from a couple of work-free, email-free, diary-free days with Nicholas & Nina in Dorset. My favourite county – the variety of landscape especially – & it was a good break.

Trump et al. inevitably high on the conversational agenda. Nicholas (a judge) suspects that, on appeal, he may win with his executive order, i.e. the travel ban, on the grounds that it doesn't *explicitly* discriminate against Muslims. Tommy (their eighteen-year-old son) follows it all closely & mentions that recently at midnight (presumably US time) Trump randomly tweeted, 'MAKE AMERICA GREAT AGAIN!', with no surrounding context & as if he could think of nothing else to say but somehow could not resist the compulsion to tweet. More generally, this week has given the gratifying (if ultimately scary) impression of the wheels falling off the Trump administration. At the start, the enforced resignation of the national security adviser (too close to Russia – but what did the Pres know? Just possibly a Watergate for our time...), & yesterday an erratic, bullying, blustering, self-pitying press conference, legitimately raising the question of his mental stability, even the possibility of a man on the edge of a nervous breakdown. For myself, I doubt it – it's sometimes the supreme egotists who have the supreme if distorted sanity – but you never know.

The Shots away at Wrexham tomorrow. Hard to be optimistic – I can't remember ever winning there; they're on a good run; last Sat's closing debacle will surely have left its scars – & I'd be more than happy with a point, which at least would keep going the post-Christmas undefeated run & also keep us more or less in contention for that almost ludicrously coveted (given that then only a 1 in 4 chance of going up) 5th spot.

Back to Trump. Again & again in his press conference he returned to the mainstream media (including the BBC) – their agenda, their 'fake news', their 'very fake news' & all that. That whole approach is so patently wrong, anti-truth & deeply self-serving that I've tended to downplay it in my head – as a temporary if irritating distraction that, because of its ludicrousness, won't be around long. Now I'm not so sure. Millions of people clearly *do* get their 'news' from other sources, many of them wholly one-eyed, that perhaps it actually will become a permanent fact of life that the mainstream media is largely bypassed. And of course, in terms of encouraging a dispassionate, well-informed democracy (surely the ideal of a free press etc.), that mainstream media often falls way, way short. Eric Blair, you should be alive at this hour.

Saturday 18 February

Not surprising I can't ever remember the Shots winning at Wrexham – in twenty (!) previous attempts before today, we hadn't. But today, mercifully, was different. No goals at half-time, followed by a dominant second-half performance & running out comfortable 2–0 winners (goals by Rendell & Jim Kellermann, who is starting to become a significant, ball-winning midfield presence). No change in position (7th, having slipped down during the week), but definitely – along with Dover, Barrow, Macclesfield & now Gateshead – in the mix for 5th, while one or two of the top four (including Forest Green) are starting to look conceivably catchable by the chasing pack. And the Shots now unbeaten in eight.

Top of the Vanarama remain Lincoln, who today in the Fifth Round of the Cup went to Burnley & won 1–0, apparently quite deservedly. And should Sutton vanquish beleaguered Arsenal on Monday, well, that would be two non-league teams in the quarter-finals. Presumably it's not going to happen, but if ever a giant was ripe for the taking, this is the moment.

I should just add something about the listening experience this afternoon, because of its enforced shades of 1966. No Radio Surrey, but covered by Radio Wales, & I listened to the last four minutes of the first half & then most of the second, including Shots taking the lead. Then Wolfie (staying with us) came down from his extended nap & I turned it off. He was a bit sad, in need of distraction, so I found myself quite happy to take him off to a different room – essentially because, after last Saturday, I didn't think I could bear to listen to the Shots trying to hang on for a win, & somehow feeling that there was more chance of them doing so if I entirely absented myself. No Nancy Sinatra this time, but again it worked.

Monday 20 February

A Shots anniversary today, but I'm not sure I quite have the heart – even after thirty-eight years – to give it the full monty. 20 February 1979, a midweek evening, & following a post-ponement the Shots (Fourth Division) at home to Shrewsbury (Third Division) in Fifth Round of the Cup, the furthest since the 1930s that the Shots had got to. Ultra-resonant for me, with in their different ways Aldershot & Shrewsbury being 'my' two places (prep school in Shrewsbury 1959–64, my grandparents moving there in 1964, & by 1979 my father & stepmother living in my grandparents' house), & this the first time I'd seen them play each other. So OK, just the bare facts. The Shots, starring a goal machine called John Dungworth, largely on top through the match. No goals at half-time. Dungworth scoring around midway through the second half, but Shrewsbury almost imme-diately equalising. And then, around the 90-minute mark, Dungworth firing (volleying?) spectacularly home – only for the Shots, a minute or two later, to try to play the ball out of their penalty area, lose possession & see the faultily placed goalkeeper (Glen Johnson, otherwise a hero in the Cup run) cruelly lobbed. Amidst very considerable competition, I think my worst-ever moment as a Shots supporter.

I went the following week to the replay at the Gay Meadow. 1–1 after 90 mins (Dungworth again), Shots hitting the post in extra time, Shrewsbury then scoring twice to win 3–1.[80] On the train back to London the following morning, I remember catching a glimpse of Wembley's Twin Towers, gleaming mockingly in the sunlight. While when, twenty-six years later, the Shots had the opportunity for revenge, playing Shrewsbury in a play-off final (at Stoke) for promotion to the League, it all went horribly wrong in the penalty shoot-out (not helped by the Shrewsbury goalie being allowed to be way off his line).

The Trump presidency is one month old today. On Saturday evening he did a rally in Florida, organised not by the White House but by his election-campaign team. It had as an event, as David Warren remarked to me even before it happened, an unmistakable fascist feel. And as usual, he laid into the media, with the crowd baying for the media's blood. Trump may be thin-skinned, but he's also a not unintelligent man. And my guess is that on his part there's something deeply cynical going on here.

Tuesday 21 February

I've only just come across Trump's tweet last Friday: 'The FAKE NEWS media (failing New York Times, NBC News, ABC, CBS, CNN) is not my enemy, it is the enemy of the American people!'

And from yesterday, on the *New Yorker*'s website, this closing para from a piece by George Packer:

An authoritarian and erratic leader, a chaotic Presidency, a supine legislature, a resistant permanent bureaucracy, street demonstrations, fear abroad: this is what illiberal regimes look

---

[80] Shrewsbury in the Sixth Round played away at Wolves. The TV highlights (on YouTube) are another reminder of what pitches could be like in that era: a sea of mud, with barely a blade of grass to be seen.

like. If Trump were more rational and more competent, he might have a chance of destroying our democracy.

A striking passage – but of course begs several questions, not least about the bureaucracy, which surely in practice could go either way.

Packer also has this to say about the Republicans, from whom so far since the Inauguration barely a squeak of protest:

Perhaps Party leaders are privately searching their souls; perhaps, as with the old Bolshevik Rubashov, in Arthur Koestler's *Darkness at Noon*, ideology and power have rendered them incapable of independent moral judgement. Whatever the case, history won't be kind to them.

History! Depends of course on who is writing it… But in a larger sense, yes, he's absolutely right.

History not quite made by Sutton last night, but a plucky effort, losing 2–0 & hitting the bar. Highlight came near the end. Their goalie on the bench was the middle-aged & dramatically overweight goalkeeping coach. Once Sutton had used their third sub (Dan Fitchett, ex-Shots), he knew he was spared – & took the opportunity to tuck into a substantial pie, a process that the close-up camera lingered on, plus plenty of 'what would Wenger make of that?' from the commentator. Wasn't there a renowned 20-stone goalkeeper in football's early days?[81] Certainly, among contemporary keepers, I always find Man Utd's David de Gea disconcertingly slender for the position of custodian.

Two deaths in today's papers. The Radio 4 presenter Steve Hewlett (cancer, fifty-eight), who died at Chelsea's Royal Marsden 'whilst listening to Bob Dylan with his family'. (*Which* Dylan? I think 'Every Grain of Sand' might suit me well enough in those fading moments of consciousness. Certainly nothing too upbeat or noisy. Conceivably 'Desolation Row' – that line about

---

[81] William ('Fatty') Foulke kept goal between 1894 and 1907, mainly for Sheffield United (with one England cap). Reputedly, he weighed 24 stone by the end of his career.

the girl thinking death quite romantic... & Ezra & Old Possum fighting in the Captain's Tower...) The other death is an England batsman of the 50s & 60s, Peter Richardson – who as a practical joker particularly targeted the undeniably pompous E. W. Swanton, so his *Times* obit is grist for the book I'm just starting on with Stephen Fay.

Stop press: turns out that the pasty-eating episode was a premeditated stunt to win a bet. Should have guessed. And apparently, with talk of an FA 'probe', the guy has resigned. While further breaking news is that Gary Waddock & his assistant were approached by a League club, but that they have committed their future to the Shots... Certainly I'd be sad if Waddock left.

Wednesday 22 February

Shots not in action last night, but various rivals were – & from a Shots perspective the results went uniformly badly. In 8th place now, & it's clearly going to take this current run of form continuing steadily if we're going to stay in contention.

Something rather alarming has been happening in the last few days. I look at photos of Trump and, yes, I still feel a strong measure of loathing, fear, distaste. But also, at some level, a grudging respect, a sort of 'you've got to hand it to him' feeling. Is there any chance that this could turn into the merest bat's squeak of affection? My God, I hope not. (The trigger moment may have been glancing at a clip from *Saturday Night Live* & seeing Alec Baldwin do his Trump impersonation & feeling just slightly turned off by the implicit virtue-signalling aspect of the whole exercise. Lucy last week said something similar – to do with smugness – when she saw a bit of another *SNL* sketch, viz. the rather brilliant female impersonator of Trump's hapless Press Secretary.[82] Put another way, it's so easy to be carping on the sidelines).

---

[82]   Melissa McCarthy as Sean Spicer.

Thursday 23 February

The bat's-squeak moment is over. Lucy told me yesterday the story of Trump buying (80s? 90s?) the Florida country house that he turned into a country club & now uses as his presidential southern retreat. It had a fine library full of first editions, etc. – a library that he trashed in order to convert it into a bar, complete with a large, commissioned portrait of himself in tennis whites.

Friday 24 February

Results in from Copeland and Stoke – the Tories win in former (first government by-election gain since 1982, when another north London left-winger was Labour leader); Labour hold off UKIP's Nuttall in latter. Which, given that Nuttall had been severely holed by all his palpable untrustworthiness on the still understandably emotive Hillsborough issue, more or less leaves Labour in a state of continuing stasis. Presumably the party's moderates, plus those reluctantly facing up to the undoubted reality that Corbyn could never win a general election, will bide their time until next year – when, two years out from a general election (assuming, as seems probable, that May doesn't call a snap one this year), the prospect of a 2020 wipe-out will be fairly imminent reality. Of course, Corbyn & Co. will do their best to ensure that he's succeeded by a Corbynista. At which point, if that happens, there surely has to be a split, & some kind of middle-ground regrouping in British politics – there must be a limit to how long nature can continue abhorring a vacuum.

Main football news is that Ranieri has been sacked by Leicester's Thai owners – less than a year after his truly remarkable triumph, & apparently a players' revolt (complaints about him becoming too distant, etc.). A shame. I'd wondered at the time, i.e. when Leicester not only won the title but by a full 10 points, whether he shouldn't have voluntarily left then, but perhaps the lure of the Champions League was too strong. Overall, it feels like a tacky decision.

Football-related (if only in my mind) is news of the death of Alan Aldridge, the Beatles illustrator. I nearly mentioned him at the end of last month. The occasion would have been a fortieth anniversary, i.e. of Monday 31 January 1977. It was a lunchtime game on AstroTurf (unyielding & unpleasant in those days), somewhere near the Caledonian Road, between my team, Battersea Park, & the *Sunday Times*. I was playing up front on the right, Aldridge was marking me at left-back, & true to his working-class background, notwithstanding his long blond hair & all the intervening hippy stuff, he proved to be a take-no-prisoners operator, absolutely *not* the sort of defender I enjoyed playing against. Anyway, by half-time they were 5–0 up. But in the second half, & I state as plain unvarnished historical non-alternative fact, we came back to win 7–6 with a hat-trick from yours truly, mainly drifting to the more congenial pastures of the left. The moment I treasure came near the end, with the outcome still in doubt. We had a corner on the right, I went over to take it (being never a threat in the air, except once at Tottenham Marshes around this time, when in the course of a 10–1 defeat I nodded home from a corner past our startled keeper), & would normally have swung it over. But just before doing so, I spotted out of the corner of my eye John Moynihan, quite close to me on the corner of the box & – I remember how the image came to me even at the time – looking like a big, friendly dog with his tongue hanging out & hoping for a bone. John was far from a great footballer – indeed, was far from a great football writer – but he was such a thoroughly nice, decent, inarticulate man that people, including me, were fond of him. So almost out of pity, plus perhaps some imp of perversity, I played it short to him – whereupon he managed some sort of cross &, miraculously, a goal resulted. I've also a faint memory, but maybe it is only a shadow memory, of shaking Aldridge's hand at the end & him being in a pretty foul, graceless mood. If that's so, I don't really blame him.

Back to the football present. One stray thought from a few days ago that I'd like to jot down. Given the strong anti-London mood that was surely part of last summer's Leave vote, might the outcome have been different if the FA had decided – as I hoped at the time they would – to replace the dilapidated Wembley stadium with a new national football stadium somewhere in the Midlands or even in the North? I actually think that particular counter-factual has some plausibility to it.

And tomorrow, the Shots are at home to Bromley. It feels a very long time since that warm August evening in south-east outer suburbia when the Shots so feebly let that two-goal lead slip, revealing the ultimate lack of steel that in the end is likely, I suspect, to see us falling short. But as to tomorrow, well, all the usual anxieties, but I predict a reasonably comfortable 3–1 win. Anything less than a win, given the form of the others, would be a significant blow.

Sunday 26 February

As George Formby almost sang, it turned out nicely... Shots on top virtually throughout – Bromley threatening only two or three times – & two goals shortly before half-time (Nick Arnold with a fortuitously overhit cross, Shamir Fenelon with a well-placed daisycutter), followed by another soon after (Jake Gallagher header – collector's item), effectively clinched it, with Matt McClure sealing it shortly before the end with a sweetly hit left-footer from well outside the box. Lots of good football – on the ground, quick interchanges, plenty of pace & purpose – so generally a pleasure to watch, apart from a rather stagnant phase midway through the second half. Most eye-catching was Idris Kanu down the left: a seventeen-year-old causing havoc, & I guess it is actually a realistic possibility that in a year or two's time the Shots might be able to cash in & make a lot of money by selling him.[83] Anyway, the Shots now up to 6th, though as usual a little deceptive because of the question of games played. It's away to Eastleigh on Tuesday evening. The Shots have never

---

[83]   In the event, Kanu was sold to Peterborough United of League One in August 2017 for an undisclosed fee. Somewhere in the £100,000–£200,000 range was the general feeling at the time.

beaten them, & on paper this must be the moment – a terrible run of form since their rather lucky win at Aldershot in November, at least one manager sacked, & they seem unable to score at home... All of which, inevitably, makes me deeply nervous... Lucy & I have thought about going, but decided against – just a bit too far on a Tuesday night at the end of February. But in theory, post-Eastleigh, we're going to see the next seven Shots matches, home & away.

Trump has declared outright war on the parts of the mainstream media he dislikes, even to the extent of excluding some from White House briefings. I know it's repetition, but he is a man without a democratic instinct in his bones. Sometimes I forget about it for a few hours, but I still get a sense of shock when I remember that he is the President of the United States. He, Bannon & the others are also systematically exploiting crude & angry nationalist instincts. And, in what can only now be a war to the death, there must be at least a 50–50 chance that they're going to win. A reputable new poll shows that, when asked to choose between Trump & the media as the more truthful purveyor of news, 45% of Americans go for Trump & only 42% for the media. Sure gives me a chill.

Over the coming weeks & months, so much now depends on the mainstream conservatives. Either they stand up for democracy, pluralism & press freedom, or they don't. The signs so far remain at best mixed. Of course I care about his policies as such, especially about immigration, but ultimately it's this 'process' issue that I care about most. And apart from the odd bit of Vanarama downtime, I'm continuing to find it almost obsessive – the sort of obsession that makes one want to scream at people who ought to get it but for some mysterious reason don't.

Monday 27 February

Interesting moment near the end of yesterday's League Cup Final. Amidst much speculation about his future, & being surplus to Mourinho's requirements, Rooney was on the touchline, preparing to come on as a sub, a few minutes from the end of normal time, with Man U drawing 2–2 against Southampton. This would surely be his moment to make a purposeful, heartfelt statement. At which point United's replacement talisman, Ibrahimovich (four years older), scored. Cue unrestrained & clearly genuine celebration from Rooney, i.e. a deeply embedded team ethic triumphs over the individual. Impressive in its way. More generally, Southampton somewhat unlucky to lose, & of course I was willing the result to go the other way. But certainly a better game than the sterile, dreary affair in 1976, notwithstanding its 'fairytale' ending. Though perhaps I'm prejudiced – it was when I was starting to get disenchanted with top-level football.

Tuesday 28 February

Last night's *Newsnight* had a lengthy item about our increasing mistrust of (& disdain towards) experts, majoring of course on Gove's infamous remark during the Referendum campaign (which in a new interview he semi-rowed back from). My feelings are mixed. Instinctively I don't care for latter-day economists (the experts nearest to my own concerns): their arrogance, their sense of priesthood, above all their model-driven lack of interest in human variables, & so it doesn't dismay me that twice in recent years they've come so spectacularly unstuck – first over the financial crisis (almost completely failing to predict it, let alone stop it happening), then with their scare predictions about the immediate consequences of Brexit. It also matters that I'm not an academic & inevitably feel some chippiness towards them, though much less (mellowing? more comfortable in my own achievements?) than used to be the case. BUT on the other hand... My belief in the importance of learning, of scholarship, of knowledge, of accumulated experience is absolute. Yes, 'common sense' matters. But to place it at the apex, to claim that it is the supreme arbiter of policy & action, as some populist politicians (Trump downwards, or is that upwards?) are now doing, is crude, philistine & potentially hugely dangerous – a know-nothing arrogance just as bad as if not worse than a know-all arrogance.

Last night's programme also had an interview with Iain Duncan Smith, in the wake of John Major's speech attacking the triumphalism & intolerance of the Brexiteers towards the 48%. 'The revenge of the little man' was how Lucy put it afterwards, & that's exactly right.

Shots at Eastleigh this evening (I'm writing this at about 3.30 in Lombard Street's Pret a Manger). As already stated, I'm nervous. On paper, there for the taking. But in practice? As usual when conflicted, I fall back on a 1–1 prediction. Whatever, it'd be nice if one or two of the other teams stumble.

Five-man barrier

Wednesday 1 March (St David's Day + Ash Wednesday)

Well, it was tense & absorbing. Got back home at about 8.10, i.e. 25 mins into the match. No goals – Shots very much on top – but Kellermann already sent off (no complaints from Shots-supporting commentators). Shots remaining on top, with a goal from Kanu (again outstanding) just before the break. Second half much more even, & finally, in about the 80th minute, Eastleigh equalising. Shots at the death the likelier to score, but it finished 1–1. A pretty heroic effort from the ten men, and with both Barrow & Dover losing away (Macclesfield & Gateshead not playing), I guess it has to count as a point gained at least as much as two dropped. Still in 6th place – with the usual caveats – & it's now ten games unbeaten, i.e. since Chester before Christmas. Next Saturday is home to Cup quarter-finalists & Vanarama leaders Lincoln – feels like the biggest game of the season so far, & my guess is a 3,000-plus crowd. Genuinely exciting.

From the Major speech, this quote about the post-Brexit rise of anti-immigrant sentiment:

I caution everyone to be wary of this kind of populism. It seems to be a mixture of bigotry, prejudice and intolerance. It scapegoats minorities. It is a poison in any political system – destroying civility and decency and understanding.

Good stuff from a, for all his touchiness, much underestimated man. He also called the Referendum result a 'historic mistake', plus had this about the dire emerging geo-political situation now confronting Britain after that wretched decision:

Outside the European Union, we become far more dependent upon the United States and – for four and possibly eight years – upon a president less predictable, less reliable and less attuned to our free market and socially liberal instincts than any of his predecessors.

It's the authentic voice of the better sort of Conservative, & I only hope we'll hear more of it. I remain doubtful.

The Royal Society of Literature publishes today the results of an extensive survey of British reading habits & attitudes to literature. 1,998 respondents named an author whom they associated with literature. The three most mentioned names were Shakespeare, Dickens & J. K. Rowling. Some way down the list, tying on seven mentions each, were those nicely complementary titans, Leo Tolstoy & Jilly Cooper. Some 20% of those surveyed were unable to name anyone.

Thursday 2 March

Trump's State of the Union speech on Tues night. First ominous signs since the Inauguration of a more consensual (or at least making vaguely conciliatory noises), father-of-the-nation figure starting to emerge.

Owen Jones reflects in today's *Guardian* on Labour's plight. What he clearly wants is Corbyn, sooner rather than later, to pass the baton to a more electorally viable left-wing leader (no names mentioned) – for fear that unless he does so, the chances of any authentically socialist project achieving power in Britain will be holed for at least a generation. Jones ends:

Either we have a country riddled with hatred and fear, a playground for billionaires that slashes support for the working poor and disabled people, that runs down and flogs off the services we depend on – or we become a country run in the interests of the real wealth creators: working people.

Is it really such a binary choice? I don't believe so. So many obituaries have been written in the last year or two for old-fashioned social democracy, but it is interesting that there's a significant twitch of life from the Social Democrats in Germany. And if David Miliband were to return from across the herring pond, something dramatic could happen here. Yes, markets need to be regulated – absolutely – but any dispassionate reading of the twentieth century, indeed of the modern world, makes it abundantly clear that, in most but not all areas of life, some sort of market mechanism is indispensable.

At the National Theatre there is something new called *My Country: A Work in Progress*, focused on last year's referendum & largely comprising extracts from seventy long interviews with 'ordinary people' (my quote marks) across Britain. The director, Rufus Norris, is reported as having been struck by how convinced all the interviewees (on both sides of the argument) were by the correctness of their own position & how reluctant they were to listen to other viewpoints. 'With the death in belief of the great them – whether they are politicians, kings and queens or experts – what do we believe in? We believe in ourselves. Cameras now are only used to take photos of ourselves – not of anything around us. We know we are in an age of extreme selfishness.' Later in the interview (Tuesday's *Guardian*), Norris does, however, name one person whom people *do* listen to: the editor of the *Daily Mail*. 'How can we have an unelected person steering the country this way? Paul Dacre. Who the fuck is Paul Dacre? Why does he have so much influence?' While as for 'that fucking liar in America', he adds temperately, the only answer for liberals like himself is 'to sharpen our teeth'.

There's an obit today of the Yorkshire batsman John Hampshire, who had the misfortune for so many years to play his cricket with Boycott. 'Geoffrey and I speak now if we see each other,' he said shortly before his death from cancer. 'There was a time in the late Seventies when we didn't. We fell out. There's been that much written about it – I just let it float over my head now. My time is short, and I don't want to be wasting my breath talking about all that.' Haunting words. 'My time is short…'

Friday 3 March

Lucy this morning found a cream cracker behind the settee – truly.

Lincoln tomorrow. It's been a looming fixture for a long time, & I've generally felt confident, but suddenly less so. It sounds from the Waddock interview (regularly on the Shots website, each Thursday morning) that one or two might have picked up injuries at Eastleigh, plus of course Kellermann starts his suspension (four matches). My worry is that the Shots are going to be a bit light in midfield. Still, there must be a decent chance that Lincoln are going to be somewhat patchy & preoccupied before their momentous date at the Emirates a week tomorrow (& on Tues they only drew 1–1 at home to still bottom-of-the-table York). The likeliest result on paper is I guess a draw, but on balance I'm plumping for a 2–1 win for the Shots. Not with any great conviction, but encouraged by my decent run of predictions lately. Whatever happens, it should be quite an occasion.

Sunday 5 March

And it was. Three and a half thousand (including 500 away supporters) saw tense, absorbing, toe-to-toe stuff – but no goals. Most of the chances falling to Lincoln – a physical, uncompromising outfit, showing precious few signs of holding back a week ahead of their big day – but the Shots had their moments. Too nerve-racking actually to be enjoyable, & I was happy enough when the referee blew the final whistle. Other results on the whole not too bad, & the Shots remain in 6th. Ten games to go, & I guess that chances of the Shots staking a play-off place are about 1 in 5, though looking at the fixtures it doesn't look too bad a run-in. On Friday I looked up the bookies' odds of promotion as such – & 25 to 1 was somewhat disheartening if probably realistic. Still, it's March & we're unbeaten in eleven & in contention: no complaints there.

A couple of footballing ghosts came up yesterday. The minor one was Eamonn McCabe, the photographer, who according to the Saturday evening Radio 4 arts review programme (which we often listen to on the way back from a post-Shots cup of tea with my mother & stepfather in Farnborough) is about to start a three-part TV documentary series on the history of photography. In the early 80s I played a bit for Nine Elms Dynamos, a Sunday team in which Eamonn was a fierce defender. My main memory of the Dynamos is that there was a midfielder whose shirt had the number 8½ – a nice touch.

The more resonant ghost came through reading Blake Morrison's *Guardian* review of a memoir by Sam Miller called *Fathers*. The fathers in question were his supposed father, the literary critic Karl Miller, & his actual father, Tony White. Strange in the *Guardian* to see a mention of Battersea Park the football team, which Tony played for much longer than I did. In his forties when I knew him in the mid-70s, he was a crude, rugged defender whom I (like I guess everyone else in the team) warmed to hugely – for his total commitment on the pitch & his great friendliness off it. His backstory has already, before Sam Miller's book, been given in Joan Bakewell's autobiography: the most talented actor of his Cambridge generation – went to the Old Vic, with the world at his feet – but then reacted strongly against the insincerity of it all – & for the rest of his life had all sorts of odd jobs, none with career prospects. That life ended in the winter of 1975/6. I missed that season (living in Yorkshire), but what seems to have happened was that one very cold Sunday morning a match went ahead on a frozen pitch (the Scrubs?) that shouldn't have, that Tony broke his leg & that a month later he died of an embolism. I'll definitely try to get hold of the book. But here I should, as a coda, mention something else – namely, in what was practically his last piece of published writing before he died, Karl Miller wrote for the *LRB* a fairly dusty, unenthusiastic review of my *Modernity Britain* book covering the late 1950s. George, my son, called it 'arsey', & though I wouldn't quite go that far... Still, I suspect I'm in decent company.

As for the lying, self-aggrandising tweeter, he's now accusing Obama (a 'bad' man) of having tapped his phones during the election campaign. Probably a predictable diversionary ploy, to try to take the heat off the steadily engulfing Russian situation, but Lucy's verdict is blunt & maybe not wrong: 'He's mad.' Meanwhile, his supporters are starting to hold 'Spirit of America' rallies. A potentially very scary (white) nationalist movement is now well under way, with their guy in office. And military spending being boosted... and generals & ex-generals at his side... On any rational basis, it remains wholly impossible to predict how this is going to play out. Outside personal stuff, I've never been so apprehensive in my life.

Back, if only to keep sane, to football. Nobby Stiles is apparently in a poor way (dementia?), & mention of that in a paper the other day reminded me of a story that always amuses me. In an early match in the 1966 World Cup, against France, he was apparently lucky not to be sent off, following at least one reckless tackle against a particular French player. Someone asked him afterwards what had got into him. 'He called me Norbert' was his reply (the name pronounced of course in a French way with a French accent). Well, what option was there but non-verbal retaliation?

Wednesday 8 March

All that was written on a stopping train from Tottenham Hale to Cambridge. (Have I mentioned my stroll round the former while waiting for the train? A bleak, harsh, inhumane sort of environment, featuring the Tottenham Hale Retail Park & a general lowering of spirits, of any possible reaching for the stars.) On the train itself, near where I was sitting, a middle-aged woman came up to a man who was in a four-seater space & asked if he wouldn't mind moving, because there were three others of them coming up the train (this was the front carriage), including as it turned out a baby. The man thought about it for quite a long time, not looking best pleased (as in all honesty I wouldn't have been in his position), before eventually saying, 'Why not?' Why not indeed… It somehow seemed a hopeful paradigm of how, in what feel like harsh & intolerant times, that underlying Orwellian decency of the British will win through.

Cambridge itself, incidentally, provided a shock. I hadn't been there for five or six years, & as I came out of the station it seemed that I was walking into Canary Wharf – I hated it. But the visit itself I really enjoyed, seeing old friends, walking a lot, looking at Phyllis Willmott's diaries at Churchill Archives Centre. On Monday I had lunch with a fellow-historian, Piers Brendon, who told me that because of his preoccupation with what's currently going on in the world, he had been keeping a diary since the start of the year. Perhaps everyone's doing it? 'A drug on the market,' as they used to say in Lombard Street in the 1890s about cheap money.[84]

I'm sometimes not quite convinced about the *Guardian*'s Zoe Williams as a political commentator, but I much liked a para on Monday:

Brexit is the new Falklands: in the 1980s that war was described by the left as a distraction, a bellicose bauble to keep the attention away from much more important and lasting acts of government. That was true, but only half the story: it was also the way to appropriate a language of patriotism for a government that was the opposite of patriotic, utterly committed to breaking the bonds of nationhood that might make a person

---

[84] 'Lombard Street' was traditional shorthand for the money market in the old, pre-Big Bang City of London; while as for 'a drug on the market', one encouraging dictionary definition is 'a commodity no longer in demand and so is commercially valueless or unsaleable'.

in the Cotswolds care about a person in Liverpool who lost their job.

That struck me as a helpful way of looking at true patriotism: trying to create a country in which the Cotswolds *would* care about what was happening on Merseyside. And on that caring score (or an equivalent version), I certainly fall well short – as indeed I did in the 80s themselves.

Trump-watch. A clip yesterday on the BBC website showed him with schoolchildren who were on a tour of the White House. Extrovert & ebullient – a hug with a child – an exhortation to them to work hard. That father-figure thing: it's starting to happen.

Saturday 11 March

On the 9.03 train to Leeds that is just pulling out from King's X (from Platform 0 – a personal first). Should be a good w/end. Lucy & I meeting up at Guiseley for lunch at the Wetherby Whaler with two old friends, Pete Bevington & Mike Baynham. And then three of us, with Mike dropping out, heading to the big match. Guiseley in as good form as the Shots – they're doing remarkably well for such a small club – & it's going to be tight. A draw probably the rational forecast, but it's a game the Shots need to win.

Lincoln play at the Emirates late afternoon. Here's a recent quote from their manager, Danny Cowley: 'Everyone keeps asking if this is the biggest challenge of my life. It's not. The biggest challenge is to get results at Aldershot.' Curiously, Lincoln began their Cup run (fourth qualifying round) by overcoming Guiseley: 0–0 at Sincil Bank, then 2–1 in the replay.

Sunday 12 March

Mike didn't make it, but the WW easily lived up to expectations – apparently the original Harry Ramsden, & a capacious, friendly place with pleasing décor & a lot of choice in the menu. Perhaps perversely, Lucy & I both plumped for the cheapo 'Senior' menu: fruit juice or soup/fish & chips/trifle or ginger sponge pudding or something else (an ice-cream float? anyway, we shared a trifle). Guiseley itself seemed an attractive small town, & at the ground I very much liked the fact that supporters weren't segregated. But as to the match itself... Shots definitely the better side in the first half, & a fine save by the home keeper to deny a goal after a sweet move, but goalless at the break. The Shots were pressing early on in the second half – at which point, 53rd minute, a slip or something (I couldn't quite tell) put the Guiseley striker clean away, completely against the run of play, & he scored a well-taken goal. After which, the Shots continued to have most of the play, but apart from one move that led to a post being hit, failed to create much in the way of real chances. Guiseley held on, indeed missed a chance or two of their own near the end as the Shots committed men forward, & it finished 1–0. The end of the unbeaten run (eleven matches). But I still enjoyed the afternoon – certainly far more than Mrs Lincoln enjoyed the play. And lovely to spend it with Pete.[85] He last saw the Shots in about 1967 or 1968 – we watched a 1–1 home draw against Bradford City, with Jack Howarth missing a hatful of chances. Last night we stayed with Lucy's Leeds friends Janis & Roger, & I'm scribbling this first thing in the morning. I haven't seen other results, nor a table. The assumption has to be that Guiseley not a mortal blow but still of course a significant setback. The Imps I gather lost heavily at the Emirates.

Tuesday 14 March

Highlight of Sunday was a long walk in the Yorkshire Sculpture Park. Lovely, inspiriting setting, plus benign spring weather. In the wood on the side of the lake is a creation by David Nash made

---

[85] He and his brother Johnny were my co-founders of *Soccer Digest*.

of coal. Originally called in 2010 'Black Steps', he renamed it the following year 'Seventy-one Steps'. And as I walked up them, & then looked down, I found it impossible not to think of my seventy-one nights in hospital in 2012 & feel an overwhelming sense of gratitude. 'Life is Good' is the title of a Natalie Merchant song, & there are moments when one can only nod quietly & savour the sheer if fleeting privilege of being alive.

Train journeys gave a chance to press on with Philip Roth's *The Plot Against America*. My only previous Roth is *The Human Stain*, which I found impressive rather than enjoyable, but this so far is terrific – both the autobiographical (presumably) detail about his Jewish childhood in New Jersey & the counter-factual narrative of Lindbergh (isolationist, nationalistic, anti-Semitic, pro-Nazi) defeating FDR in a landslide in 1940 & becoming President. On the train back from Leeds I also read the *Guardian*'s interview with Bernie Sanders. 'We have a president who is a pathological liar... Trump lies all the time and I think that is not an accident, there is a reason for that. He lies in order to undermine the foundations of American democracy.' And Sanders describes Trump's method as being to put out the message that 'the only person in America who stands for the American people, the only person in America who is telling the truth, the only person in America who gets it right is the president of the United States, Donald Trump'. And by contrast: 'George Bush [junior] was a very conservative president, I opposed him every single day. But George Bush did not operate outside of mainstream American political values.' Sanders also called on Republicans to join the resistance to Trump. Yet unfortunately, apart from a few honourable exceptions, that doesn't seem all that likely – at this stage anyway – to happen. And Theresa May remains adamant that the state visit to the UK will go ahead. That ludicrously premature offer was a stupid, stupid thing to do.

I gave a lecture last night at the British Library, with Peter Hennessy (whom I barely know) in the chair. He could not have been kinder or more generous, including in his opening remarks. In the autumn of 2006, some six months before the publication of *Austerity Britain*, I reviewed for the *TLS* his book on the Fifties.

Some of the review was quite harsh: not in wholly bad faith – I'd still defend the substance – but partially so. Essentially I was saying, over a decade after the publication of his prize-winning *Never Again*, 'Look out, folks, there's a new kid in town.' It was in its way quite a virtuoso piece of writing. But I now look back on it with a sense of shame – & soon afterwards, I vowed that in future I would never review a 'rival' book.

Friday 17 March

St Patrick's Day – the day of my confirmation, by the Bishop of Shrewsbury, fifty-three years ago. Feels in every way so remote. Yet still of course in some sense that twelve-year-old boy.

It's been quite a week out there. Here are a few headlines from today's *Times*: 'No new independence vote for Scotland before Brexit' (about May refusing Sturgeon's demand for a vote by spring 2019); 'GCHQ ridicules White House over claims it spied on Trump'; 'Trump targets aid and arts in budget to boost military'; 'Europe breathes easier as Dutch halt Wilders' march' (the Dutch elections undeniably a moment of huge relief, of 'pushback', but will the example be followed this spring in France, *the* crucial election surely of 2017?); 'Bulgaria deports lone Afghan children'; & from that lovable Philippines leader, 'Duterte sacks opponents of death penalty'. There are moments when it all seems too much to take in, to reflect on, & perhaps because I'm feeling rather oppressed by the Bank of England endgame – fielding numerous queries from the admittedly excellent copy editor – this is one of them. I also feel completely impotent to do anything significant about anything, plus generationally now a 'back marker'; one of the old timers, who had his chance – but WHEN exactly?? – & now it's gone.

Not the first time I've written this, I'm sure, but the Shots face a season-defining week. Home to Sutton tomorrow; home to Dagenham (third in the table) on Tuesday evening; away to Macclesfield (one of the quintet chasing 5th spot) a week tomorrow. Minimum requirement, to stay in the hunt, has to be

5 points, which in practice means a win tomorrow almost indispensable. After last Saturday – not exactly a bad performance, but not great either – it feels quite possible that this is where the season starts decisively to fall away. Obviously it could go either way. But on balance I tip the Shots to win tomorrow – maybe even a relatively comfortable 2–0. Though even that would still leave two very stiff tests immediately ahead.

Apparently, after the match at the Emirates last Saturday, the Lincoln squad called for a hoover in order to clean up their dressing room – whereas Arsenal, after their Cup tie at Sutton, had left the place a complete tip.

Sunday 19 March

Well, 2–0 to the Shots it indeed was, but 'relatively comfortable' not *les mots justes*. Playing against the wind in the first half, Shots seemed barely able to get across the halfway line – Jake Cole made a few excellent saves & blocks – until almost on the stroke of the interval a nicely executed breakaway (including a fine diagonal pass by Jake Gallagher) seemed to end with the Sutton defender haplessly slamming the ball into his own net. Second half more even, but Shots still creating disappointingly few chances – until in injury time, with Sutton inevitably throwing men forward, Anthony Straker (rare appearance, on as a sub) engineered a skilful move down the left, ending with a cross to the unmarked Bernard Mensah in the middle, & the unprotected keeper didn't really have a price. Elsewhere, the rival teams did irritatingly well – doubly irritating, because they'd all been struggling somewhat at half-time – & the Shots stay in 7th. Home to Dagenham on Tuesday is now an intriguing prospect. For several months they've been one of the unbroachable top four, but they lost yesterday at Barrow – & if the Shots were to win, we'd be 2 points behind them (i.e. eminently catchable), though having played a game more. The real worry meanwhile is Gateshead, who I think have now won seven on the spin & lie in 5th. It doesn't help that on Tues they're at home to Guiseley, i.e. very winnable. Even if the Shots were to get a point apiece from the next two difficult games, that might not be enough to stay genuinely in contention. But a win against Dagenham...

Yesterday afternoon also notable for a half-time breakthrough. As usual we sat in the second row of the South Stand (the side of the ground where I first sat & where in recent years I have returned to after a long spell on the north side – a return also partly governed by better loo access, plus not looking straight in the sun, plus better protection against rain), & as usual we intermittently wondered what to do about food & drink at the interval. In the event, Lucy went to the stall by the corner flag as one enters the ground towards the south side & got a sausage roll, while I went to the snacks part of the bar behind the South Stand, run by a very nice guy, & got a KitKat plus cup of tea. All of which we shared on returning to our seats. Perfect.

One other thing. Heather, the pleasant, middle-aged woman who sits in front of us, is a truly dedicated Shots fan, going to *all* the matches, home & away. But unlike me, who gets all tensed up as the Shots for instance try to preserve a narrow lead, it struck me yesterday how by contrast she seems relaxed & able to appreciate any humorous aspects of the situation. She's also unfailingly positive in her attitude & would only not be if she felt the players weren't trying their hardest. In short, she seems to be a wholly admirable supporter, & getting to know her a little has been a real bonus since Lucy & I first got chatting with her at the Chester match early last year.

Chuck Berry has died. A magical moment in that Wim Wenders film *Alice in the Cities*, but otherwise never really meant much to me. I think it might be of him performing in Wuppertal. Where, as it happens, the British sculptor Anthony Cragg has lived since shortly after that film (presumably no causal connection?). At the Sculpture Park last Sunday, I watched an interesting German documentary about him: interesting partly because it always is watching a master craftsman (any type, any genre) at work, but mainly because of one or two things he said. He described his work as 'a dialogue with the material', i.e. as opposed to coming from any preconceived ideas. In short: 'I am not a conceptual artist.' Feeling much the same about my own stuff, I liked that very much. In the end, it's about a sensibility – in my own work, *my* sensibility, whatever that is – reacting to raw source material & seeking to create some sort of satisfying shape-cum-narrative. So at a rather uneasy time – with my post-war project currently on sabbatical leave – I found that helpful. How one clutches at straws, trying to locate 'objective' correlations with one's own personal myth.

Tuesday 21 March

As so often, scribbling on a morning train to Waterloo. The big news is that Martin McGuinness has died. Of course, IRA bombs shadowed much of the 70s & 80s in London, even the 90s. In late 1983, the night before the bomb at Harrods, I even in casual conversation with friends of Lucy predicted there was about to be one. We were living in Chelsea (grotty basement bedsitter in Oakley Street, where according to Ferdinand Mount 'everyone' lives at one stage or another), & I well remember hearing on that Saturday afternoon the ominous dull thud in the distance. But the closest connection came in early 1972, soon after Bloody Sunday. I was at Oxford, my father and stepmother were living in Aldershot (7 Knollys Road), & one day, when fortunately they weren't at home, their windows were blown out as a bomb exploded (killing seven) just down the road.[86] A few weeks later, on the way to Skye with friends, we stopped off at Pete McQuay's home in Blackburn. His father, a doctor, looked at me & said rather solemnly, 'Well, David, what about Aldershot?' It took me a moment – actually, more than a moment – to realise he wasn't asking about the fortunes of Aldershot FC.

That particular institution played its final match a quarter-century ago yesterday: a 2–0 defeat at Cardiff, after an utterly awful, confusing, can-it-really-be-happening period of

[86] The bomb, on 22 February 1972, targeted the officers' mess of the 16th Parachute Brigade. Of the seven killed, six were female cleaners.

several weeks, indeed months, as the financial situation rapidly deteriorated. I went to one of the last home matches – standing on the East Bank, where I hadn't been since adolescence, & watching in a funereal atmosphere a 3–1 defeat against Mansfield – & then, five days after the Cardiff match, heard on the radio early one evening, as I stood outside the LSE library (having brought a transistor with me), that the Shots had been wound up, that it was all over, that we were the first club since Accrington thirty years earlier to have left the League mid-season. Of course, quite soon a new club was formed – Aldershot Town – & a phoenix arose from the ashes. That was 1992, & five promotions lay ahead, before the Shots returned to the League in 2008.

Now of course we're out of the League again, but for the first time since the drop (& near-death experience) in 2013 looking in some sort of shape to return to it. Having watched the last two performances, I'll be pleasantly surprised if we beat Dagenham tonight. In fact, my main hopes are pinned on the sheer length of their return journey from Barrow on Saturday. My best guess has to be a 1–1 draw. But I could live with being pleasantly surprised.

Wednesday 22 March

The morning after the night before, & I'm living very happily with a pleasant surprise. A truly blistering first half from the Shots – pace, invention, control, the lot – that made Dagenham look very ordinary indeed. Two goals (Fenelon-cum-defender from a Mensah cross; Mensah from an Arnold cross), & it could easily have been more. Second half much more even, but after Dagenham pulled one back slightly luckily, McClure sealed it near the end with a fine left-foot finish. Nick Arnold named man of the match, much to Lucy's satisfaction. I like him a lot too: tough & combative, but plays football. 'We're on our way' was the East Bank's steady chant, & it felt like it. Intriguingly, Dagenham's current semi-slump has brought 4th position into play – so it's now six teams in contention for those two remaining play-off spots (4th & 5th). No one is going to catch Forest Green, Lincoln (who are faltering) & Tranmere in the top three places. The only fly in the ointment is that the Shots have still on the whole played more games than the others – indeed, it's probably helpful at this point to set out the business end of the table:

	Played	Goal difference	Points
Forest Green	38	33	75
Lincoln City	35	33	72
Tranmere Rovers	36	23	70
Dag & Red	38	17	67
Gateshead	39	26	66
Aldershot	39	19	65
Dover	37	14	63
Barrow	38	17	62
Macclesfield	35	12	57

So, seven games left for the Shots, starting on Saturday with a trip to the Silkmen, a massive eight points behind but with an equally massive four games in hand. We're hoping to be there, on our way to a few days in the Lakes, but still one or two uncertainties. Meanwhile, our son-in-law Graham has just sent an email message that extrapolates the final table on the basis of form over the last eight matches. In it the Shots finish a heartbreaking 6th with a very creditable 78 points, but a point behind Dover. And Forest Green take the title with 93 points. Anyway, it's barely a month from now until all will be crystal clear, one way or the other. My own aim is just to enjoy – & be grateful for – the excitement.

Friday 24 March

That was written on Wednesday morning. That afternoon, a middle-aged, UK-born convert to Islam ran amok on Westminster Bridge – first with a vehicle, then with a knife – &

four people died. Parliament was clearly in his crazed sights. Uncertain at this point whether it will prove to have been one of 'those' events – in some sense defining – or will fairly soon be semi-forgotten. My mind when the news came through was still preoccupied (apart from the mountain of B of E queries) with McGuinness – specifically, whether (as I'm inclined to think) it is fair to condemn him (whatever that means) because his 'conversion' from violent to peaceful methods was essentially strategic, as opposed to remorseful & Tolstoyan. If his change had been of the latter type, would Tebbit still have spoken of his hope that a specially warm part of hell was being reserved for him? Hard to know.

Still hoping meanwhile to see the Shots at Macclesfield tomorrow. Two teams in form, & should be a good encounter. I'd be happy enough with a point – & on balance, that's my prediction. Especially given that, on paper, this looks the hardest of the seven remaining matches, apart from away to Tranmere on Good Friday.

We're staying tonight with Cilla in north Oxford &, on a fine spring late afternoon, have just had a pleasant walk around affluent suburban streets.[87] Feels like the very heart of Remain territory – indeed, even the odd sticker from last summer lingering in windows. Sadly, this city with which I have such an ambivalent relationship still living up to its reputation as the home of lost causes.[88]

---

[87]   Cilla Sheringham, widow of Micky Sheringham, still much missed. In around 1995 their son Sam kindly donated to our son George (ten years younger) his no longer cutting-edge Championship Manager '93 – a defining moment in George's childhood.

[88]   'How so?' asks my editor about that ambivalent relationship with Oxford, especially the university. Well, suffice here to say that I was fairly miserable during my first year as an undergraduate there, in part because I seemed to be surrounded by over-entitled old Etonians; that I came to love the beauty of the place; and that most of my work as a historian has in some sense been a reaction against traditional Oxford assumptions as they still obtained in the early 1970s and perhaps are still not entirely dead (the vulgarity of money-making, the irrelevance of the everyday lives of 'ordinary people'). It was Matthew Arnold, a great man but not devoid of those assumptions, who characterised Oxford as 'home of lost causes, and forsaken beliefs, and unpopular names, and impossible loyalties'. Even so, who knows? Just possibly, in the long run anyway, Remain might turn out not to be a lost cause.

Saturday 25 March

This evening we're at a Premier Inn in Macclesfield – partly not wanting to try to find in the dark our remote Lake District cottage, partly because we've heard about Macclesfield's legendary Treacle Market, apparently a crafts market that happens on the last Sunday of the month.

The football went well. Not a sparkling performance by the Shots, but determined & competent. A cagey, goalless first half, then after the break two well-taken goals – Kundai Benyu (after beautifully weighted through ball from Mensah), then McClure after the keeper parried a Jake shot. In the end, despite the odd hairy moment (though not many), a surprisingly comfortable 2–0 win. So, after an intensive week, nine points from the three games – a full 4 points more than I would have been reasonably satisfied with. Season-defining? Well, perhaps – & at last, the Shots are in that elusive 5th place, though still broadly speaking having played more matches. Six to go, everything to play for, & let's just hope that April doesn't prove to be the cruellest month.

Monday 27 March

First thing on Monday morning, & we're ensconced in our reasonably snug National Trust cottage near Lake Windermere. Weather good, & a very enjoyable walk along the edge of the lake yesterday evening as it began to get dark. First time I've really encountered the unlovely modern phenomenon of dog-owners having left the neatly bagged poops of dog shit hanging from random twigs in random trees – faintly Dali-like in effect, & I feel much the same about it as Orwell felt about Dali: not quite the thing... The Lake District itself I barely know. A memory of stopping off in March 1972, as a bunch of us from Oxford drove up to Skye (the same expedition as the conversation with Pete McQuay's father), but only a shadow, unreliable memory. Definitely came here for a couple of days in June 1986, when Laurie was barely a year old. We didn't have a car, & my main memory is of us being dropped by a bus a mile or two from Ruskin's house & me pushing her in a buggy along a country road in the steady rain. So it's exciting to be here, & I've started to read Margaret Drabble's 1966 critical book on Wordsworth. I like it a lot: directly engaging with the poetry itself – not too technical – & that poetry's connection with 'life'. Perhaps because she made such a strong impact with those four early novels, & those novels were so zeitgeisty, her body of work as a whole remains seriously undervalued. I'm particularly thinking of her mid-1970s novel *The Needle's Eye* – to my mind the *Middlemarch* of its era.

At a service station yesterday – the legendary modernist one near Lancaster where I'd never been before – I picked up *The Non-League Paper*. The front-page story refers to the Shots having 'finally broken into the top five'; there's a nice Waddock quote ('We have a confident, close-knit group of players, who get on very well with one another and have over-achieved, for sure'); & a rather deflating match report ('quality, tempo, accurate passes and highlights were all in short supply … in a coma-inducing first half'), with the game as a whole getting one star out of five for entertainment value – perhaps fair enough for the neutral spectator, but it didn't feel quite that way in the immediate afterglow of victory.

There's also a story in the paper that has made me think a bit about the history of my relationship with Chelsea. It's been complicated, & goes something like this:

1960s. Not much on my radar, but a definite fondness, largely because of Jimmy Greaves's amazing goalscoring exploits just as I was getting keen on football.

1970. The epic Cup Final encounters with Leeds, when I was definitely rooting for the fortunate, undeserving southerners.

Rest of 1970s. The London team I watched most often (though not that often), & perhaps because I never dared to stand in the Shed I had a fondness for the Bridge, including that funny wooden stand near one of the corner flags.[89] A phase

---

[89] At Stamford Bridge, the terrace known as the Shed End was, until its demolition in 1994, home to Chelsea's uncompromising ultras.

that culminated (1979 I think, but maybe 1980) in going to see a friendly between Chelsea & China – not much of a contest (4–0 to the West), but in a Tennysonian, cycle-of-Cathay sort of way the resonance of the fixture was irresistible.[90]

Most of 1980s/90s. Indifference shading to negative, largely because of my dislike of the rebarbative Bates.

Late 1990s. George getting keen on football – Chelsea briefly becoming his team (because of a girl at his infants school being called Chelsea?) – Chelsea themselves having Gullit + Zola, two truly wonderful players – & for me a flickering revival of my '1970' feelings.

Since the early 2000s. Essentially hostile. Once I'd grasped how Abramovich had obtained his billions, any lingering fondness disappeared – a hostility compounded of course by Mourinho. And that's basically where I still am, except I have to acknowledge three complicating factors in recent years:

1. A grudging admiration for John Terry.
2. An unstinting admiration for Eden Hazard.
3. The awkward fact that Chelsea have actually been quite generous to the Shots in recent years – playing youth matches at the Rec, plus even donating their pitch when it was due to be replaced (& it's undeniably a fine surface).

HOWEVER, the story in yesterday's paper fortunately allows me to return to old-fashioned Johnsonian hate.[91] Basically, Chelsea have bought from AFC Wimbledon (who naturally want to get back to Plough Lane in SW19) the Kingsmeadow ground just down the road from us – the ground that Kingstonian had foolishly sold to AFC over a decade ago & then paid a small rent to continue to play at. Chelsea will use the ground for their youth & ladies' teams – & are not willing to allow Kingstonian to use

---

[90] A real puzzle, according to online research. Not about the date (Friday 13 August 1979) but about the scoreline, apparently 3–1 to Chelsea, not 4–0. Ah well, always 4–0 in my mind... Either way, it was a final Chelsea appearance for Blues legend Ray ('Butch') Wilkins, in front of a meagre crowd of 8,098.

[91] 'Dear Bathurst was a man to my very heart's content; he hated a fool, and he hated a rogue, and he hated a whig – he was a very good hater!' (Samuel Johnson).

it also, which makes them homeless. AFC have done the decent thing – giving £1 million to Kingstonian – but Chelsea haven't. 'A Rocky Road Ahead for Ks' is the story's headline, & so it is likely to prove for what the paper also calls 'one of Non-League football's most famous names'. It's a real shame. And less than twenty years since Kingstonian under Geoff Chapple – who I always felt should at some point have managed the Shots – won the FA Trophy in two successive seasons.[92]

Tuesday 28 March

Lots of walking yesterday, & generally pretty good: that seductive mix of views, of greenery, of water. Just the two blemishes: a disgusting, overpriced lunch (an ill-chosen as well as ill-cooked stew) at the pub next to Beatrice Potter's house (captive market & all that); & on the other side of the lake, in Bowness, an unavailing search for a chemist that revealed a town almost entirely bereft of 'normal' shops & almost entirely devoted to tourism, which I always find faintly demoralising, quite apart from what it might be like to live there. As usual on holiday, a search also for the *Guardian*. For a long time looked likely to be unsuccessful, until finally a copy turned up in ... Bargain Booze. Of course – why didn't I think of that first?

With the British government about to trigger Article 50, formally beginning the process of leaving the EU, we watched last night a special edition of *Question Time*. Three Remainers (Nick Clegg, Alex Salmond, Keir Starmer), three Leavers (Suzanne Evans, David Davis, Melanie Phillips), & generally arid, predictable stuff: few confessions of ignorance or uncertainty or ambivalence, & even fewer attempts – whether from the panellists or the audience in Birmingham – to try to discern a bigger picture than the internal market or how much we'll

[92] Kingstonian FC, continuing to play in the Isthmian League, shared Leatherhead's ground for the 2017/18 season, before moving to Tolworth, just off the A3, for a ground share with Corinthian Casuals, an even more famous name. Happily, as I write, they have just made it to the Second Round proper of the FA Cup.

pay or what should be the level of immigration. All of those are significant of course, but none of them are what really matter. What does? Well, how about: is the decision to leave essentially proxy for becoming a less tolerant, meaner-minded society? does our leaving make Germany dangerously dominant in an unbalanced Europe? are we now horribly dependent upon the US & China, the two giants, & both with values that now seem seriously different from what ours should be? I suspect (though am not certain) that we're in the process of committing an act of significant economic self-harm; but I know in my bones that, in ways that transcend economics, we're doing something truly damaging & foolish.

Thursday 30 March

Back in New Malden, & fifty-eight years to the day since I first watched Aldershot. Easter Monday, 1959, home to Gillingham, & my father took me from Headley Down. The Shots on a run of lean form, struggling in the first season of the old Division Four, but that particular day winning 4–2. If I have a memory, & it's a very vague one, it's of the ball going high in the air when the goalies kicked out of their hands. But an attachment, which soon became unbreakable, was formed.

Friday 31 March

We're not in the event going to make it to Solihull tomorrow – even though it's 'Tour of Duty' day, that annual away match which Shots supporters make a special effort to get to. It's certainly extremely tight in the Vanarama. Lincoln, Forest Green & Tranmere all vying for the top spot, i.e. automatic promotion, with not much to choose between them. For the 4th & 5th spots, I think it's now down to five teams, with Macclesfield (who lost again on Tuesday) probably out of contention. This is how it looks going into April:

	Played	Goal difference	Points
Dagenham	39	18	70
Aldershot	40	21	68
Barrow	40	20	68
Gateshead	40	26	67
Dover	39	17	66

And here are their latest odds (Sky Bet) for a top-five finish: Dagenham 4/7; Shots 6/5; Dover 7/4; Barrow 2/1; Gateshead 9/4. As for tomorrow's match, the Shots are 21/20 to win, with the draw at 23/10 & Solihull at 5/2. I'm nervous. Shots have won their last three, Solihull lost their last two – if I had to bet, it would be on the draw.

The BBC's website page on the Vanarama carries a story about the 'incredible' return to football of Gateshead's J. J. O'Donnell, two & a half years after being diagnosed with a rare foot condition. Reading the piece, it's clearly time to put to rest this particular bygone. I can't quite forget the shameless cheating, the satisfied grin; but it's what professional footballers do – even occasionally those wearing red & blue – & he was only twenty-two. So, not that it makes the slightest difference to anyone, all hard feelings are now officially declared over.

This week's *Economist* has a brilliant farewell by the current 'Bagehot', with the columnist moving on to Berlin from his UK berth after five years in post. He is generally gloomy. 'A low-rent, bilious referendum has begotten low-rent, bilious politics' – a process in which 'the force of the referendum, a McCarthyite mood in the Brexiteer press and a prime minister whose original support for Remain seems more baffling by the week [have] combined to neuter the legislature'. And he notes how 'hundreds of parliamentarians filed, dead-eyed, through the lobbies granting Theresa May the untrammelled power to conduct and conclude exit talks most of them believe will do Britain harm'. The columnist also reflects on the Referendum's 'cultural legacy' – which 'created the ugly precedent that someone's view on things like trade, immigration and financial regulation are matters of policy second and expression of his very faith in the nation first. This elision of Brexit and the national interest has curdled British politics.' What really makes the piece, though, is the final paragraph – a paragraph that Walter B himself would have been proud to compose:

> Beyond the headlines and TV studios, Britain's everyday impressions are mostly those of a homely and mingled place, not a bitter and binary one. The blare of pop songs on shop radios, the church bell across the marshes, the simian whoops and cackles on market-town high streets of a Friday night. The shared shrugs and sighs after a train has waited too long at a station for some misery-unleashing fault not to have materialised. The vinegar-haddock-urine smell of seaside towns; the perfume-booze-sweat crush of commuters travelling home from booming cities. The saris, shiny suits and waxed jackets, the hipster moustaches and old-school mullets. The emergence from a car park or railway station to be confronted with a scene of architectural horror – or unprepossessing and unexpected gorgeousness.

Actually, this isn't remotely what Walter Bagehot (for all his many qualities) could have written. But if Orwell was still alive and firing... Than which, in terms of this sort of impressionistic feel-of-the-nation reportage, no higher praise.

Jake in excelsis

Sunday 2 April

No Solihull, so George & I went to see the Ks as they enter their final month at Kingsmeadow. Home to Leatherhead (also in deep relegation trouble) & entering the match with 2 points from the previous ten games. A scrappy sort of affair for the most part, with the visitors, perhaps predictably enough, winning with two second-half goals (though Ks did pull one back near the end, but too late). Highlight was probably the notably well-written match programme, full of gallows humour & a degree of frankness that one doesn't normally encounter in the genre. I feel very sorry for them. About to lose their ground, & one wonders how many of this hard core of say 250 supporters will next season make the regular journey to Leatherhead (about six miles away). If it even registered on their radar, which I'm sure it doesn't, Chelsea should be ashamed of themselves.

Meanwhile, on George's phone, reassuring news came steadily through from the West Midlands: a comfortable 2–0 win for the Shots, both goals coming from Kundai Benyu, whose loan period from Ipswich has been extended (subject to recall) until the end of the season.[93] Michael was there, & he rang later on to say that the Shots had been so dominant that it was actually quite a boring match. Tougher tests ahead, of course. Elsewhere, Dagenham & Dover both won, Gateshead & Barrow both lost, so there's now a bit of daylight between the Shots & those last two. (Macclesfield won, I should report, but I still feel they've got too much to do.) At the top, Forest Green managed to lose at home to North Ferriby – & indeed are now only 4 points clear of the Shots, though with a game in hand – so it's looking like Lincoln or Tranmere for the automatic promotion place. All very tantalising, & I'll try over the next few weeks not to spend too much of my time gazing at the table & working out all the possible permutations.

An article on the online *New Yorker* is arguing that bemusement-cum-pleasure at its incompetence is now replacing fear as the default position of liberals towards the Trump administration. Maybe. But I remember my mother telling me once that that sort of condescension was how Berliners originally viewed Hitler & his gang of fellow-hicks. Incidentally, seeing a video the other day that briefly featured Steve Bannon looking at Trump suddenly & irresistibly reminded me of Albert Grossman hovering around Dylan in *Don't Look Back* – the two string-pullers, a strong physical resemblance, & neither of them a nice man.

At Waitrose yesterday morning. Elderlyish couple (well, actually, my sort of age) approaching the newspaper rack. Wife: 'I now can't remember what I forgot.' Husband: 'You should have that on your T-shirt.' At which point, without a moment of hesitation, they reached for their copy of the *Telegraph*.

---

[93] I realise in retrospect that I failed to say enough about Benyu. Still in his teens, and possessing truly silky ball-retaining skills as well as good vision and the proverbial eye for goal, he dominated midfield during the second half of the season and was Aldershot's outstanding outfield player. The season over, he was signed by Celtic on a four-year contract, but has so far been unable to make an impact.

Tuesday 4 April

Dagenham helpfully lost at Lincoln last night – that 4th spot is definitely in play.

I'm conscious that I've had little to say or report recently about the domestic political situation – I guess the general hopelessness has left me rather weary & fatalistic. So the current issue of the *New Statesman* may perhaps serve, for me anyway, as some sort of timely wake-up call. The cover sets out a series of propositions – 'Wanted: An Opposition. The Labour Party has collapsed. A hard Brexit is looming. Who will speak for liberal Britain?' – & inside there is plenty of matter. It might be worth it, at this particular moment of widespread (i.e. among my kind of people) pessimism, to jot down some of the more interesting-cum-quotable thoughts/propositions. So here goes:

> In the 1970s, as those who would later be called Thatcherites set about dismantling the postwar consensus and creating a new economic settlement, the sense of intellectual ferment was thrilling. There is no comparable sense of intellectual excitement on the Corbynite left. It's as if Corbyn has nothing of substance to say. (*Jason Cowley*)

> It's the chicken-and-egg conundrum of British politics: we need a new party to change the electoral system; we need to change the electoral system to get a new party. Otherwise, we are stuck. That's why things come back in the end to the Labour Party, the decaying tree under whose shadow nothing can grow. (*David Runciman*)

> One gets the distinct impression that Jeremy Corbyn and his acolytes would prefer the purity and posturing of permanent opposition rather than the messy, compromised business of government. They offer ineffectuality and disdainful

superiority dressed up as a kind of saintly decency. (*Stuart Maconie*)

The voice of liberal Britain sounds like a far-off, self-referential whine. No one will care who speaks for it or what it says, unless the speakers turn their gaze from the mirror in which they have been admiring themselves for decades. (*Hilary Mantel*)

The solutions seem much more moderate than I ever would have expected. It's 'middle people' like Emmanuel Macron who seem to offer hope. (*Marina Warner*)

How disgraceful is it to be told that Labour hates the Liberals more than any other party? Could we please have a new party that considers us the people? (*Carmen Callil*)

I've always taken that phrase of Larkin's, a 'frail travelling coincidence', as a great definition of a nation. But it needs to know the direction of travel. Everyone wants to belong, to be part of a story. When some cultural grandee [Ian McEwan] announces that 'the air in my country is very foul' he's really saying, 'You people are not part of the story. You're the mob, not the people.' In that atmosphere it's hardly surprising that people who bother to offer a story – whether it's drain the swamp, or the West is Satan – gain ground. (*Frank Cottrell Boyce*)

The reason why some liberals think there is a crisis of democracy is that they have, for once, lost an argument. They are used to winning things. (*David Goodhart*)

Faith is too important to leave to the religious. Patriotism is too important to leave to the nationalists. Emotions are too important to leave to populist demagogues. (*Elif Shafak*)

What the left needs now is a new story that it can tell with passion and clarity and good sense and charisma. It ought to be a story that articulates a new vision of hope and inclusiveness, a story that shows the confidence and rich benefits of a diverse and creative Britain. A story that shows Britain is at its greatest when it faces the world with bigness of spirit...

The left needs a new story to enchant the age and open up the future. (*Ben Okri*)

Thursday 6 April

'A foundation of shared values and shared interests': so the other day declares Liam Fox, our International Trade Secretary, about our relationship with the Philippines, whose thug of a President, Rodrigo Duterte, has launched a wholly extra-judicial war on drugs so far killing some 7,000 people. In the wake of our triggering of Article 50, it is all part of this week's co-ordinated 'global Britain' initiative – in effect, putting us in bed with many of the world's most hateful & least democratic regimes. What a pretty pass. Brexit may or may not turn out to be economic folly, but in a broader and ultimately more important sense – the defence of liberal democracy, indeed of enlightenment civilisation – we are now becoming part of the problem, not the solution. I find myself ashamed to be British. And ironic that the Brexiteers should now be dependent on the forces of globalisation to salvage the consequences of a decision that in many ways was a cry against globalisation.

Perhaps I'm just in a bad mood. There doesn't seem much – putting the resurgent Shots to one side – to take pleasure or satisfaction in at the moment. And much to be afraid of. My mood not improved by the experience yesterday of visiting the Evelyn Grace Academy, the secondary school in Brixton where George is currently teaching. Holiday time, so what struck me most was the building itself – Zaha Hadid's first completed building in England, & winning for her the Stirling Prize in 2010. The *Architectural Review* that year was lavish in its praise. 'Layered and loveable interiors ... a tour de force ... curving corridors and volumetric variations ... this is architecture that treats its pupils like adults, and expects them to behave like it.' Except, according to George, in most functional ways it simply doesn't work very well. While to my eyes it seemed a brutalist, unwelcoming, inhumane concrete monster – harsh & unforgiving. Inevitably my mind turned to the school in Hunstanton, Norfolk that was the flagship creation in the mid-1950s of the Smithsons: like Evelyn Grace it won the plaudits but in daily practice was fairly useless; & again similarly, it was the product of arrogance, of an indifference to small-scale human concerns and needs. Modernism has so much to answer for. And somehow it seemed appropriate that opposite the entrance to the staff car park was James Joyce Walk: a memorial to the twentieth-century modernist who almost single-handedly took literature in the wrong direction.[94]

David Loffman is meant to be coming round – our current Thursday-evening project is working our way through the Pink Floyd oeuvre (a distinctly mixed experience) – but just time to look ahead to the Shots at home to relegation-threatened Torquay on Saturday. I'm anticipating a keen contest, but on current momentum have to assume a home win – 3–1 perhaps? More generally, I'm finding that part of me wants this season to go on for ever because it's been so absorbing & in recent months gratifying (but would that immersion have been quite the case if I hadn't been keeping this diary? not sure), while an almost equally big part of me could do with a long break soon from all things Vanarama because I've been expending so much nervous energy (again, because of the diary?) on something that really doesn't matter very much. What was that Yeats line about poetry (as opposed to rhetoric) coming out of a quarrel within oneself?[95] A true & wonderful thought, but my conflicted state not exactly producing poetry in this case.

Sunday 9 April

Yesterday afternoon a keen contest indeed – fraying tempers under a warm sun, a noisy crowd, much at stake for both sides, & in the

---

[94] Joyce was of course a supremely gifted writer. Yet when I quite recently re-read *Dubliners* (first time for many years), I could not but wish that he'd gone on to become a novelist writing in a similar idiom – they'd have been wonderful novels. Equally, though, I don't deny for a moment that creative writers have to do what creative writers have to do.
[95] 'We make out of the quarrel with others, rhetoric, but of the quarrel with ourselves, poetry' (W. B. Yeats, 'Anima Hominis').

end perhaps a surprise that no one took an early bath... Shots mainly on top early on, but failed to capitalise, & then on about 25 minutes Torquay went ahead with a slightly fortuitous but well-taken goal. The second half a thoroughly tense affair: Shots clambering back in about the 70th minute with a Kundai Benyu free kick (he's now scored the Shots' last four goals) & that's how it stayed, though not before some 12 or 13 minutes of added time included the Shots goalie Jake Cole being stretchered off – looked maybe serious, but apparently nothing worse than a badly gashed shin (not that that sounds fun). Shots stay in 5th place, but Dover won away & are level on points with a game in hand. Gateshead & Barrow are both faltering, so my feeling is that it's down to us or Dover for 5th (especially as Forest Green & Dagenham are now clearly going to occupy 3rd & 4th – while at the top, incidentally, Tranmere put 9 past hapless Solihull Moors). Significantly, Dover not only have that game in hand, but a somewhat easier run-in. They could still make it even if we beat them on Easter Monday. We can't make it *unless* we beat them that day. Anyway, that's how I see it... All that said, actually I had a mini-epiphany while returning to my seat for the second half. Which was that I was entirely happy if the Shots stayed at this level, as long as they were playing decent, competitive football, winning at least as many matches as they were losing, & attracting economically viable rather than huge crowds. I appreciate that the club's management cannot but have ambitions – after all, historically we're still essentially a League club – but actually I don't mind pottering along in the higher reaches of the Non-League. The journey, not the destination, & all that.

As usual in this diary, it seems slightly weird to pivot from the Shots to Trump, but I must. Two or three days ago, in the midst of hosting the Chinese Premier in the dignity of a Florida resort, he sent 'targeted missiles' into Syria, following pictures of the victims of an attack by chemical weapons almost certainly ordered by Assad. Most people see the attack as justified in itself, but strikingly at odds with his pre-office pronouncements about the folly of intervention in Syria, notwithstanding many other 'beautiful babies' having lost their lives as a result of Assad's wickedness. The good news is that perhaps he's moving away from 'America First' & towards internationalism. The bad news is that he's taking action in an impulsive, ego-driven way – as well as perhaps motivated by an urgent tactical need, as investigations into his links continue, to distance himself from Putin. His action will play well across middle America. And watching his 'beautiful babies' speech justifying it, a speech delivered with the palpable sincerity of a showman (think Hughie Green), I found my father-of-the-nation premonitions – with all their potential authoritarian possibilities – stirring again. Hard not to be dreading the next big terrorist attack on the States. It'll happen – & Trump won't be the loser.

Tuesday 11 April

Yesterday's *Times* (like Saturday's) didn't include my letter to the editor. It was so short that I can quote it in full: 'Your editorial criticises Labour's policy of imposing VAT on private school fees as "socially divisive". Whereas the existence of private schools isn't?' I didn't really think they would print it, but I was still a little disappointed. And more generally, to continue in Pooterish vein, I've yet to succeed in getting a letter published there – having started some time in the late 60s when I suggested the north of Scotland as a suitable location for London's 'third airport'. A total of perhaps four or five failed attempts? And perhaps, rather like scoring a century, it ain't never going to happen.[96]

If it had been included, my letter might have nicely complemented a piece in the paper's football section by Matthew Syed – 'Football's fundamental fairness offers signpost to a different, better world: The game's level playing field is in sharp contrast to cosy connections and nepotism in wider society'. In the main body of the piece, Syed argues that it is purely through merit (involving a high degree of application), as opposed to

[96] Eventually it did: earlier this year (2019) a letter, co-written with Francis Green, about the private school problem.

nepotism or favouritism, that players get to the top – & that those players have often grown up in hard, difficult environments. The argument strikes me as basically sound, though doesn't address the question of whether superior resources (e.g. through private education) can also make a difference, thereby undermining the 'fundamental fairness'. There are some signs that may be starting to happen. And of course, football's *larger* structure is grossly unfair & inegalitarian – probably getting worse by the day.

Saturday's *Guardian* had a fine, cherishable piece by Matthew Engel – a favourite writer (intellect/warmth/humour/idiosyncrasy) – about county cricket being organised increasingly on a business model, & that in the process 'something beautiful is being lost'. *The* big cricketing structural change is due to take effect in 2020, when the city-based Twenty20 competition starts & the four-day game is further marginalised.[97]

Thursday 13 April (Maundy Thursday)

A *Times* obit yesterday of Jeremy Lewis. Publisher, journalist, biographer, memoirist – he came to represent, I guess, the soul of upmarket Grub Street. I first met him at Chatto in 1989, when they were still in Bedford Square. He had a small room at the top of the building, there was a manual typewriter on his desk, & even then it felt like I was getting a last glimpse of old-style, non-corporate, non-technocratic publishing. We had a bit of general chat, & he said something about the importance of taking as long over a book as the book needs – trite in a way, but actually quite helpful. Then over the next quarter of a century a series of periodic encounters – mainly at the London Library (which, in terms of authors bumping into each other & swapping gossip/ideas, he once compared to the floor of the old Stock Exchange) or at *Oldie* lunches at Simpsons in the

---

[97] By April 2018 the prospective new competition had taken the form of The Hundred, announced by the ECB on the same day as the publication of *Arlott, Swanton and the Soul of English Cricket*, whose generally downbeat concluding remarks chimed neatly with the negative reaction of most cricket lovers, led by the *Guardian*'s Vic Marks.

Strand. We never got remotely close. He was always genial to me (as I imagine he was to everyone), & I liked him, but was somehow put off – frustrated really – by that air of bumbling self-deprecation. Perhaps also, silly though it sounds, by his physical bulk. The puritan in me scented, I guess, some kind of flabbiness – he was never, to put it mildly, a Leavis man. All that said, a few years ago we did make a more intimate connection, when it transpired that, not long after my three months at St George's in 2012, he had likewise been having cancer treatment in the same ward, though in his case as an outpatient. The last time we met, at that *Oldie* lunch in late 2013 featuring Terry Wogan & Brian Sewell, I interrogated him quite closely about his favourite novelists. Easily top was Trollope: for his realism, his shrewdness, his tolerance of the different shades of human nature. As it happens, I've just started on *The Small House at Allington*, so that seems appropriate.

The Shots go to Tranmere (second in the table) tomorrow afternoon, while Dover entertain Southport (bottom of the table & more or less doomed). So, not ideal, though I'm finding some hope in the fact that Tranmere not only played a match as recently as Tuesday evening (home to Forest Green), but lost 1–0 – which puts them 3 points behind Lincoln, who also have a game in hand. Put another way, notwithstanding those nine goals last Saturday, it may not be such a bad time to be going to Prenton Park. Even so, the horrible truth is that, given the highly probable outcome at Dover, the Shots badly need to win. Realistically, that's fairly unlikely – & indeed, in intrinsic terms, a draw would be far from shabby. Which on balance, all things considered (including presumably the absence of Jake Cole), is my far from confident prediction.

Some headlines from today's *Times*. 'Clifford pleads poverty' (I'd completely forgotten about that ghastly publicist Max Clifford, now needing money to finance an appeal against his eight-year sentence for indecent assaults on teenage girls). 'Nearly half of us can't wire a plug' (including me, I'm afraid). 'Bannon's future in doubt as president changes tack' (i.e. away from 'America First' – though whether he really is I remain unconvinced). And this from a Tesco ad in the *Evening Standard* earlier this week: 'Great offers on beer and cider. Good Friday just got better'.[98]

Today's *Times* also has an obit of Tony Benn's brother, David. He is described, as Orwell once was, as being 'conservative in everything except politics'. Question: how conceivably can that work in practice? How realistic or authentic can someone's political radicalism really be if it is at odds with everything else (e.g. food or literature or art or pastimes or indeed whatever)? I don't know the answer, but am genuinely puzzled – especially because it's a description that could, I suspect, be broadly applied to me.

Saturday 15 April

Well, a gripping, nerve-racking hour & a half listening to the commentary yesterday afternoon on Surrey local radio. The match was actually being televised on BT, so in theory I could have gone to a pub to watch it, but we've got Wolfie with us for a couple of days so that wasn't really feasible. The first half the real roller-coaster – McClure giving the Shots an early lead, Tranmere scoring twice (the first involving an error by Cole, who was playing), Mensah equalising just before the break after a McClure flick-on – while during the second period it could easily have gone either way, with both sides badly needing the win, but in fact stayed at 2–2. So a well-earned point for the Shots (& meaning only one defeat between Christmas & Easter), but simultaneously Dagenham were entrenching themselves at 4th while Dover were comfortably beating Southport to go 5th – & now 2 points above the Shots, as well as having a precious game in hand. So on the face of it not looking good. Even so, if the Shots could beat Dover on Monday – which on balance is my prediction – then I would see us having at least a 50–50 chance of getting that tantalising play-off place. But a draw or a loss, & our chances would be slim indeed. It's likely to be quite an occasion, quite an encounter.

---

[98] Tesco did subsequently apologise, but only after considerable criticism.

Headlines today are understandably dominated by what feels like the significant possibility – unthinkable though it is – of some sort of nuclear-triggered war between the US & North Korea. The latter – a top-to-toe evil regime, very far from comic – undeniably represents a real threat (we're not talking Iraq 2003 here), but it's an unsettling look-out when the rest of the world is having to put its faith in the calm, resolute judgement of Donald Trump… While on a local note, the fact that New Malden has I think the biggest Korean expat population of anywhere (mainly of course from the South, but quite a few who have fled from the North) gives a particular twist.

The *New College Record* for 2016 arrived the other day. I'm sufficiently anti-Oxford, plus mildly peeved that my friend from New College days Nicholas Underhill is an honorary fellow & I'm not, that I only really look at the obits. Only one contemporary – Alastair MacGregor (brother of Neil & an acquaintance rather than a friend but in whose car in spring 1981 I first heard 'Bette Davis Eyes' by Kim Carnes) – & the obit that caught my imagination was of someone much older, Tom Wisdom. He went to New College in 1952, graduated with 'the most modest degree then possible', & spent many years working in Norwich for the BBC's East Anglian service. The piece (by a New Coll contemporary of his) ended with these three sentences: 'He settled in his parental home of Cambridge, enthusiastically pursuing rural interests as an expert horse rider and dinghy sailor. He and I used to meet once a year, at Twickenham to see the Varsity Match. When we walked to the stadium from the station, Tom always had a friendly word with the mounted police marshalling the crowd, and never forgot to bring carrots for the horses.' A nice way to be remembered – with echoes perhaps, give or take a species, of that famous, inspiriting sentence at the end of *Middlemarch*?[99]

---

[99] 'But the effect of her [Dorothea's] being on those around her was incalculably diffusive: for the growing good of the world is partly dependent on unhistoric acts; and that things are not so ill with you and me as they might have been, is half owing to the number who lived faithfully a hidden life, and rest in unvisited tombs.'

Tuesday 18 April

I'm starting to write this entry a few minutes after Theresa May has announced her intention to hold a general election on June 8th. But first things first...

A psychologically gruelling afternoon at the Rec yesterday in front of a large crowd (not all that far short of 4,000) in pleasant conditions. Frustratingly for the spectacle, if tactically understandable in the context, Dover essentially came to park the bus & get a 0–0, hoping that their prolific goalscorer, Ricky Miller, might nick one in a breakaway. The Shots struggled during the first half to create openings, but played much better – with real confidence, fluency & inventiveness – in the second, culminating in a trip on Gallagher leading to McClure hammering home the penalty straight down the middle. Then came twenty very slow-moving minutes: Shots with the chances to wrap it up – Kanu perhaps harshly sent off – & amidst chaotic scenes in the penalty area at the High Street end, Dover missing near the end of injury time a gilt-edged chance to get their draw. So in the end a 1–0 win – entirely deserved, & it would have been almost unbearably exasperating if the outcome had been different. Which puts the Shots (with two games to play) back in 5th on 76 points, while Dover (with three games left) are still on 75. Dagenham in 4th place dropped a couple of points yesterday but are still four ahead of the Shots & will presumably scrape over the play-off line (though their final two games may not be easy). Obviously it's still in Dover's hands - & three straight wins would do it for them however the Shots fare – but at the very least it remains wonderfully open. Perhaps indeed an unrepresentative season for this diary, but no complaints here.

And so to May's *démarche* – which although entirely logical in its Labour-crushing terms was not on the whole, as far as I can see, being predicted (& certainly not by me). My instinctive feeling is that this is opportunistic, cynical & rather tacky, clothed in the fig-leaf argument that the government needs a large Commons majority in order to pursue Brexit negotiations effectively – while of course the overwhelming & wholly partisan motive is to crush Labour while it's weak. Still, even though the Tories will presumably win a thumping majority, I see some silver linings. One, obviously, is the imminent end of Corbyn. Another is the clear prospect of a major Lib Dem revival – it sounds outlandish, but I could imagine them winning up to 100 seats or even more, especially if the election turns into some kind of Brexit referendum re-run. Not sure that Farron is the ideal leader, but he's quick on his feet & has that invaluable cheeky-chappie quality. Anyway, gaming it through in my mind, I have put £10 (at Joe Coral's in Tooting) on who the next Labour leader is going to be – a 50/1 shot, & currently not in the Commons, but assuming he's keen & finds a seat, it's just possible it could play his way. I'm thinking of Ed Balls: undeniably a political heavyweight; undeniably a potential PM; & now officially, in the wake of *Strictly*, a national treasure. I'd be amazed if he's not weighing up the possibilities.

Meanwhile, before the big British story broke, the main headline on this morning's BBC website was about Trump congratulating Erdogan, now officially Turkey's strongman dictator following yesterday's rigged referendum. Predictable but completely chilling. Trump, to repeat for the nth time, is no democrat. Almost three months in, it remains wholly grotesque that he is in the White House.

I'm a bit ashamed that my Easter this year had virtually nothing of the religious about it – symbolised by the fact that when Michael asked me whether Jesus came back to life on the Saturday or the Sunday, I struggled for a moment to give the right answer. Perhaps the nearest I came to any sort of quasi-spiritual moment was during our Saturday-morning walk with Wolfie around Cannizaro Park. There's a slightly 'secret' garden there that has a bust of Haile Selassie & two or three benches. One of those benches was in memory of Angela Sasporta, 2 August 1957 to 2 May 1997. No new dawn breaking for her on that latter date – & I realised that both dates were a Friday, so a true Friday's Child…[100] Also on the

---

[100] Cannizaro Park is a fine (if underfunded) landscaped public park just to the south of Wimbledon Common. 'A new dawn has broken, has it not?' was what Tony Blair told cheering supporters at the Royal Festival Hall as the sun rose the morning after the general election of 1 May 1997 which had produced a landslide for New Labour and was about to take him to No. 10 via Buckingham Palace.

bench was the inscription 'Daniel Bray 8 December 1994' – the day he was both born & died? If so, the day after our Michael was born, which I found a very unsettling thought, mingled of course with a sense of gratitude for undeserved good fortune. All of which reminds me of how little this diary has been reflecting on death itself (as opposed to people who happen to have died in the last eight or nine months). Which is unsurprising, because I'm sure one of its key purposes is to re-engage me with the present & thereby help to keep out of sight & out of mind the unwelcome prospect. An interview the other day with Bill Nighy (a bit older than me) mentioned that he thought about it around a dozen times a day & kind of assumed that that was the same with most other people – indeed, was surprised that anyone should have been surprised by the extent of his preoccupation. And doesn't Evelyn Waugh (or one of his characters) say somewhere that *everyone* over the age of forty thinks about it at least once a day? I know I do. It's simultaneously the most important & unimportant subject. And as similarly paradoxical, I very much like the title of that Julian Barnes extended essay on the subject: *Nothing to be Frightened of*. Exactly.

Wednesday 19 April

Once reality (aka BBC website) kicked in almost first thing this morning, hard not to be preoccupied by this almost certainly wretched – & gratuitous – election. 'CRUSH THE SABOTEURS' is the *Mail*'s charming, inclusive, tolerant-of-debate headline, & more generally it feels like we're moving into a period – stretching well into the 2020s & perhaps beyond – of a virtual one-party state that takes its marching orders from the *Mail*, the *Telegraph* & the *Sun*. Given the life-chances odds stacked against them, & the overwhelmingly right-wing voting habits of the insufferably narrow-minded, selfish & complacent old (or at the very least that's how it sometimes seems), perhaps the only hope is if the young at last get it together (as the phrase used to go) – but not in such a self-aggrandisingly suicidal way as to alienate everyone else. In terms of this coming election, people are understandably talking about the echoes of 1983, but for me it also has a whiff of 1931: Labour crushed to a miserable rump (then by a 'National' government, now by a nationalist PM banging that most boring but potent of drums), & a terrible, perhaps dangerous period ahead before there can be any hope of a socially more just order. The silver linings I sought to identify yesterday don't feel all that lustrous this morning. Even a crushing defeat is no guarantee of Labour coming to its senses. And the notion of 100 seats for the Lib Dems is probably wildly fanciful.

I'm on my way to Lord's as I write this. Research in the library for the book on Arlott & Swanton, followed by the awards dinner for the cricket book prize that I've been a judge of (but am now pulling up stumps). It should be mildly therapeutic for at least two reasons. One is the almost invariable uplift to spirits as a result of sitting in the Long Room on a spring early evening, looking out at the green grass in the fading daylight, remembering some of the mighty deeds performed there, thinking about future generations emulating them, & generally feeling in touch – unimportant though cricket ultimately is – with some kind of bigger, quasi-timeless picture. The other reason is to be chatting with people from the cricket world: the great majority of them Conservative-voting; the great majority of them thoroughly decent. People, in short, trump politics. It's true – & too often I'm in danger of forgetting it.

Saturday 22 April

The Shots this afternoon play at North Ferriby United. A small place, a small club, & they're already down – predictably, I fear the worst. We'd originally planned to go & make a weekend of it, including staying in the Lincolnshire Wolds (which, ever since noting in *Archie's Last Stand* that the rather pompous amateur cricketer J. C. Hartley had retired to Woodhall Spa, I've wanted to look at), but in the event it's going to be a morning at the BL

(I'm on the train to Vauxhall) & listening to the radio commentary this afternoon. In terms of the table, it's now almost certainly going to be a top three of Lincoln, Tranmere & Forest Green, in that order, but who gets 4th & 5th is much more open. The current situation is (without goal differences, which I don't have at hand, but it's tight):

		Played	*Points*
4th	Dagenham	44	80
5th	Shots	44	76
6th	Dover	43	75
7th	Barrow	44	72

Dagenham away today at Wrexham (not the easiest game), Dover at home to Torquay (optimistic perhaps, but I could see this as a draw), & I can't remember about Barrow. In essence, with only one game left after today, the Shots really can't afford not to win. Perhaps it's helpful – but conceivably not – that during the week some ten or eleven players agreed terms for next season. Ultimately surely good news: they've played some terrific football, & particularly at this level a lack of continuity must be the bane of managers trying to build something. So, in with a real shout this season – &, looking further ahead, some not irrational optimism.

Elsewhere on the football scene, the Ks (who have had a revival & appear safe) play their last match at Kingsmeadow. And Wembley is of course the venue for the weekend's Cup semi-finals, which still seems completely wrong, even if arguably the allure of neutral, non-Wembley venues died at Hillsborough in '89. The romance of the Cup hardly helped by the participants in this year's semis: Arsenal, Man City, Chelsea, Spurs.

I'm such a print junkie – as well as Autolycus-style rootler of paper bins – that I've picked up this morning a copy of yesterday's *Evening Standard* (to which George Osborne, tactically withdrawing from the political front line, will soon be devoting his unalloyed efforts). It features this by Danny Murphy about

Dietmar Hamann, with whom he played for Liverpool some fifteen years ago:

> If we were leading with only a few minutes to go, he would be talking to us constantly. He'd tell us when to stay down after a foul, when to play a free-kick long rather than short. He'd be the man who'd remind everyone that we didn't need as many attacking players as usual in the box if we had a corner.
>
> He had the ability to receive the ball in a tight area, stick out his backside to draw a foul. It would make the rest of us laugh but it was so effective – and a couple of minutes would go by before the free-kick was even taken.

Game management, they call it now. And of course I appreciate that just to raise an eyebrow is ludicrously priggish.

The French hold their first round of voting tomorrow – & it looks very, very tight. Presumably Le Pen (helped by an Isis-backed murder of a Paris policeman), but increasingly uncertain it's going to be Macron opposing her. Given he stands for centrist liberalism (as opposed to the Thatcherite & Trotskyite alternatives), I very much hope it is. That said, I'm acutely conscious that the people who support him are, like many of those supporting Remain last summer, often from the prosperous cities, for whom life is essentially benign & who are very far from the 'left-behind' – or, as David Goodhart has recently put it in a book that's had a lot of attention, they're the 'anywheres' (cosmopolitan, etc.) rather than the 'somewheres'. (I know Goodhart a bit. Somewhat aloof? Somewhat cold-blooded? But, for all those unavoidable Wykehamist tendencies, I definitely respect him.) I was also much struck the other day – & similarly made uncomfortable – by Giles Fraser's *Guardian* piece, arguing that the Thatcher/New Labour period of liberal capitalism was now mercifully (having rotted our souls) coming to an end, given that in their different ways both May & Corbyn were pushing for a less amoral approach – an approach in which naked or even thinly disguised greed was no longer OK & in which 'the power of money' was no longer 'concentrated in the hands of a few'.

Well, it's conceivable that he's correct about May, though so far it's been words rather than actions. And of course, I'm entirely with him about the grotesque power-cum-arrogance-cum-unaccountability of big money & those who possess it, often so undeservedly. But if capitalism is, as it might well be, the necessary precondition of liberalism? Then there might have to be a price to be paid, though of course it'd be good to reduce it, i.e. through a more managed-cum-responsible capitalism. And given that Fraser is so visibly on the liberal wing of the C of E, then surely that should give him some pause for thought?

Sunday 23 April

Even though Dagenham (now guaranteed 4th place) & Barrow (now out of it) both won, where it *really* counted yesterday afternoon went remarkably well – in other words, a comfortable win for the Shots (3–0, with a brace for Mensah & one for Rendell) while Dover were going down to a 2–1 home defeat against Torquay (both of whose goals came from Brett Williams, the player who more than any other kept the Shots up three years ago, in the season where we started on minus 10 points). So it's looking good – certainly much better than this time last week – with the Shots now 4 points clear of Dover. Even so, they still have that game in hand, at home to Macclesfield on Tuesday, & if they win it the Shots might need to win next Saturday to get that remaining play-off place. But let's see first what happens on Tues before starting to work out all the possible permutations. Meanwhile, I think I should record the remarkable fact that the Shots have now lost only once – once – in their last twenty matches. An extraordinary run, & I can't quite believe it's happened.

Wednesday 26 April

Listened last night to the closing stages of the Radio Kent commentary on Dover v Macclesfield. The Silkmen 2–1 up with a quarter of an hour to go – all hope apparently gone for Dover, but then Ross Lafayette (who played for the Shots a couple of years ago & was a shining light in a poor team) pulled one back – & a frantic 6 minutes of injury time saw Dover miss two good chances & Macclesfield hit the post. So, a 2–2 draw, & that leaves Dover on 76 points, three behind the Shots & each with a game left: Shots at home to relegation-threatened Braintree; Dover away at Barrow (longest trip in the Vanarama, with the supporters' coach apparently leaving at 3am (!), because on Saturday all the matches in the division start at 12.15). In effect, given their six-goals superior goal difference, it's highly probable, if not however absolutely certain, that the Shots will get that fifth spot. I'm of course drawing up in my head all sorts of doom-laden scenarios – a 3–0 home defeat for the Shots, complemented by Dover winning by the same score, currently the most frequent – but on any rational basis the Shots should be there. Still, I won't breathe easy & all that...

The election is not much more than white noise at the moment – just a vague but persistent sense, which I don't want to examine too closely, that something horrible, mean-spirited & generally depressing is inexorably unfolding... I find a tiny bit of consolation in the battle for top spot (& thus automatic promotion) in the Vanarama South. There, Maidenhead (Theresa May's constituency) have made the running for I think almost the whole season, but with Ebbsfleet fairly hard on their heels. Last Saturday, Maidenhead had the chance to clinch it at home to Ebbsfleet – but blew it, losing 2–1 after being one up. Playing for the visitors were two former Shots favourites – Aaron McLean & Dave Winfield – & it was the latter who scored the decisive goal near the death. It'll still be Maidenhead's if they win their last match – away at Margate this Saturday – but they may yet get caught at the post... Not that, in all honesty, I remotely think anything like that's going to happen in the election. But I'll leave that topic for another day.

So yes, following Sunday's vote, it is Macron versus Le Pen in the run-off on May 7th. Of course there are plenty of negatives about him: the elite education; the investment-banking background; his remoteness from many people's struggles. He's in fact, for better or worse, a Blairite. What he's *not* is a small-minded, anti-immigrant nationalist, who quite likely is instinctively neither a pluralist nor a democrat, but at best an authoritarian populist. So it has to be fingers crossed that he wins – & that, in particular, the French left have the appropriate, historically aware sense of priorities. Unfortunately, I'm far from convinced they have. I suspect it's going to be tight. It may – forgive the possible hyperbole – be the most important European election of my lifetime.

Friday 28 April

I went with Nick Humphrey & a friend of his last night to the Dulwich Hamlet semi-final play-off against Enfield Town. A crowd of two & a half thousand – & a club that's really going places. They won 4–2, helped by some catastrophic Enfield defending, & on Bank Holiday Monday go to Bognor Regis for the play-off final (the winners going into Vanarama South, i.e. one tier below the Shots).[101] It was generally entertaining & played at a whirlwind pace, though inevitably at times a bit pinball scattergun. While, on a mercenary note, the transport to Denmark Hill was free (courtesy of my Freedom Pass), admission for seniors was £4, & the programme was £2 – all of which, remarkably good value, even prompting thoughts of a season ticket next season, if not too many fixture clashes with the Shots.

While as for the Shots, at home to Braintree tomorrow, it *should* be all right – & certainly, a very major upset if they blow it at this point. To put it in perspective: *even* if Dover win 3–0 at Barrow & the Shots lose 2–0, the Shots would *still* be in the play-offs. Lucy & George are both coming – Nick is loyally planning to – & we're taking Margaret Henry, a very nice Scottish lady in her mid-80s who goes to the same Senior Wives church fellowship group as my mother & whose husband Gordon (who died some

---

[101] Hamlet lost in the final, but were promoted the following year.

years ago of dementia – after heading too many heavy leather footballs?) was a Shots stalwart between 1956 & 1964.[102] In case of disaster, she will provide a salutary long-term perspective. Braintree themselves, incidentally, are in deep relegation trouble, in terrible form, & need to win this final match in order to avoid the drop. Logic points only one way – but logic can be the most fickle of mistresses.

I've been meaning for the past fortnight to record a couple of paras from a recent *Economist* editorial about Turkey:

> The new constitution embodies the 'illiberal democracy' of nationalists such as Viktor Orban of Hungary and Vladimir Putin of Russia, to whom Mr Erdogan is increasingly compared. On this view, election winners take all, constraints are obstacles to strong government and the ruling party has a right to subvert institutions, such as the judiciary and the press.
>
> Yet this kind of stability is hollow. The most successful democracies make a point of separating powers and slowing governments down. The guiding idea of the American constitution is to stop presidents from acting as if they were monarchs, by building in checks and balances. Even the British prime minister, untrammelled by a written constitution, has to submit herself to the courts, a merciless press and a weekly grilling in Parliament, broadcast live.

A nationalist Tory PM, with poorly disguised authoritarian instincts, being exposed to a merciless right-wing press? The travesty of democratic accountability that is PMQs? The inevitable temptation for those bewigged 'enemies of the people' to lie doggo? Agreed, we're not a banana republic yet. But we're going that way.

George has just told me, before I popped out to write this entry in Bingsoo (a pot of burdock tea, complemented by the delicious Korean speciality that is green tea cake), the news about Obama & his forthcoming $400,000 speech to an investment

---

[102] He played over 200 times for the Shots, including in his final season the famous win against Aston Villa.

bank. He's intensely disappointed (especially as someone who was an Obama volunteer in the 2012 campaign), as am I, not least because of the Blair parallels. Neither man needs/needed that sort of money – it severely damages reputations – & of course contributes significantly to the centre no longer holding... It sometimes seems that the worst enemies of liberal democracy are the liberal democrats (both words very much lower case). And it sometimes seems that those like Blair & Obama, in whom such massive responsibility has resided & almost by default continues to reside, are at best only semi-aware of just how much is at stake.

Sunday 30 April

Well, the Shots did it. Although Dover (accompanied by twenty-four travelling supporters – the true heroes of the day) won 3–2 at Barrow, it didn't matter, because the Shots took the three points at home to Braintree. Some good, fluent football – most of the team very comfortable on the ball – & in the end reasonably comfortable, with second-half goals by Evans & Mensah. A well-earned lap of honour at the end – with a definite lump in my throat as they came past the South Stand – & then the presentations, with the various player-of-the-season awards being shared by the two Jakes (Cole & Gallagher, with the very reliable keeper justifiably taking the main honours, notwithstanding my vote for the knobbly-kneed Jake G as the heartbeat of the team). After the match, we went first to Mrs Henry's, where she showed us some very evocative early 60s Shots photos (including cheerful-looking, mud-coated players in the dressing room), & then on to my mother & stepfather in Farnborough, where they were pleased with the outcome but I'm not sure quite grasped the full mechanics of the play-off system.

Now I'm having Sunday-morning breakfast in the café just below where I had an office in the late 1990s & treating myself to a read of *The Non-League Paper* (which includes the detail of an apparent rumour that the Braintree team threatened not to play because of non-payment of wages), as well as reflecting on the achievement. It seems to me a considerable one on the part of Gary Waddock & his assistant James Rowe: gathering together a squad virtually from scratch – having a mixed but far from unpromising first half of the season – & then from Christmas through to yesterday going through twenty-one matches with only one defeat. A mixture of solidity at the back (Cole, Reynolds, Evans) & quickness, agility & creativity at the front (Mensah, Kanu, Benyu). In terms of the bottom line – Shots finishing 5th on 82 points, Dover finishing 6th on 79 points – one retrospective counter-factual (pointed out to me by Michael the other day) is worth mentioning. Back on August Bank Holiday, Shots went to Dover & won 2–1, with the home side having omitted from its starting line-up Ricky Miller (who would finish the season with a remarkable forty-five goals), apparently on disciplinary grounds. If he had played kick-off that day, who knows what ultimate difference that might have made? I also find myself reflecting on this time last year when, again accompanied by Mrs Henry, we saw the Shots lose dismally at home to Southport: fourth successive home defeat, a small & dispirited crowd (two and a half thousand less than yesterday), & it really felt like a club in terminal decline. Whatever happens in the play-offs, it's now certainly not that. For which I'm – unambiguously – grateful.

Idris, almost

Tuesday 2 May

I'm so under the harrow with correcting B of E proofs – over 800 pages – against a tight deadline that it's all I can do to keep this diary going re the Shots, let alone anything else.

But in fact it's a big day tomorrow: home leg (7 o'c kick-off) of the play-off semi-final against Tranmere. This time will be the fourth time since 2003 that the Shots have been involved in play-offs: so far getting once to the final & twice being knocked out in the semis. Overall, Tranmere must start as favourites: bigger club, finished some 15 points ahead, advantage of the second leg at home. But it's quite possible tomorrow that, if the Shots play in a relaxed, confident mood, we could take say a two-goal advantage into the second leg. Though arguably possible rather than probable – who knows? Anyway, I'm looking forward to it, not least as an antidote to the Old Lady, though can't wholly banish the thought from the back of my mind that it could just be like that horrendous (& horrendously unfair) first half against Forest Green last October. I guess that's always the danger with an essentially young, inexperienced side, i.e. every now & then a complete, catastrophic collapse. The bottom line is that anything other than a defeat makes the second leg a competitive prospect. And although of course I want more, I'll settle in the end for that.

Wednesday 3 May

Two things to add this morning to my rather tired late-evening entry. First, & most importantly, that *au fond* I'm just amazed that the Shots have reached this stage. By the middle of the season, approaching Christmas, it seemed more or less beyond the bounds of possibility. And doubly amazing, of course, that what's turned out to be such a memorable season should have happened to coincide with the keeping of this one-off football-oriented diary. Second, it feels a bit feeble not to make a firm prediction for this evening. So, here goes: the Shots to win by two clear goals, with 3–1 being my actual forecast (which, if it happened to be the outcome, would be an exact repeat of the memorable encounter – probably the most memorable of the season – back in early September). But whatever happens, I'll try to enjoy the moment.

Thursday 4 May

Well, I may not be getting that phone call asking me to join the Pools Panel. It could hardly have gone worse. A slip by Kellermann leading to a very early goal for Tranmere – a wonderful move after half an hour or so leading to Mensah hitting the bar – a dreadful, head-in-the-hands (certainly my head in my hands) mistake by Cole gifting Tranmere a second soon after the break – Shots creating dismayingly little against a very big, tough, uncompromising outfit, helped by most of the referee's decisions seemingly going their way – & Tranmere sealing it with a counter-attacking, clinically taken third with about a quarter of an hour to go. The atmosphere, exuberant & thrilling at the start, understandably flat at the end. A game too far for a young team?

Too soon, after reaching the play-offs, to get into proper focus for the play-offs? Nerves? Of course it's not *actually* over – the second leg is at Prenton Park on Saturday – but, barring a highly unlikely Istanbul-style miracle, it is in effect. For myself, yes, I'm disappointed, but otherwise rather calm &, to my surprise, just slightly detached. Mainly I think because (like the players themselves?) my emotional energies had football-wise been so focused these last few months on securing that 5th spot that I had little left in the tank, when it came to it, for going beyond that? And also, I can't deny it, because I'm quite relieved at the prospect of ending very soon this tranche of diary – nine months feels like quite a long time. I've always loved the story of Henry James after his play *Guy Domville* spectacularly flopped on its first night, in personally humiliating circumstances, & the next morning he realised with a profound sense of relief, & strange calm, that his doomed attempt to become a commercially successful playwright had run its course. Not that I feel that about the Shots or (I think) diary-writing. But sometimes one just knows – & is not unhappy to know – that a particular phase of one's life is, however all-consuming it may have seemed at the time, conclusively over.

Today is, as it happens, a final Shots anniversary (& the point where until recently I'd long imagined that I'd end this diary). Friday 4 May 1973 – away at Stockport – Shots needing a point to get their first promotion (out of the old Div 4) since entering the Football League in 1932. My last term at Oxford, just over a month before Finals, & I took the train – going to the match on my own, as usual. Not a great game, not even a good one, but the Shots just about managed to eke out a 1–1 draw, helped by a fine save (low to his right) about 8 minutes from the end by Tony Godfrey, a particular favourite of mine (perhaps because he was notably short for a goalie).[103] At the end I joined the pitch invasion – never before, surely never again – & made a beeline for Jack

---

[103] I've always had a particular fondness for short sportsmen, no doubt in part because I wasn't quite tall enough myself as a sometime goalie. The book I'm happiest to have written is my biography of Bobby Abel, the England and Surrey professional batsman (and son of a Rotherhithe lamplighter) who at 5 foot 5 was so physically different, and such a different type of batsman, from his Golden Age amateur contemporaries.

Howarth, at which point I found myself having to reach up in order to slap him on the back: until seeing him so close up I had had no idea he was so big. Anyway, an exultant feeling, which just about survived an overnight coach from Manchester to London. And that Saturday afternoon I was at Wembley to see the Cup Final (again a first & almost certainly a last), with a terrace ticket courtesy of my father (i/c the Army School of Physical Training at Aldershot). Sunderland of the Second Division beat 1–0 the all-conquering Leeds of the First, & I was at the right end for both the Porterfield goal & the legendary Montgomery save (although in real time I thought that Lorimer, who seemed odds-on to score, had hit the bar direct). That evening, in a journey in an old-fashioned compartment with mellow sunlight through the window, I took the train from Paddington back to Oxford. It seemed then, as it still seems now, the best footballing twenty-four hours of my life. And I suspect I knew already – or at least had a kind of premonition – that I would never again be so wholly & straightforwardly in love with the game. Everything, in short, could only get more complicated.

Friday 5 May

The general post-match gloom has been alleviated by Mike Burns emailing through a couple of photographs he took of his TV as it played the recording of the match. Taken just before the ref mercifully blew the final whistle, the particularly evocative one – currently promoted, in a masochistic way, to screen-saver status – shows from left to right: Nick Humphrey looking as if the world is about to end; George covering his face with his hands; Lucy looking anxious; & Mike himself more resolute but slightly dazed. I'm yet again out of camera. In the row in front there's an old man who looks like he's seen it all before. I emailed it on to Andy Ward, who in his reply said he was struck by how much it showed that everyone *cared*. Which I guess is true.

The second leg at Tranmere is at 12.15 tomorrow. It's not possible, for various reasons, to go, but Michael (living in Leamington) is planning to go with some friends. I don't think they'll see a miracle, but hopefully a spirited performance by the Shots – my best guess, for the currently very minimal amount that feels worth, is a 2–2 draw. I'm hoping we're going to be able to fix it to be able to watch it at home on BT Sport. I've never seen the Shots on TV live at home, so that would be a minor ambition fulfilled. Whether it's a contest – or even remotely a contest – in terms of the tie as a whole probably depends heavily on who scores the first goal. I very much want it to be the Shots, with just an accompanying frisson of excitement. Fingers crossed.

Saturday 6 May

The match finished an hour or so ago, & it certainly felt like a very novel – & enjoyable – sensation watching the Shots (in their proper red & blue colours) live on TV in my own sitting-room. We had to pay £18 for the privilege, but well worth it. In front of a highly partisan crowd of over 10,000, the Shots began nervously, but then reasonably settled down, albeit without threatening much. Slightly unexpectedly, Tranmere took the lead after about 25 minutes: Route One & well taken, but Reynolds & Evans should surely have coped better. Then, to the utter delight of the assembled company (Lucy, me, George & an American friend of George's called Joe, who turns out to be a keen Arsenal supporter), a fine long-range strike by Mensah equalised just before half-time. 1–1 on the day, but of course still a three-goal margin. Then, quite early in the second half, not long after Tranmere had hit the post, an own goal from a corner actually put the Shots ahead. Game on, & hard at that point not to remember Michael Frayn's immortal line for John Cleese. So it proved, as knuckles in New Malden became ever whiter. The Shots on top for much of the rest of the game, but just couldn't quite deliver another goal – Rendell thwarted once by a superb save by the keeper – that would really have put it in the melting-pot. Near the end, as the clock ticked away, a bitter snort all-round for McNulty being named man of the match, after an ugly, street-wise performance by the grey-haired tank that a better, more sophisticated – & braver – referee would have clamped down on. In injury time itself, with the Shots inevitably stretched, Tranmere scored to put the issue beyond any doubt. So, 2–2 on the day (my forecast), but 5–2 on aggregate. Accordingly, it ain't going to be Wembley this year.

Overall, for all the might-have-beens, it was the better side – but also the dirtier side – that won, taking the two legs as a whole. But, for the Shots, some real honour & pride salvaged from today's performance – important to take into next season. The nucleus should be there to build on this season's sense of progress & really do something.[104] It's also been a considerable pleasure how good some of the football has been. Writing the diary has undoubtedly sharpened the intensity of my support & accompanying emotions this season, but I think anyway that it would have been a memorable & often all-consuming nine months. It feels like a long, long time since that rather unlucky 1–0 defeat away at Barrow. An epic ride, & if it doesn't seem too ludicrous to say so, I actually feel rather privileged to have been some small, noises-off part of it.

Sunday 7 May

About 9.45 in the morning – Bingsoo sadly not open yet – & The Place (where for symbolic reasons I'd like to have gone, completing this diary's cycle) doesn't open on Sundays – so *faute de mieux* it's Costa: not a favourite place, but as a house sign/name

---

[104] Yes and no as it turned out. The 2017/18 season proved ultimately a repeat of 2016/17: a final position of 5th, followed by failing to make it through the play-offs (a penalty-shoot-out defeat at home to Ebbsfleet United). But that was better than in 2018/19, when a miserable and injury-hit season culminated in relegation to National League South, the departure of Gary Waddock and his replacement by Danny Searle (whom I instantly warmed to). At which point an improbable reprieve took place in the form of Gateshead's relegation on account of financial irregularities and the reinstatement of the Shots. As I write, well into the 2019/20 season, we hover just above the drop zone; and Waddock, briefly in charge of struggling Southend United, has left following a 7–1 home defeat to Doncaster Rovers, with his team reduced to nine men. It's a cruel game.

used to say near to where we previously lived in New Malden, 'It'll Do'.[105]

A *cri de coeur* by Will Hutton in today's *Observer*. Two paras stand out:

> Britain is a country of the European Enlightenment, or so I have thought. For decades, we have muddled through without a written constitution. But the impact of a referendum that went against majority opinion in parliament, along with a desperately weak parliamentary opposition, a weaponised right-wing media and lack of mass support for the rule of law, has shown how vulnerable our civilisation is to know-nothing populism and a profoundly dysfunctional democracy.
>
> Enlightenment values – tolerance, respect for the importance of fair debate, checked and balanced government, objectivity and impartiality, recognition of international interdependencies – are being trashed. Matters could get very ugly, very fast. It is not just Europe we are leaving, but an idea of Britain.

I fear he's horribly right – of course I do, because after all this whole diary has at one level been, I suspect (though I haven't read it & don't for the time being intend to), a fearful, semi-bewildered lament. For Hutton himself, tactless man though he can be in real life, I have a high regard – & much regret New Labour's timidity in not following him down *The State We're In*'s potentially zeitgeist-capturing & game-changing stakeholder capitalism road in the mid-90s. The immediate context is Labour's abject performance in the local elections, contrasting starkly to 'Theresa' being 'On the March!' (to quote yesterday's *Mail* front-page headline), heading next month for a nationalistic, quasi-nativist, quasi-authoritarian, fiercely anti-Europe landslide.[106] Yet fundamentally, there's something even bigger at stake: civilisation – &

---

[105] The Place, the other Anglo-Korean café in New Malden High Street, was where I wrote this diary's opening entry.

[106] Well, that's how it seemed at the time. But anyway, by the time (August 2020) this diary is published, memories of the June 2017 election are likely to be moderately irrelevant. Not of course that those malign forces will have done the decent thing and quietly disappeared.

Hutton's dead right (as it were) to use that word. Of course I concede that middle-class 'progressives' have been too remote, too detached from working-class realities; of course I concede that a modest patriotism is a justified (or anyway potentially justified) sentiment; of course I have my problems with militant, self-aggrandising, morally superior liberals & socialists. But in the end one has to be on one side or the other, & I know which I'm on. Which certainly means that I'll be holding my breath later today, to see that Macron has indeed defeated Le Pen in the second round. The alternative is an inconceivably appalling thought – though, for this diary's final prediction, my guess is that she'll win in 2022. This particular history train (an image from Paul Simon's first solo album) has still got some way to roll.

If & when I do get to read these scribblings since last summer, I know I'll be embarrassed by quite a lot (including some stupidly intemperate outbursts), irritated by all the various loose ends not tied up (but perhaps that's inherent in the form), struck by what seems to have been an exaggeration of Corbyn's socialist ambitions (but not of Trump's malignity), appalled by some of the slack writing, & disappointed by the relative lack of quotidian detail (at least partly explained I'm fairly sure, as I think I've said before, by the strong wish to avoid tiresome & predictable grumpy-old-man mode). Of course, the diary's ultimate subject is the unresolved tension-cum-conflict within me: on the one hand, despair at the rise of narrow & intolerant & often anti-democratic identity politics (above all the politics of nationalism); & on the other hand, the importance to my own identity of continuing to support an obscure, small-town football club (where almost certainly the great majority of supporters voted Brexit & would not have felt unduly fussed about Trump). Perhaps that's helped me a bit to look at things through different pairs of eyes? Perhaps it isn't really a conflict, but a Whitman-style reflection of the variousness and contradictoriness of man?[107] Yes, perhaps that's it: something to embrace, even gladly. Even so, to end this

---

[107] 'Do I contradict myself? / Very well, then I contradict myself, / I am large, I contain multitudes' (Walt Whitman, *Song of Myself*).

solipsistic diary (though is there any other sort?) on a suitably solipsistic note, life might have been simpler if my father hadn't taken me to that match at the Rec almost sixty years ago. But at least those years have taught me that tribalism & decency are not necessarily incompatible – a lesson I'm now clinging on to in these darkening times.

Illustration details

All photographs taken by Ian Morsman.

Acknowledgements

I am grateful to the following for helping to transform my loose-leaf scribblings into this book: Michael Fishwick, Georgia Garrett, Greg Heinimann, Nick Humphrey, Peter James, Lilidh Kendrick, George Kynaston, Lucy Kynaston, Harry Ricketts, Honor Spreckley, Lauren Whybrow. I'm also grateful to the club's photographer, Ian Morsman, for allowing me to reproduce some of his images from the 2016–17 season. And my greatest debt is, of course, to the many players who over the years have worn the red and blue.

About the author

David Kynaston was born in Aldershot in 1951 overlooking the football ground. A professional historian since 1973, he has written extensively on post-war Britain; on the City of London; on cricket; and on the private school question. *Shots in the Dark* is his first football book.

Note on the Type

The text of this book is set in Linotype Stempel Garamond, a version of Garamond adapted and first used by the Stempel foundry in 1924. It is one of several versions of Garamond based on the designs of Claude Garamond. It is thought that Garamond based his font on Bembo, cut in 1495 by Francesco Griffo in collaboration with the Italian printer Aldus Manutius. Garamond types were first used in books printed in Paris around 1532. Many of the present-day versions of this type are based on the *Typi Academiae* of Jean Jannon cut in Sedan in 1615.

Claude Garamond was born in Paris in 1480. He learned how to cut type from his father and by the age of fifteen he was able to fashion steel punches the size of a pica with great precision. At the age of sixty he was commissioned by King Francis I to design a Greek alphabet, and for this he was given the honourable title of royal type founder. He died in 1561.

A SHOCKER-

MEN WITH THE SHOTS

No. 4
DAVID JONES

Vanarama C

ALDERSHOT TO

SOUTH STAND SEATIN

CONCESSION

SEASON TICKETS 20

ALDERSHOT FOOTBALL

F.A. CUP SPECIAL

ALDERSHOT goalkeeper Tony Godfrey.

Reading, 2

SHOTS GAIN POINT IN GAME OF SHORT TEMPERS

LAST-GASP GOAL ROBS ALDERSHOT

TRANMERE, 2; ALDERSHOT, 2

Dave Jones

Ron Davies